For Zelma Long —

    With my thanks for setting
this journey in motion originally
— and with all best wishes —

        Barbara

May 1988
New York

AMERICAN VINEYARDS

AMERICAN VINEYARDS

BARBARA ENSRUD

PHOTOGRAPHS BY CHARLES E. DORRIS

STEWART, TABORI & CHANG

NEW YORK

Text copyright © 1988 Barbara Ensrud
Photographs copyright © 1988 Charles E. Dorris

Designed by J.C. Suarès
            Jeff Batzli
Map by Guenter Vollath
Edited by Brian Hotchkiss

Published by Stewart, Tabori & Chang, Inc.
740 Broadway, New York, New York 10003

Library of Congress Cataloging-in-Publication Data
Ensrud, Barbara.
    American vineyards.

    Includes index.
    1. Viticulture—United States. 2. Wine and wine
making—United States. 3. Vineyards—United States.
4. Viticulture—North America. 5. Wine and wine making
—North America. 6. Vineyards—North America. I. Dorris,
Charles E. II. Title.
SB387.75.E57 1988   641.2′22′0973   87–9963
ISBN 1–55670–010–5

Distributed by Workman Publishing
1 West 39 Street, New York, New York 10018

Printed in Japan

88 89 10 9 8 7 6 5 4 3 2 1

First Edition

₊photo credits
page 57: © 1982 Richard Jeffery
page 61, top: New York Historical Society
page 61, bottom: Philip Mazzei Foundation
page 73, both: Courtesy Lafayette Vineyards and Winery
page 75: Courtesy Biltmore Estate Winery
pages 84, 85 (both), 86, and 87: © 1987 Matthew Kaplan
page 174: photography by Matthew Klein, courtesy of Chateau Ste.
Michelle
pages 186, 187, 189: Barbara Ensrud
pages 192, 199: Andrew Stewart
pages 195 (both), 196–197, and 198 (both): Courtesy Vinícola L. A.
Cetto

For Whit and Jay

CONTENTS

10
Introduction

32
Chapter One
Vineyards of the Northeast

60
Chapter Two
Vineyards of the South

80
Chapter Three
Vineyards of the Heartland

100
Chapter Four
Vineyards of the Southwest

122
Chapter Five
Vineyards of California

158
Chapter Six
Vineyards of the Pacific Northwest

178
Chapter Seven
Vineyards of Canada

192
Chapter Eight
Vineyards of Mexico

202
Regional Listing: Wineries and Vineyards

209
Glossary: North American Wine Grapes

216
Glossary: Wine Terms

220
Bibliography

221
Index

C A N A D A

ONTARIO

QUEBEC

PRINCE
EDWARD
ISLAND

NEW
BRUNSWICK

NOVA SCOTIA

L. Superior

MAINE

•Kentville

•Halifax

MICH.

•Montreal

VERMONT

BAY OF FUNDY

WISCONSIN

L. Huron

NEW HAMPSHIRE

Minneapolis

L. Michigan

•Traverse City

Toronto•

L. Ontario

NEW
YORK

Boston•

Plymouth
MASSACHUSETTS

Prairie
du Sac

Niagara Falls
St. Catharines

•Rochester

RHODE ISLAND

MICHIGAN

Buffalo

•Martha's Vineyard

L. Erie

Erie

CONNECTICUT

IOWA

Detroit•

Blenheim

Davenport•

•Kalamazoo

Cleveland•

•Chicago

Sandusky•

PENNSYLVANIA

New York•

NEW JERSEY

•Philadelphia

INDIANA

OHIO

Pittsburgh•

York•

DELAWARE

City

ILLINOIS

Indianapolis•

Cincinnati•

•Washington

•St. Louis

Ohio R.

WEST
VIRGINIA

Middleburg•

MARYLAND

Hermann•

•Augusta

Charleston•

Charlottesville•

•Fredericksburg

KENTUCKY

•Rolla

VIRGINIA

MISSOURI

Mississippi R.

ARKANSAS

TENNESSEE

Tennessee R.

NORTH
CAROLINA

tus•

Memphis•

•Asheville

Little
Rock•

APPALACHIAN

Columbia•

Merigold•

•Indianola

ALABAMA

Savannah R.

SOUTH
CAROLINA

GEORGIA

•Atlanta

•Jackson

MISSISSIPPI

Sabine R.

•Montgomery

LOUISIANA

•Tallahassee

New Orleans•

FLORIDA

GULF OF MEXICO

•Tampa

•Miami

UPLANDS

ATLANTIC OCEAN

N

| 0 | 100 | 200 | 300 | 400 Miles |
| 0 | 100 | 200 | 300 | 400 Kilometers |

KAUAI

OAHU

MOLOKAI
LANAI

MAUI

•Ulupalakua

HAWAII

HAWAII

INTRODUCTION

TODAY'S WINEGROWERS ON THE NORTH American continent are modern pioneers. As I heard their stories, walked in the vineyards they had painstakingly planted vine by vine, and tasted their efforts at winemaking, I was continually reminded of the early settlers and pioneers who first developed this country. Delving into the history of each region, I discovered what is seldom taught in the overview of history we get in school. History courses deal almost exclusively with the history of politics, with little time spent looking at the life and culture of those who crossed the continent, who settled the country and chiseled its destiny out of the earth. Yet it is the everyday human struggle involved in striving to achieve an aim, to realize a dream, that enlivens the study of history and touches one's feeling.

The sweep of American history is perhaps at its most powerful in the saga of the pioneers. Reading their diaries and recollections is absorbing enough, but actually traveling to various parts of the country where vineyards now stand evokes some feeling of what life must have been like as the country was being explored and settled. On the vast and desolate plains of west Texas, one is moved to ponder the raw and gritty life of the cowboy. Today grapevines grow where the cattle and buffalo once roamed, and although you do not need a six-gun or a lariat to round up grapes, tending them there is still a gritty task. In Michigan or Missouri, one can sense the solid tenacity and determination required of the Midwestern farmer turned vineyardist, but it is also possible to see how the beckoning of the wide sky urged more restless souls of the 1880s to move on. And in the fertile valleys of California, land of promise and dreams fulfilled, one sees the triumph of the vine as it covers whole valleys end to end.

I frequently allude to our pioneer forerunners in these pages. Though today there is none of the life-and-death struggle that relentlessly confronted their efforts, the same spirit of adventure, high hopes and bold dreams that enticed the men and women of the last century to continue forward inhabits twentieth-century winegrowers. The pioneers ventured into the unknown, carving out something entirely new. In a very real sense the modern winegrower is doing the same; not so much, perhaps, in California, where the vine readily took to the hospitable climate, but certainly in the rest of the country.

Like the pioneers, winegrowers have often had no one to turn to for guidance, no one who understood the specific set of givens—soils, weather, pests and diseases—indigenous to regions new to the grape. Just as a scout familiar with the Santa Fe Trail would be of limited use to pioneers on the Oregon Trail, the scientists of California or Syracuse were often unable to guide winegrowers in Michigan or Missouri or Virginia. What advice was forthcoming was often wrong. Scientists invariably urged against growing the European species *Vitis vinifera* east of the Rockies. Fortunately, some stubborn but visionary souls in places like New York, Virginia, Georgia and Texas persevered, garnering exciting results in several instances. It is gratifying to see the rapid expansion encouraged by these successes.

Winegrowing is a young industry in North America, spanning a mere five decades since repeal of Prohibition. On this continent we are only just starting to produce the quality of wines that Europe has enjoyed for centuries. Not that there has been any lack of trying from the very beginning: Efforts at winegrowing in North America commenced with the earliest European foray ashore in the New World, the arrival of the conquistadors in the sixteenth century. In 1524 Hernando Cortez decreed that ev-

Vintner Michael Johnson (OPPOSITE) *at La Chiripada Winery near Taos, New Mexico.* (PAGES 12–13): *A pergola of vines frames the homestead at Crosswoods Vineyards, a former dairy farm in Connecticut.*

11

The tool shed at West Park Wine Cellars in New York's Hudson Valley.

ery landholder in New Spain (now Mexico) plant a thousand vines for each one hundred Indian workers on an estate. Seeds and cuttings were brought from Spain to accomplish this. By 1595 so much wine was being produced in the New World that Spanish wine producers complained they were going broke and persuaded King Philip II to put a stop to it. Philip not only forbade further plantings in New Spain but ordered that existing vineyards be torn out. Nevertheless, the Franciscan fathers who traveled north, establishing missions in Texas and the Southwest, continued to plant vines in order to have wines for the Sacrament.

The early settlers along the Atlantic also attempted to grow vines from European seeds and cuttings. The Jamestown colony, Lord Baltimore's settlers in Maryland, and William Penn at Philadelphia all tried to establish vineyards, but the vines died. They then made wine from the wild grapes that grew in such abundance. These wines, with their strong, grapey flavor, were very unlike those made from the European varieties and therefore not to the colonists' taste. Early American cookbooks, however, contain numerous recipes for making wine from the Scuppernong grape (a native American variety), as well as from other fruits.

The failure of the European grape species in American soil meant that the kinds of wines that traditionally graced the tables of Europe were unavailable to Americans, and this was to have far-reaching ramifications. In the 1700s rum from the Caribbean became a readily available commodity. In Pennsylvania and Kentucky farmers turned surplus grain into corn whiskey and bourbon. Settlers along the East Coast also drank a fair amount of fortified wine from Madeira, which clipper ships picked up on their way to the Indian Ocean and eventually brought to Savannah, Charleston and other American ports, where the sea merchants traded it for indigo and cotton.

Gradually, grape varieties were developed that could survive the American climate and better withstand native insects and disease. Experimental growers like John Adlum of Mary-

land (who furnished Thomas Jefferson with seeds and cuttings for vineyards at Monticello), Ephraim Wales Bull of Massachusetts, Dr. Daniel Norton of Virginia, George Husmann of Missouri and T. V. Munson of Texas, labored to develop native varieties that would produce palatable wine east of the Rockies.

In California, however, French and German immigrants planted vinifera with relative ease, establishing vineyards in the Cucamonga district east of Los Angeles and north and south of San Francisco Bay. By the late 1800s, several parts of the United States had thriving wine industries, not only on the coasts, but in Ohio, New Mexico, Missouri, Texas, even Mississippi and Arkansas. Many American wines found favor abroad, winning recognition at such international wine competitions as the Paris Expositions of the late nineteenth century.

American winegrowers would have come a lot further a lot sooner had it not been for Prohibition. This law, passed in 1919 as the Volstead Act, prohibited the production, transport and sale of all alcoholic beverages, with the exception of those used for either sacramental or medicinal purposes. A so-called noble experiment designed to eradicate the evils of alcohol abuse, it failed utterly, fostering worse abuse as well as bootlegging, which brought about the most violent period of crime that the nation has ever known. Why did it happen? There are many who feel it would have never occurred had America been successful with winegrowing.

Prohibition was a reaction against the excessive use of hard liquor. The potent beverages—what Thomas Jefferson termed "ardent spirits"—were the prevalent alcoholic drinks of the country. There was little tradition of wine, a more moderate beverage, except in California and among certain ethnic communities, and liquor had gained a foothold in the early years of the Republic. Corn and other grains were plentiful; ease of transport made whiskey cheap and distilleries cropped up everywhere. In 1900 the number of saloons in Chicago equaled the number of grocery stores. Drunkenness had become a grave threat to home and family.

Riesling grapes are among those for which the Finger Lakes region of New York is becoming known.

A temperance frenzy swept the country, gaining momentum during an era of reform that began in the nineteenth century with the drive for suffrage, labor reform and the welfare of children. It started in the Northeast, a veritable hotbed of utopian ideals and fanatical movements, and was taken up with fervor in the Midwest. It is interesting to note that these were regions settled by northern Europeans, those of Anglo-Saxon, Scotch-Irish and Scandinavian descent, for the most part, with a tradition of strong drink rather than wine behind them. In California it was quite different. A large number of the people who settled California were from parts of Europe where wine was an accepted, indeed commonly considered the healthiest, beverage for the table. Drinking wine was not considered evil, nor was it associated with drunkenness.

Prohibition began in 1919 and lasted for fourteen years, putting virtually all wineries out of business except for the few that produced sacramental or medicinal wines. Vineyards were abandoned, in some cases their vines grafted over to table varieties or tough-skinned grapes such as Alicante Bouschet or Zinfandel that could withstand the rigors of rail shipment to the East, where they were sold to home winemakers.

When the Volstead Act was repealed in 1933, wineries in the United States and Canada (which had also enacted prohibition laws) had to start again almost from scratch. Large firms quickly released as much wine as they could, regardless of quality; some of the stuff had sat in cask for years and was moldy or oxidized. Dosed with alcohol, "refreshed" with young wines, it nonetheless was bottled and sold. There were no standards for quality or style, since few wines were imported until after World War II. The years of the speakeasy and bathtub gin had created a demand for a quick, inexpensive jolt of alcohol.

Cheap fortified wines labeled port, sherry or muscatel dominated the wine market of the 1930s and 1940s. Table wines were made by

16

a few producers—Louis M. Martini, Wente Bros., the Gallos—for those who had never stopped drinking wine (mostly Italian-Americans who, during Prohibition, had made their own). But these were generally hearty, simple blends, inexpensive wines for everyday use. Interestingly, however, wineries like Martini, Inglenook and Beaulieu in California's Napa Valley produced Cabernet Sauvignons in the early 1940s that are alive and drinkable even today.

It was really only about twenty-five years ago that the big move to better wine came about. That was when the general public first began to discover the delights of wine. Americans traveling to Europe in the 1950s became acquainted with wine in a new way—as a beverage to drink with food, as part of a more sophisticated lifestyle; it tasted good and was something to enjoy.

In California in the late 1940s and early 1950s, seminal figures in American winemaking like André Tchelistcheff, Martin Ray and

James Zellerbach began producing fine Cabernets, Chardonnays and Pinot Noirs in the style of great Bordeaux and Burgundy, paving the way for a new wave of emulators in the 1960s. By the early 1970s, a wine boom appeared to be underway. The number of wineries in California more than doubled between 1970 and 1980. The dramatic growth spread from California to the Northwest, across the Midwestern plains, to the Northeast in Pennsylvania, Connecticut and Rhode Island, to Canada, and to Virginia and points south with astonishing momentum. By 1985, wineries on the North American continent numbered almost 1,300, vineyard acreage well over the million mark. We have come a long way in a very short time, and it is due entirely to the vision, dedication and hard work of some very energetic and determined people, as we shall see in the pages that follow.

What is it that lures people into winegrowing? This ancient endeavor traces its illustrious heritage throughout the history of mankind and has

17

associations with gods and goddesses, biblical heroes, kings and popes. But it comes down to something much more immediate, I think: It is the challenge and satisfaction of producing something that gives pleasure and serves as nourishment, not just to the body but to the senses, the spirit and the imagination. Growing cotton or soybeans may be more lucrative (although not always!), but it is simply not the same as producing a bottle of wine made from grapes you grew yourself, that you can open proudly and share with friends and the world.

More often than not, individuals have gotten into grapegrowing and winemaking for the adventure, the novelty, the romance of it. The difficulties came as something of a shock. Unforeseen were the disasters—arctic freezes that could destroy an entire crop, pumps or generators that would break down during the critical moments of harvest, the myriad pests that can attack a vine, the frustration of trying to learn the ropes from a book, the tremendous financial cost involved. Like the pioneers, had they known of the pitfalls beforehand, they might never have started out. As one winemaker remarked with a rueful laugh, "Yes, I'm living my dream, but sometimes it's more like a nightmare."

The various factors with which growers must contend are taken up in each chapter. Sometimes they are peculiar to the region; more often they are variants of cold climate, humidity, diseases like rot or mildew, pests such as phylloxera. The single most challenging puzzle today, in every region, is determining which varieties will do best in particular microclimates. The subtle conditions that exist in certain exposures—a south-facing slope or the proximity of a large lake—will allow, say, Pinot Noir to ripen satisfactorily in one spot where only a few miles away it will not.

Growers are now getting more help from regional viticulturists at various universities. Although the University of California at Davis remains the leading school of oenology and viticulture, research facilities at institutions like the University of Arkansas, Mississippi State University, Cornell University, the University of Florida, Virginia Polytechnic Institute, the University of Texas and Texas A & M increasingly provide technical assistance that aids local growers.

Winegrowers also have to contend with antiquated, restrictive laws, residues of Prohibition that hamper the marketing of their wines. All alcoholic beverages are regulated by the Federal Bureau of Alcohol, Tobacco and Firearms (BATF) and are also subject to numerous state regulations. Many of these place an unfair burden on the small grower.

One of the most important developments in the last decade or so in fostering the growth of the American wine industry has been the passage by many states of farm winery bills. Starting a vineyard or winery is a capital-intensive enterprise. It takes a minimum of three years to get a decent crop from a young vineyard, another year to make, age and ready the wine for market, and sometimes a great deal longer to create demand for the product. To help the small grower, many states have issued farm winery licenses that allow small-production vintners to pay reduced taxes, to sell from the premises and to establish other points of sale direct to the consumer. They are also allowed to sell on Sundays, when most tourists are about. Many wineries sell up to a third or half of their production to tourists or local customers who buy at the winery.

The farm wineries that have sprung up across the country have had a twofold effect that is significant for the future. First, they encourage others to start their own operations. But, perhaps more important, they are helping to introduce people to wine in an agreeable way. Wine is still something fairly new to many parts of the country, still shrouded in a certain mystique and a misconceived aura of elitism that intimidates those who are unfamiliar with it. When people visit a local winery, however, much of that is dispelled. There is something about the honest toil of working a vineyard that legitimizes wine and sets it apart from previous

Vineyards alternate with hops and other crops in Washington's fertile Yakima Valley (OPPOSITE), a desert until irrigation tapped the mighty Columbia and Yakima rivers in the early 1900s. (PAGES 20–21): The Florida Mountains provide a backdrop to vineyards in the Mimbres Valley of southwestern New Mexico. (PAGES 22–23): Fall Creek Vineyards in the hill country west of Austin, Texas. Nearby Lake Buchanan (in background) helps moderate the warm temperatures of Texas summers.

19

notions about alcoholic beverages. Most American vineyards and wineries are family enterprises and, in much of the country, the winery is only a few steps from where the family lives and raises its children.

In this book I have divided the continent of North America into large geographic regions, each section embracing a fairly sizable area of the country. The Northeast, for example, includes New York, New England, Pennsylvania

and New Jersey. The South swings from Maryland to the Mississippi Delta. The Heartland comprises the north-central states and the Midwest, covering territory from the Ozark highlands to Michigan and Ohio. Texas and the southwestern states of New Mexico and Arizona are treated together, and the Northwest covers Oregon, Idaho and Washington. California gets a chapter all its own, as do both Canada and Mexico.

What emerges is a fairly broad survey of each region, highlighted with a more detailed look at specific properties. By focusing on one or two growers in each region, I try to convey something of what American winegrowers have achieved, what they are up against, what they hope to accomplish.

Choosing the wineries was not difficult. The painful aspect of the task was not being able to include more of them. The focus of this volume, therefore, is not encyclopedic; rather, it concentrates on the flavor, the look, the personal aspect of winegrowing in North America.* The visual charm and beauty of the vineyard landscape has been wonderfully captured by photographer Charles Dorris, who traveled extensively to search out images that reflect the life of American vineyards in all their variety of season and geography.

North America has yet to make its best wines, and who is to say from where these will come—Oregon, Virginia, Texas, Ontario, California? It is still too soon to judge. While in each region there are wines that are still somewhat awkward and amateurish, the exciting thing is that the wines everywhere are getting better and better, and will continue to do so. The golden age of American wine lies just ahead.

*For those readers who would like a comprehensive guide to the wines of America, I heartily recommend reading Leon Adams's *The Wines of America*.

*Snow in the vine-
yard acts as a
blanket, giving the
dormant vines a
layer of protection
against severe drops
in winter
temperatures.*

A YEAR IN THE VINEYARD

The winegrower's year is a busy one, for the active cycle of life in the vineyard is unceasing. In
the space of twelve months the vines grow, rip-
en, mature and go dormant until the process
begins again. The vine is always doing something, even in winter, when in a sense it "hiber-
nates" to protect the next season's growth from
the cold. The winegrower has year-round work
to do in the vineyard, though some periods involve little more than attentive waiting.

WINTER

It may seem odd to begin at what is usually considered to be the end of the year; but, while
many aspects of winegrowing end in winter,
others begin. The growth cycle actually starts
here, while the vines are still dormant. Buds for
the next year's crop have already formed, and
the tangle of canes left from the previous year
await pruning to make way for new growth. Before pruning, the winter vineyard looks a mess,
a snarl of wayward tendrils that trail about
helter-skelter. Trimmed and pruned, it becomes starkly neat, beautiful in its austerity.

The task of pruning is critical because it
determines the size, and therefore the quality,
of the new crop. The more clusters a vine bears,
the more dilute the intensity and character of

the fruit. Overcropping, or pruning for high
yield, is not desirable if you want wines of concentrated character, and it can have other detri-
mental effects as well. In marginal areas of cool
climate, too much fruit on the vine prohibits
ripening. Not only is poorer wine—thin, fla-
vorless, acidic—the result, but the health of
the vine itself may be endangered, since the
wood may not ripen sufficiently to withstand a
severe winter.

Timing can also be crucial. Pruning may
be undertaken as soon as the vines are fully dormant, usually in December or January. But in
areas subject to an early winter thaw followed by
freezing temperatures, such as Virginia, the
vines are pruned later to delay bud break and to
lessen the threat of damage from a sudden
freeze. Winter pruning is a tough and chilly
business, a labor-intensive process in a large
vineyard. On a bright brisk January day the
work can be exhilarating, but it is downright
painful in the finger-numbing cold of some
climates.

Each vine is pruned individually (machines that do the work are still in the experimental stage, and are costly). The old growth is
cut away and a specified number of buds per
cane are left for the current year's growth and
the year following.

The way the vines are trained—that is,
whether they stand alone or are tied to wires or
trellised—depends on the climate and the particular variety. In warm regions like Georgia,
vines may be trained high to provide better air
circulation and to keep them away from the
warm, moist earth that promotes rot. Elsewhere
they may be stretched horizontally along wires
for maximum sun exposure, and in still other
locations trained so that the fruit is shaded to
avoid sunburn.

Another winter chore is "hilling up." In
colder regions, like the Finger Lakes, Michigan
and the Okanagan Valley in British Columbia,
earth is piled up a foot or so around each vine to
protect the graft point against freezing temperatures. Winter is also a time for cleanup in
the winery and crucial winemaking tasks.

Racking, removing the new wine off the lees (the sediment that sinks to the bottom of a vat or cask in which a wine ages), often takes place in December or January. This is also a good time to blend the various lots of certain red wines, such as Cabernet Sauvignon, and run them into oak barrels for aging. If these tasks are accomplished early enough, there may be some time to relax, travel, or just coast until the vines are ready to become active again.

SPRING

As the days lengthen and the sun waxes warm, the vineyard responds like all else in nature. Sap starts moving in the vines, fattening the buds until they push open, unfolding in a delicate fringe of pinkish-green foliage. A month or so later sees the formation of flower buds, forerunners of the grape cluster. Bud break, as it is called, comes at various times, depending on the climate and the variety of grape. In the Finger Lakes district of New York, it happens

Pruning (TOP) *takes place in December at Laurel Glen Vineyard on Sonoma Mountain.* (BOTTOM): *Rootstock in a new vineyard at Chalone. The milk cartons placed around the vine stocks prevent the tender new growth from being devoured by jackrabbits and other nibblers.*

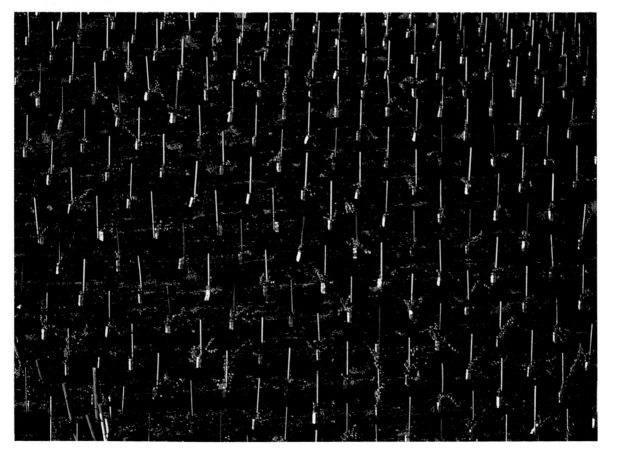

Soil nutrients being applied at Pheasant Ridge Winery in west Texas, near Lubbock.
When frost threatens, wind machines (OPPOSITE) like this one at Glenora in the Finger Lakes keep the air moving in the vineyard.

about the second week of May. In California it usually starts in March, occasionally earlier.

Spring is a beautiful time in the vineyard, but it can also be a dangerous period. One of the greatest threats to a vineyard is a late frost. Cold, clear spring nights make the winegrower nervous, especially around the time of a full moon, for these are the times when the temperature is likely to sink back down below the freezing point. Frost can be devastating to the tender young growth at this point; if the flower buds freeze they will turn black and fall off. Growers in frost-prone areas keep this in mind when establishing a vineyard by planting on slopes and avoiding flat or low-lying spots where cold air collects. When the temperatures drop below freezing on a spring night, the whole of Napa Valley knows about it. Huge airplane propellers stationed in the vineyards roar through the night, keeping the air moving and pulling warmer currents down onto the vines. Smudge pots and gas heaters are still used in some vineyards to raise temperatures. It does not always work.

The most effective protection against frost is also the costliest: sprinklers. Positioned among the vines, they spray a fine mist of water that freezes the moment it hits the buds. The action of freezing is the key, since it generates just enough heat to avoid freezing the bud as it forms a coat of ice that insulates against surrounding low temperatures.

Spring is also the time for laying out a new vineyard or cultivating an existing one, plowing under ground cover to provide nutrients to the soil, breaking up the earth for better drainage. The grower must now look for early signs of insects or mildew and take steps to get rid of them. Vines that were hilled up must be uncovered in spring, and it must be done early enough to prevent the wood from rotting in the moist warm soil.

SUMMER

June ushers in another critical time for the vine: flowering. Grapevine flowers are tiny and delicate, hardly what we think of as flowers at all.

Growers hope for warm, calm weather during flowering in order to get a good fruit set. Rain, wind or, worst of all, hail, can knock off the flowers, thereby reducing the amount of fruit. If it is cold, a condition known as shatter occurs, when the flowers burst and leave tiny hard berries that do not ripen.

The flowers give way to clusters of baby grapes and the leaves and roots produce the energy to make them grow. By mid-June the vines have a lush dense canopy of bright green. If the fruit set is heavy, the grower may go through the vineyard and cluster thin, trimming off bunches to aid ripening and promote greater intensity of flavor. If the vines show heat stress, they are irrigated. As summer warms up, humidity may become a problem; spraying to prevent mildew and rot is done on a regular schedule, and must be repeated after a rain. Spraying stops, however, some weeks before harvest is to begin.

Around August the vivid green grapes begin to change color, a part of the ripening process known as *veraison*. White varieties become translucent and take on a paler hue, becoming yellowish green or light gold. Black grapes darken to varying degrees of deep purple or midnight blue, often developing a dusty bloom on their surface. The process moves faster in warmer regions like Mississippi or Florida, beginning in late July or early August. In cooler areas the growing season extends well into October, especially for late-ripening varieties like Cabernet Sauvignon and Riesling.

AUTUMN

Harvest is the climax of the growing year and the most exciting time for winegrowers, winemakers and wine lovers. In wine regions everywhere, expectations are high and the tension in the air is palpable. The growers are out in the fields daily, checking the sugar and acidity levels of the grapes to ascertain the peak moment for picking. When the time arrives, the pickers fan out into the fields at dawn to pick the grapes while it is still cool. Mechanical harvesters,

which permit picking through the night, are increasingly used, not only in California but also in many other regions. The grapes arrive at the winery, are weighed in and dumped into the destemmer/crusher. The must, or juice, is then channeled into fermentation vats, where yeast is added. The transformation into wine has begun.

Basically, wine makes itself through the action of yeast cells (either the wild yeasts found on grapeskins or lab-developed strains that are added to the fermentation vat), which convert the grape sugars to alcohol. The challenge for the winemaker is to guide the process along, making the critical decisions at each step that will determine the style of the wine. Red wines are fermented with the crushed grapeskins, for they contain the pigments, tannin and flavoring elements that distinguish red wine from white. The fermentation usually takes only five or six days, but a winemaker may choose to leave the wine on the skins longer to pick up extra nuances of character or to soften the tannins.

For white wines, the juice is separated from the skins before fermentation, though for varietals like Chardonnay and Riesling, the juice and skins may remain in contact for some hours to give the wine more intensity of flavor. White wines are more fragile than red wines because they lack the stabilizing component of tannin, so they are fermented at lower temperatures than reds in order to protect against oxidation and to preserve the fruit aromas and flavors. Increasingly, the finer white varietals like Chardonnay and Sauvignon Blanc are barrel-fermented, which means that the fermentation takes place in sixty-gallon oak barrels. Sometimes only a portion of the juice is barrel-fermented, sometimes all of it. Though it is a lot more trouble to tend many small barrels than a single large stainless steel fermentation tank, some winemakers feel it gives the wine more interesting and complex flavor and greater aging potential. Simple whites like Chenin Blanc or Riesling are generally fermented in temperature-controlled stainless steel tanks.

Rosé or blush wines are made in the same

manner as white wines, but the juice remains with the grapeskins until it has picked up the degree of color desired, anywhere from a delicate pink, or "blush" (which is how blush wines got their name), to a deep rosy hue.

The next step after the fermentation process is a period of aging before the wines are bottled. Wines that are meant to be consumed quickly, when they are young and fresh, may spend only a couple of months in a settling tank, either a stainless steel vat or a large oak cask. The better wines, like Cabernet Sauvignon, Chardonnay, Pinot Noir and certain others, are aged in wood, either oak casks or small barrels (which are usually of sixty-gallon capacity). Oak lends additional flavor and complexity to the wine. Simpler whites and rosés are only rarely aged in oak, since the primary emphasis is on the fruit. The bigger whites, such as Chardonnay and Sauvignon Blanc, are aged in oak for anywhere from three months to a year. Red wines remain even longer, sixteen to twenty-four months, as a rule.

Some harvests are more hectic than others, especially when heat spells hasten the process and everything ripens at once. When the crunch is on, vineyard and winery crews operate around the clock. It is exhausting, but the adrenalin flows and keeps spirits high. When the grapes are in and the vats are filled with new wine, it is time to celebrate with a harvest feast. The wine flows liberally, and the fruits of past labors are quaffed in toasts to the new vintage.

CHAPTER ONE

VINEYARDS OF THE NORTHEAST

AMERICA'S POTENTIAL FOR WINEGROWING WAS first recognized in the Middle Ages. Eric the Red's son Leif and his band of Vikings scanned the shores around the year 1000 and found grapevines to be so abundant that they wrote "Vinland" on their maps. This suggests that the Norsemen plied the coast in summer, when the luxuriant growth of the vines was easy to spot and identify. How far they ventured down the coast is uncertain, but some five hundred years later another group of Europeans also became encouraged by the abundance of wild grapes that flourished at many points along the entire length of the Atlantic coast. It is well known that the Mayflower Pilgrims put in at Plymouth because they had run out of drink as well as food, "... our victuals being much spent, especially our beere."

The Northeast, which for our purposes encompasses New England, New York, Pennsylvania and New Jersey, has played a vital role in the history of American winegrowing, and has done so in the face of great odds. The first settlers tried to establish vineyards the moment they landed. John Winthrop, first governor of the Massachusetts Bay Colony, attempted to grow vines from cuttings brought over by ships that followed the Mayflower, but the vines soon died. People thought it was the severe cold that killed the European vines, and that was indeed part of it, but it took another two hundred years to discover that the vine's worst enemy was not the cold, but a little bug known as phylloxera, a root aphid that avidly dines on the tender roots of the European species. Over the ages, American vine species like *Vitis riparia*, *Vitis rotundifolia*, *Vitis aestivalis* and *Vitis labrusca* developed tough roots impervious to the bug. But *Vitis vinifera*, the European species whose Latin name literally means "the winemaking vine," was vulnerable. Still, the settlers persisted in their winegrowing efforts by turning to native species when vinifera failed. By the early 1800s, grape scientists had come up with hybridized labrusca varieties that withstood the cold better and were more resistant to pests and diseases: Catawba, Delaware, Isabella, Niagara, Ives and others. The infamous Concord, which was to give Eastern wines a reputation for "foxiness" (an aggressive wild grape aroma and flavor that comes from a component known as methyl anthranilate) they have yet to live down completely, was developed in New England by Ephraim Wales Bull. Named for the Massachusetts town where Bull lived, it was offered to local nurseries in 1854.

Vineyards of the Northeast share the problem of poor image that has come from cultivation of the native labrusca species. Americans may like this flavor in grape juice, jams and candy, but it becomes too exaggerated when grape juice is fermented into wine. For years, wineries of the Northeast ameliorated the taste with wines from California or with water. It was not until the mid-1950s that new notions of which grapes could survive in cold climates emerged, first with French-American hybrid varieties (French varieties developed on cold-hardy American rootstocks, commonly referred to as French hybrids) and, later, with the traditional European, or vinifera, varieties.

It is these developments that have made winegrowing in the Northeast viable (if not yet very profitable). The 1970s ushered in a growth

Among the winegrowers that are beginning to succeed with the vine in New England is Crosswoods Vineyards, near Stonington, Connecticut, which was founded in 1978.

spurt in the industry, which was followed by a setback in the early 1980s in some regions (upper New York State, for example). But as can be seen in the young wineries featured in this chapter, many regions have made rapid strides in producing wines to please discriminating palates.

NEW YORK

New York has the longest tradition of winegrowing on a major scale in the East, which, in recent years, has been more of a burden than a blessing. No winemaking region in the country is in a greater state of flux and transition than New York, its biggest difficulty being the effort to wrench free of a reputation for unpalatable wines, the "jelly-jar" image created by wines made from Concord, Catawba and other grapes more suitable for toast spreads than table wines. Erasing a poor image is far harder than building a new one from scratch, and it has been easier for places that had no modern winegrowing tradition, like Texas or Virginia, to gain acceptance for their wines than it has been for New York's classic wine regions—the Finger Lakes and the Hudson Valley—to change negative perceptions of their wines.

This is unfair. The changes over the last ten years are as dramatic in New York as they have been in some of the country's brand new wine-producing regions. A renaissance in New York winegrowing is already underway with a strong trend toward vinifera varieties. Some excellent wines—Chardonnay, Riesling, sparkling wines, even Pinot Noir—are being made. But how long will it take wine drinkers to realize it? One of the greatest obstacles is the Eastern wine market. The East Coast corridor, with its large metropolitan centers—Boston, New York, Washington, Miami—has such an influx of imported and California wines at competitive prices that wine drinkers exhibit little interest in wines from New York, New England or elsewhere in the Northeast. Local markets for the wines are often quite good, but in the cities it has proven impossible to gain the inroads that would provide the wines with exposure and rec-

ognition; yet without such recognition they are not taken seriously. This is a problem that should be ameliorated with time, as the wines gradually become better known, and consumers recognize their quality. Meantime, the wineries must survive and try to exand, but it is a tough job for small producers.

THE FINGER LAKES REGION

The Finger Lakes region certainly offers the challenge. Winegrowing here goes back to the 1820s. Of New York's four wine regions—the Finger Lakes, Erie-Chautauqua (which includes the Niagara Peninsula), the Hudson Valley and eastern Long Island—this is the largest in area and the most scenic. Its name derives from the uniquely shaped bodies of water that extend south of the New York Thruway between Rochester and Syracuse. "Fingerprints of the Great Spirit," the Indians called these elongated lakes set among the hills and woodlands of western New York. Some hold that they were gouged from the earth thousands of years ago as the last glaciers retreated; others claim that ancient upheavals created deep fissures that were further carved out by cataract plunges similar to those that rage over Niagara Falls. There are eleven lakes, varying in length from ten to forty miles. The three most significant in terms of grape-growing are Keuka, Seneca and Cayuga.

The lakes are large enough and deep enough to have a moderating effect on the climate of the region, making it excellent for fruits and other crops. The Indian tribes that made up the powerful Iroquois League in the seventeenth and eighteenth centuries grew corn, grapes, peaches and apples here. Soldiers who had fought in the French and Indian Wars returned to the area to settle, and a young clergyman was the first to plant vineyards in 1828. Other settlers began to plant vineyards and make their own wines. By the 1860s the first commercial wineries were established around Hammondsport, a town near Keuka Lake that became the first wine center of the East. Some of New York's largest wineries, Taylor, Great Western and Gold Seal (closed in 1984), were established here during those years.

From the beginning, the emphasis was on sparkling wines; New York even became known as the "Champagne District of America." The wines were made mostly from Catawba and other labrusca varieties, but they developed quite a following. Table wines and fortified dessert wines were made as well. A strong industry developed in the late nineteenth century, and despite their flavors, which were so different from those of European wines, New York wines won medals at the Paris Exposition of 1900. Already, however, the move toward Prohibition had begun. A large portion of New York grapes, especially Concord, began to go to juice companies that sprang up, like Welch's, founded by the Welch brothers, who were fanatically against wine. Prohibition effectively destroyed the wine industry in New York as it did everywhere in the country. Of the fifty wineries in the Finger Lakes before Prohibition, only six reopened their doors in 1933. Gradually the industry revived and recovered, however, and well into the 1960s New York continued to produce most of the domestic champagne sold in America.

The seeds of change in the American wine market were sown about this time, as more Americans discovered European wines, and California began producing wines from the same grape varieties grown in Europe. New York might have moved ahead sooner had it listened to Dr. Konstantin Frank, a Russian-born immigrant who arrived in the United States in 1947. A viticulturist by trade, he headed for the Finger Lakes to pursue his calling, grapegrowing. He insisted that grapes like Chardonnay, Riesling, Muscat, even Cabernet Sauvignon could be grown in the Finger Lakes, but New York scientists at the State Agricultural Experimental Station in Geneva said it was impossible. Dr. Frank knew better because he had grown these varieties in the Ukraine, where winters were far colder than those in New York. The only man who did listen was Charles Fournier, who had come from France's Champagne

Ornamental ironwork at West Park Wine Cellars in New York's Hudson Valley.

district in 1934 to make sparkling wines at Gold Seal. Dr. Frank joined him there and together the two men planted experimental plots of Chardonnay and other vinifera, eventually producing New York's best sparkling Blanc de Blancs.

In the early 1950s Konstantin Frank began acquiring land on the western shores of Keuka Lake, where he planted an all-vinifera vineyard. People thought he was crazy, and his feisty, stubborn, outspoken zeal did not enhance his popularity. Vindication came in 1957, however, as Leon Adams describes:

In February 1957 came the crucial test. Temperatures on the lake slopes plummeted to 25 degrees below zero. Some of the hardiest labrusca vines—the native varieties—were frozen and bore no grapes. But on the first Chardonnay and Riesling vines that had been grafted on hardy roots, fewer than a tenth of the buds showed any damage.

Konstantin Frank, who died in 1985, is hailed today as the father of vinifera winegrowing east of California. In 1964 Dr. Frank opened his own winery, Vinifera Wine Cellars, where he produced Rieslings, Chardonnays and other wines that were considered remarkable and sold for the same prices as their counterparts from Germany and France. Sometimes the wines were not so special, since Dr. Frank was more interested in viticulture than in winemaking, and he spent a great deal of time and energy railing against French hybrids, which he felt were a waste of time and produced wines little better than the labrusca. But he managed to prove undeniably that the Finger Lakes could produce wines of exceptional character, especially whites.

In 1986 I came across a bottle of Dr. Frank's 1975 Riesling that I had forgotten I had. Thinking it surely was oxidized, I almost threw it out, but decided to chill it and see. To my amazement the wine was superb: Off-dry, more Germanic in style than any American Riesling I had tasted, it was like a *Kabinett* Riesling from the Rhinepfalz. The wine had the flowery aromas typical of a fine Riesling, but more significant were its depth of flavor and complexity of character. Far superior to any of the drier Rieslings produced in California, it was over ten years old. That wine convinced me of what is possible in the Finger Lakes. If the industry can survive the struggle to forge a new identity, its greatest period lies ahead. Wines I have tasted since have only reinforced this feeling.

Changing trends, however, had a disastrous effect on the region. Still in the grip of native varieties like Concord, Delaware and Catawba, the Finger Lakes got left behind in the wine boom of the 1960s and 1970s. Consumers turned to wines from Europe, California and other regions whose products were better with food and were more to their taste. The large wineries like Taylor, Great Western, Widmer and Canandaigua, however, continued to purchase labrusca varieties from Finger Lakes growers, encouraging only gradual expansion into cold-hardy French hybrids like Seyval Blanc, Aurora, Ravat, Vidal and Chancellor. As long as they could sell their grapes, growers were re-

luctant to pull out existing vineyards and replant with hybrids and particularly vinifera, which were riskier to grow, lower in yield and difficult to care for. The day finally came, however, when the large firms no longer wanted the native grapes. They saw the declining market for these wines and began importing wines from California by the truckload. Finger Lakes grape prices began to slip, plunging to an all-time low in 1984 and 1985. Varieties like Delaware that once had brought four hundred dollars a ton were sold for one hundred dollars. It was a bleak time; vineyards were plowed under or simply abandoned as some growers went broke.

An intrepid few, however, had seen the handwriting on the wall. Small growers and wineries had begun experimenting with Riesling and Chardonnay and found, like Dr. Frank, that the vines could survive. It was risky, though; yields from these varieties were low, which meant small production, and the vines demanded a great deal more care and labor in the vineyard than did French hybrids or labrusca varieties. This made for tough going financially, and it was impossible to compete under the same restrictive laws that governed the big wineries, with their vast distribution networks and capital resources. In 1976 the state legislature passed a farm winery bill that gave a break to the small wineries. This law, which limited production to 50,000 gallons, reduced license fees and taxes, and permitted wineries to sell their wines on the premises and to remain open for business on Sunday. It was the most positive thing that could have happened to New York's wine industry. In the decade after the bill was passed, some fifty new wineries opened in every region of the state. The Farm Winery Act essentially launched a new era for New York wine. Though small, the wineries' impact was large. They were the ones making the new and stylish wines that won attention from critics and consumers.

Winegrowing in the Finger Lakes will never be easy, but it rarely is in the marginal areas that often produce the best wines. For some winegrowers in this region, merely surviving is a triumph. That is so, at least, for Peter Johnstone of Heron Hill, a winery overlooking Keuka Lake not far from Dr. Frank's vineyard. Johnstone was a New York City advertising executive who vacationed in the Finger Lakes one summer and fell in love with the region.

Johnstone purchased twenty-five acres here in 1968, planted the traditional Concord and Catawba, then promptly proceeded to rip them out. In 1971 he began replanting the vineyard with Riesling and Chardonnay, but soon realized that he had made a poor choice of site for vinifera. A saddle in the ridge above Heron Hill acts as a conduit for cold air, sending it streaming down the mountainside in winter. "We're ten degrees colder than my neighbor and we never know how we'll survive the winter," said Johnstone. "The good Lord takes 80 percent of the buds on the vine. We get no more than two tons—sometimes only a ton and three quarters—of fruit per acre."

That is low, even for vinifera, which, in more favorable spots around the region, yields up to three or four tons per acre. Johnstone must bury his vines—referred to as "hilling up"—most winters to protect them, demonstrating one of the reasons why growing vinifera in the Finger Lakes is a labor-intensive process.

Heron Hill makes crisp, appealing wines. Johnstone grows only Chardonnay and Riesling, but buys hybrid grapes from other growers to meet production capacity. Most winegrowers in the Finger Lakes hedge their vinifera bets by growing French hybrids, which not only are hardier, but also produce bigger yields, resulting in more wine to sell. This helps a great deal with cash flow, and people like them. Some of the wineries' bestsellers are hybrid blends that are light, fruity, inexpensive. For example, Peter Johnstone's partner is John Ingle, whose vineyards on Canandaigua, the next lake to the west, bear French hybrids like Seyval Blanc and Ravat in addition to Chardonnay and Riesling.

Heron Hill produces about 15,000 cases of wine a year under two labels, Heron Hill and

Some of the steepest hills in the Finger Lakes region surround Keuka Lake. Heron Hill Vineyard occupies the western slopes above

Midday harvesting at Heron Hill (TOP) yields lug boxes full of grapes, such as their Riesling (BOTTOM).

Otter Spring, the difference between them being stylistic. Heron Hill wines are fermented entirely in stainless steel and tend to be drier than those under the Otter Spring label. Some, like the Reserve Chardonnay, are aged in French oak. Heron Hill Rieslings have about 1 percent sugar, though they taste almost dry because of high acidity. Otter Spring Rieslings are lighter but sweeter, and are made only from what is known as free run, the juice that runs off as the grapes are crushed before pressing. They are charming and delicate wines, sweet but not overly so, again because the sweetness is balanced with high acidity, which keeps them fresh and crisp. Heron Hill made its reputation with Riesling and makes two or three Rieslings each year, including late-harvest dessert Rieslings that have the honeyed character of noble rot (*Botrytis cinerea*), the same mold that plays a crucial role in the production of the great sweet wines of Germany and Sauternes. Botrytis mold is destructive to most grape varieties, but on certain ones, Riesling, Muscat, Gewürztraminer, Sauvignon Blanc and Sémillon among them, it works a miraculous transformation, and the wine becomes a luscious sweet nectar with aromas of honey, apricots and peaches. Ideal conditions for botrytis are humidity followed by warm, dry weather during harvest, and these occur frequently in the Finger Lakes. We shall meet this beneficent mold again in other regions.

Peter Johnstone plans to expand production at Heron Hill by investing in new equipment that will give his wines more finesse, and by hiring an experienced winemaker to relieve him of at least some of the job. He also wants to experiment with other vinifera, mainly reds like Cabernet Sauvignon and Merlot.

The New York wines that have made the greatest impact outside the state come from around Seneca Lake, the deepest of the Finger Lakes and one of the longest. It is only forty miles from Keuka by car, but the microclimate is quite different. The slopes bordering Seneca are gentler, so the vines are much closer to the water. Dr.

Nelson Shaulis, the Cooperative Extension Service viticulturist for the state of New York, called this "the banana belt" of the Finger Lakes because Seneca Lake right here is at its deepest and widest, so it never freezes like Keuka does. Glenora is a tiny hamlet on the west side of Seneca near the little town of Dundee. Remnants of the lakeside village, which was once a thriving lakeport, remain, but it is now mostly filled with summer homes. The game of Monopoly was developed in one of the old buildings down by the water, and the original playing board still hangs over the fireplace.

Gene Pierce, founder and co-owner of Glenora-on-Seneca, has his home down by the lake, some three hundred yards below the winery. It was mid-November when I visited Glenora. We looked out over vineyards covered with the first snow of the season. The past and the future of the Finger Lakes lay right there, a juxtaposition of the old and the new. Immediately below the winery is an old Concord vineyard, planted in 1943. Next to it is an even older

stand of Catawba, planted around the turn of the century. Beyond that is Gene Pierce's best Riesling. Bottled separately from the other Riesling produced by Glenora and labeled Spring Ledge Vineyard, it is Glenora's most consistent medal winner. This wine has the delicate flowery fragrance typical of good Riesling; it has about 2 percent residual sugar, which makes it lightly sweet, but high acidity keeps it crisp and fresh. As we tasted it, I asked Gene what he would serve with it. "Bosc pears and Brie," he replied. An excellent combination, I agree, but I also feel it is the kind of wine that is delightful to drink just on its own: light, clean and appealing.

Aiming for precisely that style, Glenora uses very little oak for aging, as little sulphur dioxide as possible and no other preservatives (such as potassium sorbate). Freshness, crispness and clean simplicity are the hallmarks of these wines, all of which are white. Most of them are off-dry or lightly sweet, except for the Chardonnay and the sparkling Blanc de Blancs, one of the country's best sparkling wines. It is about 95 percent Chardonnay, the rest Pinot Noir, a bright, brisk wine that greatly impressed the French winemakers who recently came to Glenora as part of an experiment.

A couple of years ago a wealthy Frenchman, encouraged by the quality of Finger Lakes grapes, proposed the idea of sending over a French winemaker to produce a French-style dry white from Finger Lakes grapes. Pierce found the idea interesting and the first wine, labeled Château Liberté (in honor of the Statue of Liberty centennial), was made in 1985. A bone-dry blend of Chardonnay, Seyval Blanc and Cayuga, the wine proved popular, so in 1986 an additional 5,000 cases were made. If success continues, production may go to 40,000 cases.

Glenora, now at about 15,000 cases, has been eager to expand and is in the process of merging with one of the younger wineries on Keuka Lake, Finger Lakes Wine Cellars, whose wines are quite similar in style to those of Glenora. Combined production will be about 30,000 cases annually. The style of the wines may also change a bit, moving toward more richness under new winemaker James Gifford, who was trained in California and favors somewhat riper grapes and more use of oak. Gene Pierce also has plans for a new vineyard across the lake, where they will plant Merlot and Cabernet Sauvignon. Neither has been truly successful in the Finger Lakes to date because the growing season is rarely long enough to ripen them. On Seneca, however, prevailing winds are from the north-northwest, bringing warmer air off Lake Ontario. "The warmer air creates a kind of thermos effect," Gene said. "If there is any place you can do Cab or Merlot around here, it has to be there, right next to this hot water bottle of a lake, which doesn't freeze."

A few miles up the road from Glenora are the vineyards and winery of Hermann J. Wiemer, who was the first to plant vinifera grapes on the banks of Seneca Lake. If anyone can be said to have inherited the mantle of Konstantin Frank in the East, it is Hermann Wiemer. Born and raised in Bernkastel, Germany, the most famous wine town on the Mosel River, he is a member of the third generation of a family of grapegrowers. Wiemer came to the Finger Lakes in 1968 to be a winemaker at Bully Hill on Keuka Lake. Bully Hill was at that time producing wines mostly from French hybrids, but Wiemer was convinced as soon as he saw the Finger Lakes that early-ripening vinifera varieties like Chardonnay, Riesling and Pinot Noir would do well. He recognized that Seneca Lake had better soil and microclimate for wine grapes than Keuka, so he bought land there and planted experimental plots of hybrids and vinifera in 1973. The vinifera grapes, mostly Chardonnay and Riesling, proved hardier in some instances than the hybrids.

Wiemer has since become an outspoken exponent of vinifera in the Finger Lakes. Though not as vociferously against hybrids as Dr. Frank, Wiemer is nevertheless highly critical of them. "These are not the wines that people want to drink," he insists. "The market proves that. People know more today and are demanding better wines, wines of the quality that comes from vinifera. We'll never get anywhere as long as people associate New York with odd-tasting wines." Naturally there is argument on this point, since a number of quite attractive wines are made from French hybrids.

Wiemer's first vintage was 1979: a Chardonnay and an off-dry Riesling. These wines won immediate acclaim and were among the first Finger Lakes wines to appear on wine lists at some of New York City's best restaurants. Hermann Wiemer's Chardonnay is crisp and clean, the flavor enhanced with a light touch of oak from barrel aging. He likes to fool people with his sparkling wine, labeled Finger Lakes Champagne Naturel. Bone dry, very finely balanced, it is made entirely by the *méthode champenoise*, but from all Riesling grapes instead of the traditional Chardonnay and Pinot Noir.

In addition to Chardonnay and Riesling, he grows Pinot Noir, Gewürztraminer and the true variety of Gamay that grows in Beaujolais.

Wagner Vineyards, with its distinctive octagon-shaped winery (TOP), *also operates a small restaurant named for owner Bill Wagner's granddaughter.* (BOTTOM): *Sparkling wines at Hermann J. Wiemer repose in riddling racks, a critical step in the traditional French method of creating champagne.*

Wiemer is most excited about Pinot Noir, which he feels has a real future in the Finger Lakes. When I tasted his 1986 Pinot, drawn from barrel in the cellar, I could understand why. For years, American winegrowers have struggled to make Pinot Noir with the finesse and savory flavors of the best red Burgundy. It has been an elusive quest, though in recent years some very excellent wines have emerged. It would surprise many wine lovers if the quest for exceptional Pinot Noir led to Seneca Lake, but the 1986 wine was most persuasive. The aromas had that enticing sweet spice of fine Burgundy; the flavors were round and delicate but not thin like so many American Pinot Noirs. It was a very attractive wine, with enough tannin to give it the structure it needs for aging. There is not a lot of it, a mere 2,000 cases that will be sold only at the winery.

Wiemer left Bully Hill in 1980. He now owns ninety acres of vinifera on Seneca Lake. In addition to the winery and vineyard he has a thriving nursery business, supplying grafted vinifera stock to wineries all over the United States. Working with local Mennonites as laborers, he has developed a technique that is 95 percent effective for grafting vine cuttings onto rootstock. Texas winegrowers, his best customers, find Wiemer's cuttings more reliable than those from California. Further, since it is much easier to plant a rooted cutting than to first plant rootstock and then graft the desired variety onto it, Wiemer's cuttings are labor saving.

On the opposite side of Seneca, another success story is Wagner Vineyards. Bill Wagner has grown grapes for thirty years on the eastern side of Seneca near the town of Lodi. He started with native grapes and French hybrids, later adding Chardonnay and Riesling, building to his present 135 acres of vinifera and hybrids. The handsome octagon-shaped winery of red pine and hemlock was built in 1975.

Wagner lies in one of the warmest locations in the Finger Lakes region. It stands above the deepest part of the lake, where warmer

Riesling grapes (LEFT) *display signs of the early stages of* Botrytis cinerea, *the mold that makes luscious, honeyed sweet wines.* (RIGHT): *A carboy of just-fermented Chardonnay.*

winds from the northwest give an extra couple of weeks' ripening time. Employing more California techniques (such as oak aging, lees contact and barrel-fermentation) than any other Finger Lakes winery, Wagner produces primarily Chardonnay and Seyval Blanc. Both are made in a rich, full-bodied oaky style, quite different from most New York wines, which tend to be leaner, crisper and more austere.

Wagner Seyval Blanc is in a class by itself. The most widely grown of the French hybrids, Seyval is the Northeast's workhorse variety among whites, fairly neutral in flavor and thus subject to a wide variety of interpretations. Wagner's Seyval is barrel-fermented; that is, fermentation takes place in an oak barrel instead of a large stainless steel tank. This technique is frequently employed with Chardonnay, to which it gives a rounder, more interesting flavor dimension, but it is an unusual technique with Seyval. Wagner's rich-flavored, oaky wine, however, has prompted a few other Eastern wineries to try the technique.

Wagner Chardonnay, also barrel-fermented, is made from riper grapes than are most New York Chardonnays. This stylistic preference results in a rich, oaky, full-bodied wine similar in style to California Chardonnays, though not as dry. Wagner Chardonnays tend to have a barely perceptible sweetness that many wine drinkers find appealing. Wagner Riesling and Gewürztraminer, both lightly sweet, are quite good, and its Pinot Noir, first produced commercially in 1986, is highly promising. One of the nicest ways to sample Wagner wines is at the winery's restaurant-café. Wagner also has a tasting outlet and retail store in New York City.

ERIE-CHAUTAUQUA

Though the Finger Lakes is the best known of New York's wine regions, the area with the largest vineyard acreage is the Erie-Chautauqua wine belt some 150 miles to the west. Over half of New York's grape production comes from here, the greatest part of it Concord, Catawba and other labrusca varieties. Some 1,700 of the state's 2,000 vineyards are located here—mostly small, family-owned properties averaging 35 acres or so. Wine coolers such as Seagram's Golden Cooler and Canandaigua's Sun Country absorb an enormous quantity of grapes from the area, largely labruscas.

Some feel, however, that in terms of climate Erie-Chautauqua is even more amenable to vinifera varieties than the Finger Lakes. "I am very bullish on vinifera here," says Dr. Robert Pool, associate professor of viticulture at the New York State Agricultural Experimental Station at Geneva, who cites the moderating effect of the Great Lakes—Erie and Ontario—in keeping temperatures warmer for a longer growing season. The soil, he adds, is similar to the Graves district of Bordeaux—gravelly, nutrient-poor and well drained. Dr. Pool is currently working with small estates in the region to determine which of the vinifera varieties will perform best at each. Wineries like Woodbury and Chadwick Bay have already done well with Chardonnay, Riesling and sparkling wine from vinifera varieties.

Chadwick Bay has no vineyards of its own but buys French hybrids and vinifera from local growers. The Woodbury family have been fruit growers in Chautauqua County along the shore of Lake Erie since 1910. They first planted vinifera varieties in 1966 on a gravel beach ridge formed centuries ago by glacial deposits. Pleased with the vineyard's quality grapes, in 1979 third-generation Gary Woodbury founded Woodbury Vineyards, which has some fifty acres devoted to wine grapes. In addition to Chardonnay and Riesling, Woodbury grows Pinot Gris, Pinot Noir, Gewürztraminer, Cabernet Sauvignon and French hybrids such as Seyval Blanc, Léon Millot, Vidal and Maréchal Foch. One of their best wines is the Blanc de Blancs, a sparkling wine made entirely from Chardonnay.

THE HUDSON VALLEY

The Hudson Valley wine region lies fifty or so miles north of New York City and is the oldest wine-producing area in the state. Huguenots planted vines in the early 1700s around New Paltz, and in the 1780s a cluster of vineyards thrived at Marlborough-on-Hudson. Newspapers of the nineteenth century, such as *Harper's Weekly* and *Frank Leslie's Illustrated Newspaper*, published numerous articles about the burgeoning wine industry along the Hudson, with illustrations of the harvest and the loading of grapes and wine barrels on riverboats.

Mark Miller, proprietor of Benmarl, one of the leading Hudson Valley wineries and the first established here in the modern era, tells the story of the Hudson Valley vineyards in his charming book, *Wine—A Gentleman's Game*. Miller notes that the mid-Hudson corresponds in latitude to Rome, giving it a long ripening period very suitable for wine grapes.

There were some 13,000 acres of vineyard in the Hudson Valley by 1900. The vines periodically succumbed to mildew, however, and gradually the valley growers converted their vineyards to orchards. The region became noted primarily for apples, pears and other fruits. Today, the Hudson Valley is a delightful place to visit, and an easy day's excursion from New York City. Farmstands offer an abundance of local fruits in autumn, including apples we do not often see in supermarkets, like Northern Spy, Cortlands, Pippins and Macouns. The tide is again turning in the Hudson Valley, however; in recent years vineyards have started to supplant orchards on both sides of the river. The two largest wineries are Brotherhood Winery, which is not run by a brotherhood but by a corporation, and Royal Winery, which produces a large line of kosher wines under the Kedem label.

The twenty-two wineries in the Hudson region of today are situated both on the western bluffs overlooking the river and in pretty little valleys east of it. Most of these are small, family-owned operations, many of which were

Wagner Vineyards (TOP) *puts mechanical technology to work* (BOTTOM) *at harvest time.*

started as hobbies by artists, doctors and businessmen. French hybrid varieties constitute the largest plantings in the Hudson Valley at the moment, primarily Seyval Blanc, Aurora and Vidal among white varieties, with red-wine grapes being represented primarily by Chancellor, Maréchal Foch and Baco Noir. Benmarl has produced good blended red wines, like Marlborough Village Red and Hudson Region Red; round, fruity, smooth, they make very nice accompaniments to beef or lamb. The Hudson is most noted for whites, however, and for Seyval Blanc in particular. It turns up in a variety of styles: crisp, lean, dry Muscadet-like from Cottage Vineyards; off-dry, fresh and fruity from Clinton Vineyards; round and fuller bodied from Benmarl (made "in the Burgundian style we aim for with most of our wines," says Mark Miller; that is, full-bodied and aged in French oak). Clinton even makes a sparkling wine from Seyval that is sprightly, dry and quite good.

Vinifera grapes are grown on a very limited basis in the Hudson Valley. In the late 1970s Benmarl began to grow some Chardonnay and Pinot Noir, and Ben Feder of Clinton Vineyards, a specialist in Seyval Blanc, started experimental plots of Chardonnay and Riesling. On Christmas Eve 1980, temperatures plunged some fifty degrees to register below zero. Following the long autumn of mild temperatures, during which the vines had not hardened enough to withstand the freeze, the sudden drop in temperature froze the vines and killed them. The "Christmas Massacre," as it is commonly referred to, decimated the 1981 harvest for many growers throughout the state. Ben Feder lost all the buds on his Seyval Blanc and made only apple wine that year. His vinifera vines were totally wiped out, and he has not replanted them. Such catastrophes are not frequent here, but history suggests that severe freezes strike about once every fifteen years.

This blow may have discouraged some growers from planting vinifera, but new efforts indicate that the interest is still there. The brightest new spot in the Hudson Valley is devoted entirely to Chardonnay, which is grown on western slopes above the river at West Park Vineyard. Owner Louis Fiore, having spent time in the Hudson Valley, had dreamed of owning a farm and making wine—the kind of wine he had enjoyed during a stay in Belgium and travels in France. In 1980 he acquired 800 acres at West Park that had originally been part of a dairy farm owned by the Christian Brothers of Ireland, who have a monastery nearby. Fiore decided he wanted to make only Chardonnay and staked out his first vineyard in 1981, harvesting his first commercial vintage only two years later.

West Park is small, with a production of some 2,400 cases a year. Fiore would like to double that eventually, but he and Nelda Bennett, West Park's viticulturist and winemaker, have their hands full with current production and intend to expand slowly. The winery complex has the quaint look of a typical Hudson Valley farm. The original dairy barn houses the tasting and sales room, the laboratory, and rows of oak barrels used for aging Chardonnay. A

large dining room, which was built on an upper level and is popular for local private parties as well as Fiore's special wine dinners, resounds with music and laughter on summer weekends. The oldest building, a 130-year-old hay barn, was restored in 1986 to be the winery's champagne cellar, where West Park's sparkling *cuvée* is made. The cellar's thick stone walls, built into the hillside, create an ideal cool environment for aging the wine.

This is a marginal area for Chardonnay. "We absolutely have to go by the book," says Nelda Bennett. "You can't make mistakes. If it says spray [against mildew] on the fourteenth day, you can't wait. If it rains that day, you must do it the day after. You run into trouble if you get off the track." On the hill above the winery, visitors can catch a glimpse of the Hudson through the trees. The river has a significant effect on the microclimate year round. It moderates the cold in winter, making it five to ten degrees warmer than New Paltz, which is about six miles inland. The vines have proved hardy so

Patricia Lenz feeds ripe Merlot grapes to Julia Child, her pet Nubian goat.

*Peter Lenz (at right)
and winemaker
Gary Galleron
bring in Merlot at
Lenz Vineyards on
Long Island's North
Fork.*

far, though there has been no repeat of the Christmas Massacre to test them. The soil rarely freezes below twenty degrees, but as a safeguard they hill up the vines here as do the growers in the Finger Lakes. Pruning is done very late—in March when the danger of severe cold is past. "It's two months of work crammed into three weeks," Fiore told me. "We wish we could start earlier, but it is too dangerous."

Spring frost is blessedly rare here, another advantage of being close to the river, which sends warm air up the hill. The climate is just severe enough to stress the vines a bit and force some interesting flavor into the grapes. "You need stress to get character," remarked Bennett. "They get it in Europe with poor soil, in California by lack of water. Here, it is the cold temperatures."

Fiore's vineyard and winery helpers are students from the Culinary Institute of America in Hyde Park, just across the Mid-Hudson Bridge. The students also prepare meals for lunches and dinners at the winery, giving West Park a good exposure to America's future chefs. The students learn a lot about wine in the process, so it is a fortuitous exchange of talent and opportunity.

West Park Chardonnay has already given a much-needed boost to vinifera in the Hudson Valley. The first three vintages made excellent wines, steely and elegant, somewhat like classic French Chablis in style, with a touch of oak that gives it nice complexity. Lou Fiore sells half his production right from the winery to local residents and Hudson Valley tourists.

LONG ISLAND

New York's newest wine region is on Long Island, out at the eastern tip where the island forks, around Sag Harbor. The North Fork, long an agricultural area, once boasted 60,000 acres of potato fields, along with other crops including cauliflower, pumpkins and corn. Agriculture began losing ground to real estate development in the 1960s, but this trend has been slowed by the advent winegrowing.

Alex and Louisa Hargrave are Long Island's wine pioneers. They planted a vineyard in 1973 consisting of forty acres of Cabernet Sauvignon, Merlot, Pinot Noir, Riesling, Chardonnay and Sauvignon Blanc. It took a few years for the wines to gain acceptance, but as the vines matured the wines got better, luring others into winegrowing. Today there are more than a dozen vineyards on the North Fork, and a few on the South Fork in the Hamptons.

Patricia and Peter Lenz were visiting Bordeaux when they got the idea of starting a vineyard. "If you close your eyes and blink," said Patricia, "you think you're on Long Island—with the same pines, the same scrubby, flat landscape and a breezy maritime climate. We understood then why the Hargraves had thought it possible." The Lenzes had operated a highly successful restaurant in Westhampton Beach called A Moveable Feast, which they sold in 1979. They then began looking for another venture. The Lenzes considered moving to Napa Valley, but settled on the North Fork because they liked life on Long Island and felt that its cooler climate is more akin to Bordeaux and Burgundy.

It also presented more of a challenge. "We would have been just another winery in California," said Peter. "Here there is a chance to prove something." They planted the vineyard in 1980 and within five years the wines of Lenz Vineyards were on the wine lists of a dozen top restaurants in Manhattan. The Lenzes make three varietal wines—Chardonnay, Gewürztraminer and Merlot—plus a red blended from Cabernet and Merlot called Lenz Reserve, and a small quantity of sparkling wine.

The most exciting aspect of Long Island's entry into winegrowing is the potential for red wines here, one of the few places in the Northeast where red vinifera like Cabernet Sauvignon and Merlot are successfully grown. The Long Island growing season is up to two weeks longer than it is upstate, so later-ripening varieties can be cultivated. In fact, the vines are so vigorous that they control them by using European spacing, planting a third more vines per acre than is

typical for this country. Competing for nutrients limits the yield and results in more concentrated fruit and hardier vines.

Long Island's most critical problem is hurricanes. The wind can rip the leaves or shower them with salt spray, either of which halts the ripening process. Torrential rains can destroy the grapes, or dilute them severely. In 1985 a splendid harvest was in progress when Hurricane Gloria whirled through. Power was knocked out at some wineries at a time when wineries are often active around the clock, and the wind and salt spray affected some of the Merlot and Cabernet. Fortunately, the hurricane did far less damage than was feared.

Merlot does particularly well on the North Fork, and several wineries make good ones. Lenz Merlot has the deep color and assertive berryish character that makes Merlot such an appealing wine. It is excellent with lamb, perfect with duck, rich and satisfying without being too tannic. Lenz Gewürztraminer is dry and crisp, made in the Alsatian style particularly favored by Peter Lenz, who is of German heritage.

The Lenzes have plans to expand, for there is growing demand for their wines as well as for those of other Long Island wineries. North Fork residents seem highly pleased with this turn of events. They lived in dread that the area would lose its agricultural identity and be swallowed up by the condos and shopping malls that have overrun much of the South Fork. But with the number of vineyards on the rise, the region's agricultural future seems assured.

NEW ENGLAND

The vine does not flourish in New England, though not for want of trying. In 1629 Governor John Winthrop planted a vineyard on Governor's Island in Boston Harbor, using vines brought over on the Mayflower II. They died, of

Autumn bounty on Long Island's North Fork, near Peconic Bay (OPPOSITE). A magnum of Lenz Reserve. The winery's best red, it is made from a blend of Cabernet Sauvignon and Merlot.

Cabernet Sauvignon grapes (LEFT) *at Chicama, the only vineyard on Martha's Vineyard. Despite its name, the island off Massachusetts called Martha's Vineyard is better known for lobster than wine. In West Tisbury, a miniature lobster boat* (OPPOSITE) *serves as a weathervane for a house on the harbor.* (PAGES 54–55): *Lowering clouds over Crosswoods Vineyards herald one of the major threats to winegrowing in the Northeast, autumn rains, which can both dilute flavor and character and cause rot.*

course, and successive attempts down through the years also failed. The Canepa family launched New England's modern era in winegrowing by starting the White Mountain winery in New Hampshire in 1964, but finally ended the long struggle against the cold by closing down in 1986. Hope springs eternal, however—New Englanders are still trying, and are meeting with greater success farther south.

In 1971 former Californians George and Catherine Mathiesen planted the first all-vinifera vineyard in Massachusetts at their summer home on Martha's Vineyard. In view of the name of the island this would seem altogether appropriate. When Bartholomew Gosnold discovered the island in 1602, it was flourishing with wild grapes; he named it for his wife, or his niece, depending on which history book you read. The Mathiesens had the feeling that vinifera might thrive there, and took the chance.

The cuisine on the island revolves around fish and shellfish, so they planned their wines with that in mind, planting mostly Chenin Blanc. The winery's name, Chicama, is an Indian word from an old deed naming one boundary of the property "Chicama path."

Being six miles out in the Atlantic has its advantages. The ocean fends off the cold Canadian winds that stream down in winter, while it cools the summer's hot winds. Winter temperatures seldom fall below five degrees; the summer's rarely rise above ninety. There are some disadvantages, too. Surrounded by water, the island gets a lot of fog, which delays ripening if it hovers about too long. The shorter growing season—mid-May through September some years—also makes it difficult to ripen some varieties. It is too cold for Zinfandel, but Chenin Blanc, and the early-ripening Chardonnay and Pinot Noir, do well enough. "The surprise for us has been Cabernet Sauvignon," said Mathiesen. "It is the last to ripen, but seems to have found a nice home on the Vineyard."

Chicama buys grapes from Long Island to blend in some of their wines, to give them extra color and fruit. Connoisseurs may do a double-

take spotting Chicama's estate red, labeled Martha's Vineyard Merlot/Cabernet. A continent away Napa Valley's Heitz Cellars produces a Cabernet whose label also bears the name Martha's Vineyard; it is a rich, multidimensional wine that is world-famous. When Mathiesen requested an official appellation of "Martha's Vineyard" (after the island) from the U.S. Bureau of Alcohol, Tobacco and Firearms, Heitz opposed the application but lost. So there are two Martha's Vineyard Cabernets, but they are alike in name only. Chicama's Cabernet is light and pleasant enough, but the white wines, Chenin Blanc, Gewürztraminer and a sparkling Brut called Sea Mist, are Chicama's most successful wines.

David Tower founded Commonwealth Winery in Massachusetts in 1978, but originally had to be content with making wine from grapes purchased from New York, New Hampshire or Connecticut. Nonetheless, Tower had faith that somewhere in Massachusetts wine grapes would grow. Today, largely due to his steadfast efforts, a dozen vineyards are found in southeastern Massachusetts around Fall River and New Bedford. French hybrids and vinifera such as Riesling, Chardonnay and Pinot Noir do fairly well here. The southeast-facing slopes are warmed somewhat by coastal winds, but the vinifera still occasionally suffer winter damage. When the canes freeze and split, crown gall, a virus common in vineyards east of the Rockies, sets in and eventually destroys the vine. Nothing can be done once crown gall erupts in a vine. It simply has to be replaced.

Commonwealth Winery is in Plymouth, overlooking Plymouth Rock and a replica of the Mayflower II. It is Massachusetts's largest winery, producing 15,000 cases annually. Tower's best wines are crisp, lightly sweet whites, such as Vidal Blanc, Riesling, Seyval Blanc and Cayuga. His Massachusetts Chardonnay, from young vines, is rather austere at the moment but shows potential for good Chablis-like character. Cape Cod is famous for its cranberry bogs, so Tower also makes a delicate cranberry—apple dessert wine that is so popular, particularly around Christmas, that he can hardly keep it in stock.

Farther down the coast is Sakonnet Vineyards. Although it was the first of Rhode Island's commercial wineries to open since Prohibition, it has been in business only since 1975. Owners Jim and Lolly Mitchell started out with Seyval Blanc, Chancellor, Foch and other French hybrids, later adding vinifera such as Chardonnay and Riesling to their fifty-acre vineyard. The blended table wines, fancifully labeled America's Cup White and Rhode Island Red, are attractive and a good value. Rhode Island has two other wineries with vinifera vineyards: Prudence Island Winery, on the island of that name in Narragansett Bay, and Diamond Hill Winery, near Providence; both are quite small, producing only about 1,000 cases annually. Prudence Island, however, has made something of a name in New England for ripe and flavorful Chardonnay.

Connecticut is home to a small but enthusiastic group of winegrowers, scattered throughout the state. One of the better-established wineries is Crosswoods Vineyard near Stonington. In the mid-1970s, Hugh and Susan Connell were living a typical suburban life with their young children in Bedford, New York. Hugh commuted to New York every day, Susan was active in a variety of pursuits—showing horses, gourmet cooking, tennis—and the children were involved in a multitude of activities. Family life was getting short shrift. So one evening Hugh

sat everybody down to discuss what they could take up that would involve the whole family. They considered all sorts of things, mostly those having to do with agriculture, since they all liked growing things. Hugh and Susan were drinking wine at the time and Hugh suddenly looked at his glass and said, "Why not a vineyard?" The more they talked about it, the more they liked the idea. Unlike others who already had land and started by growing grapes on it, the Connells began by looking for land suitable for grapes. They spent two years doing climatic studies within a two-hundred-mile radius of Bedford and, in 1981, chose a hilltop site in North Stonington.

It is a typical Connecticut setting, close to the whaling communities of Stonington, New London and Mystic, on a landscape marked off by low stone walls—some that were laid a century ago, and others that developed with clearing of the land for the vineyard. Against all advice from eastern viticulturists they planted vinifera. They would never make it financially because of low yield, they were told, so they added a few acres of Vidal Blanc, a French hy-

brid. But yields on Chardonnay, Gewürztraminer, Riesling and Gamay were far above expectation and they now sell most of the Vidal to other winemakers.

The winery is a converted dairy barn, a large, imposing white structure that dates to 1850 and is mostly underground. Tall stainless steel fermentation tanks stand in the cellar where cows once came to be milked, and rows of French oak barrels are stacked in an adjacent room. Visitors to Crosswoods can look down on this center of activity from the ground-level tasting room. The Connells hired California winemaker Walter Schug as consultant, and also sought viticultural advice from France.

The vineyard has excellent southern exposure, with the good air drainage that is essential to healthy vines. Constant wind, averaging ten miles an hour, brushes cold air down off the hill and helps dry out the vines after rain or dew. The maritime climate is similar to that of the North Fork of Long Island, which is only twelve miles away across Long Island Sound. Based on the North Fork's success with Merlot, the Connells planted it in 1986.

During the last Ice Age, retreating glaciers left New England soils with the good drainage needed for the propagation of the vine as well as with ample material from which to construct the region's famed stone walls (TOP).

Birds sometimes find the luxuriant foliage of grape vines an appealing spot for nesting (BOTTOM).

Crosswoods has hit its stride in a relatively short time and production is now up to 5,000 cases. The Connells have narrowed their focus to concentrate on two varietals, Chardonnay and Merlot, and they produce estate wines of each. But they also buy additional grapes of these two varieties from Ressler Vineyards on Long Island, and designate that vineyard on their label. Crosswoods also makes small amounts of estate-grown Gamay (the true Burgundian variety) and Gewürztraminer in superior vintages. By 1990 Pinot Noir will be part of the roster as well. One of their most delightful wines is Scrimshaw White, a crisp, appealing blend of Chardonnay, Riesling, Gewürztraminer and Vidal Blanc.

Connecticut has several other vineyards that are also doing well with a mix of French hybrids and early-ripening vinifera like Chardonnay, Riesling and Pinot Noir. Haight Vineyard in Litchfield was the state's first bonded winery, and among the state's other wine-growers are Hopkins Vineyard in New Preston,

Hamlet Hill Vineyards in Pomfret, DiGrazia Vineyards and Winery in Fairfield County and Clarke Vineyard in Stonington.

PENNSYLVANIA AND NEW JERSEY

Two Northeastern states that are showing great promise for wine grapes are Pennsylvania and New Jersey. Pennsylvania drinking laws are some of the most restrictive in the country and wine can be sold only through state-owned stores, but growing grapes is far easier. Pennsylvania's wineries are found mainly in the southern half of the state, from Chadds Ford near Philadelphia to south of Pittsburgh. Along with several others along Lake Erie, they number over thirty. Lancaster, York and Chester counties in the southeast have the greatest concentration of vinifera vineyards, but most grow French hybrids and a few varieties of labrusca as well. Some of Pennsylvania's best wines come from Allegro Vineyards, Chaddsford Winery, Fox Meadow Farm, Naylor Wine Cellars, Nissley Vineyards and York Springs Winery. Southeastern Pennsylvania, which usually enjoys a relatively long and warm growing season, has had success in recent years with Chardonnay and shows great promise for red vinifera, including Cabernet Sauvignon.

New Jersey has a mere handful of wineries, located mostly in the rural southern sections of the state. Tewksbury Wine Cellars, Alba Vineyard and Tomasello Winery are the largest, all of which grow some vinifera in addition to hybrids. Up-and-coming names include Four Sisters Winery—named for the four daughters of an Italian family—Gross' Highland Winery, and Kings Road Vineyard.

Perhaps the most encouraging aspect of the Northeast's progress with the grape is the fact that many of its wineries and vineyards were started in the 1980s. They are young, but they are growing in both size and impact. There is a definite trend toward vinifera varieties, particularly in warmer areas such as eastern Long Island and southeastern Pennsylvania, where Chardonnay, Cabernet Sauvignon and Merlot are becoming more impressive with each vintage. The better French hybrids, however, such as Vidal Blanc, Seyval Blanc and reds like Chancellor and Maréchal Foch, will not quickly disappear. As northeastern winemakers gain experience with these varieties, the wines are increasingly more stylish and attractive. The German Riesling also has its best chance here for producing wines of real character and depth. A great deal more can be done with Riesling in the Northeast; it is a grape capable of producing a variety of styles that have barely begun to be explored by winemakers.

Marketing is a major problem for the Northeast. Getting attention in the major metropolitan cities, where competition from imports and California wines is very strong, is difficult and the results often discouraging. The better wineries, however, appear to be making gains through special tastings held in places like Philadelphia, New York and Boston. These spurts of publicity help attract interest on the part of consumers. Northeastern wines generally do well locally; this is important, for it can generate an ever-widening ripple effect that increases familiarity with the wines and encourages further growth of the market.

CHAPTER TWO

VINEYARDS OF THE SOUTH

IN THE EARLY CHILL OF A NOVEMBER MORNING in Virginia, two men walked over frost-whitened hills near Charlottesville. The taller man, wisps of reddish hair visible under his worn felt hat, led the other to the top of a south-facing slope and gestured toward a nearby hill. They stood there, talking, nodding, intent on their discourse as the day grew brighter.

The year was 1773; the setting, Monticello. Thomas Jefferson led Filippo Mazzei across the November-chilled hills of his estate, pointing out possible vineyard sites for Mazzei's brave aspiration to grow wine grapes and olive trees in Virginia. As they headed back for breakfast that morning, the two men had little notion of the problems that would beset them—the same problems that Virginia wine-growers face today and have only recently begun to conquer. Mazzei was of the opinion, however, that "the best wine in the world will be made here," and later wrote to George Washington, saying, "This country is better calculated than any other I am acquainted with for the produce of wine."

Jefferson had invited Mazzei to Monticello by pure chance. Born and raised on a wine estate near Florence, the Italian had spent twenty years in London as a wine merchant and importer of such goods as olive oil, lemon trees, cheese and preserved fruits. A cultivated man of broad interests, Mazzei became acquainted with Benjamin Franklin, who in turn introduced him to several Virginians then living in London. Listening to their account of the "well-governed colony" and persuaded of its congenial climate, he eagerly made plans to go to Virginia and to establish a large plantation of vineyards and orchards. Efforts to finance the grandiose scheme—which involved collecting some ten thousand grapevines from Burgundy, Champagne, Tuscany, Portugal and other noted regions—failed. Undaunted, Mazzei modified his original plan and was soon on his way, with a scaled-down quantity of vines, lemon trees, olive trees, and a complement of ten Tuscan viticulturists hired to work the vineyards.

The group landed in Virginia in the fall of 1773. It was in Williamsburg, where Mazzei stayed with Francis Eppes, Jefferson's brother-in-law, that he met several political figures of the day, including Jefferson and George Washington. Mazzei was bound for Augusta County, Virginia, to look at possible vineyard sites, prompting Jefferson to invite him to stop by Monticello in Albemarle County on the way.

Jefferson must have been intrigued to hear of Mazzei's plans. An avid gardener himself, Jefferson was greatly interested in the idea of growing grapes and Mediterranean fruits in Virginia. Out on the frosty hill before breakfast, Jefferson showed Mazzei an adjacent tract of land that might be suitable for his purposes. Mazzei was delighted with the look of it, and Jefferson gave him two thousand acres to start his project. Writing about it some years later, Jefferson noted Mazzei's excitement about the southeastern exposure of the slopes, with their "lean and meagre spots of stony and red soil, without sand, resembling extremely the Cote of Burgundy from Chambertin to Montrachet, where the famous wines of Burgundy are made. I am inclined to believe he was right in preferring the South Eastern face of this ridge of mountains."

The west facade of Monticello (OPPOSITE), *the renowned Charlottesville, Virginia, home of its designer, oenophile Thomas Jefferson* (TOP). *Filippo Mazzei* (BOTTOM).

Thomas Jefferson's appreciation of good wine and food, his keen interest in agriculture, particularly as it pertained to foodstuffs, are well documented. His voluminous correspondence and diaries contain numerous references to wine, and these grew more frequent after his sojourn in France. In 1784 he was appointed Minister Plenipotentiary (i.e., ambassador) to France, succeeding Benjamin Franklin. Jefferson became quite a connoisseur in France, making special forays into Bordeaux, Burgundy and other wine regions, where, being innately discriminating, he acquainted himself with the best. He drank the *premiers crus* of Bordeaux seventy years before they were so named in the Classification of 1855. In 1786 he placed orders with his wine merchant in Bordeaux for quantities of Château Margaux, "de la Fite," "hautBrion" and "Diquem," while other correspondence mentions great Burgundies like Montrachet, Chambertin, Clos Vougeot. During a journey through the Rhine Valley, he visited some of the great German wine estates, and even partook of Riesling one morning at breakfast. On his return to America in 1789, he became unofficial wine advisor to George Washington, stocking the presidential cellars in Philadelphia and at Mount Vernon.

When Jefferson himself became president in 1801, invitations to his Epicurean dinners at the Capitol in Washington were much sought after. Such gatherings were a natural outgrowth of his experiences in Europe, where politics often commingled with the pleasures of the table. During Jefferson's tenure as president, the table was supplied by his best cooks from Monticello as well as a French chef, and filling its goblets were the finest wines he could procure. Heads of state, ambassadors, cabinet members and other persons of importance gathered regularly at his "round table." Jefferson often conducted certain affairs of state at these dinners, believing that a more relaxed and less formal atmosphere than that found in the chambers of State was more conducive to achieving his aims in governing the country.

Thomas Jefferson had a grand vision for winegrowing in America. His belief in wine as a healthy beverage, and his experiences of life abroad where wine is a natural part of daily life, led him to conclude that winegrowing was definitely something that the republic should pursue. In a now-famous statement from an 1818 letter to a Monsieur de Neuville in France, he maintained that: "No nation is drunken where wine is cheap; and none sober, where the dearness of wine substitutes ardent spirits as the common beverage. It is, in truth, the only antidote to the bane of whiskey." Nevertheless, Jefferson's efforts at growing imported European vinifera species failed again and again, despite his persistence. The famous Garden Book, which he kept from 1766 to 1824, indicates that he tried at least six times to establish vines at Monticello.

Mazzei's efforts met with no greater success. In 1774 he arrived at his new estate—which he named Colle, the Italian word for "hill"—with his troupe of viticulturists. The following spring the planting began at Colle and Monticello with several varieties of *Vitis vinifera*. Everything appeared favorable—the mild climate, the rocky red soil similar to that of the Côte d'Or in Burgundy, the sunny slopes with good drainage. But that very first year a devastating frost occurred in late spring. The Garden Book entry for May 5, 1774, reads: "a frost which destroyed almost everything . . . the leaves of the trees were entirely killed. All the shoots of vines." Undaunted, they tried again over the next few years; though some of the native varieties survived, vinifera species succumbed to winter cold, or to humidity that caused fungus and rot, or to as yet unidentified pests like phylloxera, the root-eating aphid that would later destroy European vineyards.

Mazzei, who became a naturalized citizen of Virginia within a year of his arrival, was a man of ideals as well as a man of the soil. When war broke out, Mazzei joined a militia unit, though he never actually saw combat. In 1778 Washington, Jefferson and Patrick Henry were among those who commissioned him to go to Italy to raise funds for their cause. During his absence, the vineyards at Colle were trampled and destroyed by a troop of Hessian cavalry. Jefferson wrote of this later: "Thus ended an experiment which, from every appearance, would in a year or two have established the practicality of that branch of culture in America." Mazzei came back to Virginia only briefly after the war and then returned to Europe, where he remained until his death in Pisa in 1816.

Thomas Jefferson was way ahead of his time as a winegrower. Although he was frequently away from Monticello during the critical years of vineyard effort, his tremendous interest in cultivating the vine continued. In 1816 he wrote to Maryland grape breeder John Adlum requesting cuttings of the Alexander grape, a red variety that had impressed him in 1809: "Am I too unreasonable in asking once more a few cuttings of the same vine? I am so convinced that our first success will be from a native grape that I would try no other."

VIRGINIA

Jefferson was not the first to attempt growing wine grapes in Virginia. There is evidence that vineyards were planted at Jamestown; in 1710 German settlers from the Rhine Valley attempted to establish vineyards along the Rapidan River west of Fredericksburg, but the vines succumbed to fungus and black rot. By the 1880s, however, native grapes were providing Virginia with a small but thriving wine industry, the state having become famous for the Virginia Seedling, a variety developed by Dr. Daniel Norton of Richmond. It produced a claretlike red wine with none of the "foxy" flavor of most domestic varieties. Eventually renamed for the man who developed it, the Norton is a grape we shall hear more of in "Vineyards of the Heartland" (Chapter Three). Before Prohibition wiped out Virginia's young wine industry, and even for a time thereafter, Virginia's most famous wines were Captain Paul Garrett's Virginia Dare, made in red and white versions from Scuppernong grapes.

It was in the early 1970s, however, that Virginia's wine industry took a leap forward into the modern wine era, and since then the state's progress with the grape has been most exciting. Winegrowers today still face the problems that defeated Jefferson—winter cold, killing spring frosts, soil parasites like phylloxera and other pests, humidity, which promotes mildew and black rot—but modern technology and advances in viticulture have helped solve most of them.

The potential for red wines in Virginia seems particularly bright. Merlot and Cabernet Sauvignon, for example, already show good flavor and an attractive fruit expression that is leaner in style than California wines, but fruitier than those from Bordeaux; these wines demonstrate the prospect of developing a regional distinction all their own. Sparkling wines also appear to have a future in Virginia. Ingleside Plantation Winery, a winery near Fredericksburg, has produced a Brut and Blanc de Noir that compare favorably with good California sparkling wines.

Virginia vineyards are scattered through much of the state, in the Piedmont just west of Washington, D.C., in the valleys of the Blue Ridge Mountains and the hills west of Fredericksburg; they are found in the Roanoke Valley and, of course, right in Jefferson's backyard, the rolling wooded hills of Albemarle County. Vinifera species—including some of those that proved frustrating for Jefferson, such as Cabernet Sauvignon and Chardonnay—make up the most significant portion of Virginia's vineyards, though French hybrids and native species are also planted, sometimes within the same vineyard.

Virginia's modern pioneer with vinifera was Mrs. Thomas Furness, who, at age seventy-five, established the first commercial plantings of vinifera at Piedmont Vineyards in the hunt country of northern Virginia. Mrs. Furness, who died in 1986, became impressed with Dr. Konstantin Frank's work with vinifera in New York and planted Chardonnay and Sémillon at her estate near Middleburg in 1973.

Good Chardonnay is also produced at near-

by Meredyth Vineyards, where cattleman Archie Smith owns a fifty-five-acre vineyard of hybrids and vinifera. His son, Archie III, is the winemaker. Meredyth Chardonnays and Seyval Blancs were some of the earliest to attract attention outside Virginia. Riper and fuller bodied than other Virginia wines, they are more akin to a California style.

Europeans have shown interest in Virginia as wine country. The young industry received a great boost in the mid-1970s when Zonin, a large Italian wine company, purchased the Barboursville estate northeast of Charlottesville. Searching for vineyard sites in the United States, Zonin determined that, with proper pest control, Virginia would be excellent for vinifera. Before that, the primary emphasis had been on French hybrids such as Seyval Blanc, Vidal Blanc, Foch and Chambourcin, all of which had proved successful in other parts of the East. Zonin devoted several million dollars to developing Barboursville Winery, producing some very good wines, particularly Chardonnay.

In 1978 Dr. Gerhard Guth, a surgeon from Hamburg, sought advice about soil, climate and topography from Professor Helmut Becker of Geisenheim in Germany. In 1979 Dr. Guth brought German viticulturist Joachim Hollerith to Virginia to assist in establishing Rapidan River Vineyards, a wine estate that ultimately will consist of 250 acres of White Riesling, Chardonnay, Gewürztraminer and Pinot Noir. The French also have begun to take an interest in Virginia. Prince Michel Vineyards at Culpepper is a joint venture between Virginian N. B. Martin and Jean Leducq of Paris. Begun in 1983, the vineyard is 110 acres, with further expansion planned. Prince Michel recently acquired Rapidan River, which will continue to operate as a separate entity. Joachim Hollerith is wine director for both wineries.

Belgian oenologist Jacques Recht, winemaker at Ingleside Plantation Winery, was the first to bring French expertise to Virginia, quite serendipitously as it happened. Recht worked for several years with the renowned Professor Ribéreau–Gayon at the University of Bordeaux and at Château Beychevelle in the Médoc prior to becoming professor of oenology at the University of Brussels. He and his wife left Belgium in 1980 to sail around the world in a catamaran he built himself. The voyage brought the Rechts into Chesapeake Bay and up the Potomac River, where they met Carl Flemer, proprietor of Ingleside Plantation. Flemer was looking for a winemaker and persuaded Recht to stay and help with the grape crush. Recht, who has consulted for several of Virginia's young wineries, firmly believes in the future of vinifera in Virginia, especially red varieties. He produces excellent Cabernet Sauvignon at Ingleside that shows every indication of aging like a fine Bordeaux, as well as good sparkling wines from Pinot Noir and Chardonnay using the traditional Champagne method.

The greatest concentration of Virginia wineries is found in Jefferson country, Albemarle County, in the vicinity of Charlottesville. A fine example is Oakencroft Vineyard, founded by Felicia Warburg Rogan, one of the most dynamic figures in the Virginia wine industry. Aware of efforts only at a few nearby vineyards such as Montdomaine and Chermont, she and her husband, John, happened to meet Lucie T. Morton, an East Coast viticulture specialist who was consulting for local growers. Lucie Morton arrived at Oakencroft one day with twenty-five vines, which were planted in the spring of 1981. Encouraged by their success with these, the Rogans added more vines the next year. Soon after tasting the first batch of wine made from their own grapes, the Rogans decided to plant more vines, beginning their venture into making wine on a commercial basis in 1983.

Oakencroft's winemaker, Deborah Welsh, was part-time gardener at the estate when Lucie Morton arrived with the fateful grape cuttings. Pitching in to help with the vineyard, she became interested in wine and soon joined the ranks of amateur winemakers who have developed their skills by practicing them.

Oakencroft Vineyard may be the only win-

Originally laid out in 1807, Jefferson's Northeast Vineyard was replanted in 1984 in strict adherence to the original owner's famous "Garden Book." Apple, peach, and other fruit trees are also planted on the east-facing slope.

Cabernet Sauvignon grapes (TOP) *ripen in Oakencroft Vineyard, Charlottesville, Virginia.* (BOTTOM): *Vineyard mascot: Acorn of Oakencroft. Felicia Warburg Rogan inspects young Cabernet Sauvignon vines planted in 1985* (OPPOSITE), *two years after she founded Oakencroft.* (PAGES 68–69): *A predawn mist rises from the pond fronting Oakencroft's winery.*

ery in existence whose label depicts cows, but it is appropriate, since it reflects the winery's setting on a working farm. John Rogan's registered polled Herefords freely roam the 250-acre estate, right up to the split-rail fence a stone's throw from Oakencroft's columned veranda. The winery, roughly half a mile away, was once a smokehouse used for curing hams and bacon. Expanded in 1985 into a handsome native-stone structure with the quaint look of a country farmhouse, it comes complete with a pond in front that is home to a gaggle of geese.

The first vines were planted up near the house, beyond the rose garden, but the main ten-acre vineyard, planted in 1983, is behind the winery on a hill chosen for its exposure and good air drainage. This is essential in Virginia's humid climate, where, at times, not a breath of air stirs for days. Oakencroft makes three varietal wines, Chardonnay, Seyval Blanc and Cabernet Sauvignon, all of which are grown on the estate. A little Merlot is also grown for use in a "house" wine or to be blended with Cabernet if the quality is suitable.

One particular danger for Virginia vines is unpredictable temperature changes, which threaten the cold-tender vinifera, especially those early varieties like Chardonnay that are apt to break into bud during a winter thaw. January 1985, for instance, saw ten days of sixty- to seventy-degree temperatures—always a dangerous occurrence, since an unseasonable spurt of warm weather causes the sap to start running and the wood to soften, leaving the vines vulnerable to a sudden freeze. On a Sunday in January of that year, the vineyard was hit by the worst freeze in a hundred years. Temperatures dropped to sixteen degrees, the sap-filled trunks froze, and split when they thawed, paving the way for crown gall: "Our number one enemy," says Deborah Welsh. Crown gall bacteria live in the plants but usually erupt only at points of injury on the vine trunk. As the gall swells it hardens the inner tissues and the vine eventually dies. Another danger for Chardonnay and other early-budding varietals is late frost, which, as happened in 1986, can come as

Oakencroft's Cabernet Sauvignon is the perfect complement for a meal featuring Virginia ham and an apple tart dessert.

late as mid-May. "It's agonizing when it happens," says Felicia Rogan. "You see the frost roll in and cover the oranges and you know what it's doing in the vineyard. You feel so helpless. This is why we'll never have it easy with Chardonnay in Virginia."

As a kind of hedge against such catastrophe, Oakencroft grows Seyval Blanc, a white French hybrid bred to withstand the cold. In years when the vinifera crop is reduced, hybrids offer something on which to fall back. Oakencroft's dry, crisp Seyval, however, is quite good in its own right.

Though severe winter cold is still one of Virginia's worst problems, there are ways of combating it. As in the Northeast, vines may be "hilled up" in winter. To delay bud break until the danger of a freak winter thaw is past, the canes are not pruned of the previous year's growth until late February. Many other problems that Jefferson faced have largely been solved as well. Vines are now grafted onto native American rootstocks that are resistant to phylloxera. Fungicides are used to prevent mildew and rot.

Albemarle County vineyards also suffer from wind, either too much or too little. To promote better air circulation when the air is stagnant, the vines are trained on double trellises. On the other hand, the region is close to hurricane country, and, though high winds can be a problem, the greatest damage from hurricanes is the rain they bring at harvest. In August 1985, Hurricane Danny dumped between five and six inches of rain on Oakencroft, just as the Seyval was about to be picked. This stopped the ripening process cold, but the grapes had to be picked before they deteriorated. Because they had not reached the desired sugar levels, Oakencroft decided to chaptalize (add sugar before fermentation to increase body, a common practice in the cooler regions of Europe), and managed to produce an attractive wine.

Virginia's chief advantages for winegrowing are its warmth, which usually allows sufficient ripening, and the good red earth that Filippo Mazzei found so promising in 1773. These conditions make Virginia one of the most favorable spots in the East for producing red wines, such as the richly colored Merlot and Cabernet.

"Give us ten years," says Felicia Rogan. "It will take that long for us to know what our vines can really do. The whole idea of a farm winery is that we produce good, drinkable regional wine. I want to emphasize Oakencroft wine as something grown in Virginia, made in Virginia, a quality product from a working farm."

Felicia Rogan has had a singular impact on Virginia winegrowing. Delving into Jefferson's writings about winegrowing, she recognized at once the historic significance of reviving his grapegrowing efforts. Putting her considerable energies to work, she organized the Jeffersonian Grape Growers Society, which now has over a hundred members. The Society sponsors winemaking and viticultural seminars and publishes a quarterly newsletter of industry news. Each October the group sponsors the Albemarle Harvest Wine Festival. Held at Society headquarters—John Rogan's Boar's Head Inn in Charlottesville—this weekend gala draws more aficionados each year. The highlight is its Bacchanalian Feast, a lavish multicourse banquet accompanied by Greek music and troupes of Greek dancers, worthy of the famed Roman banquet giver Trimalchio. More important, in 1984 the Jeffersonian Grape Growers applied for the viticultural area designation under the name *Monticello*. As of 1984 all ten wineries within the boundaries became entitled to use this appellation.

The development that would have pleased Thomas Jefferson most of all, however, is the revival of vineyards at Monticello. His long-held dream appears to have been fulfilled at last. In 1984 Jefferson's Northeast Vineyard, originally planted in 1807 (the Garden Book cited twenty-three varieties planted that year) was replanted under the direction of Peter Hatch, superintendent of grounds and gardens. In the fall of 1984, twenty-one modern versions of the 1807 varieties were planted on terraces facing east, just below the garden wall.

The vineyard is small, about one-quarter acre, its vines trained on split-rail fencing six feet apart. It is a handsome arrangement, with vines curling and draping along the weathered rails much as they must have done in Jefferson's day. Peter Hatch and his garden crew followed sketches for the vineyard plan from the Garden Book. Nomenclature of the original varieties was confusing, however, for in Jefferson's day some bore fanciful names like "Great July" or "Queen's grape." With the help of Lucie Morton, who is also an ampelographer, or grape cataloguer, most of the modern incarnations were tracked down. They include Cabernet Sauvignon (Jefferson's "Black Cluster"), Chardonnay, Pinot Blanc, Chasselas, Aleatico, Sangiovese, Muscat and Pinot Noir, as well as native varieties like Scuppernong. According to

Planted on east-facing slopes above the cattle barns, the Oakencroft vineyards are bathed in the rising sun. The 250-acre estate also raises registered polled Herefords.

Hatch, the vineyard is thriving, with the first crop due in 1987. There are no plans at present to make wine, since Jefferson did not make wine himself. But the temptation is there. "Perhaps we will sell the grapes," says Hatch, "or concoct a unique Monticello vintage of seventeen varieties."

MARYLAND

Virginia's flurry of wine activity over the last decade may at present capture the lion's share of attention for Southern vineyards, but there is plenty going on elsewhere in the South. Prior to the success of vinifera in the 1970s and 1980s, the grapes that proved most encouraging to would-be winegrowers in this part of the country were French hybrids—which were first developed on significant scale in Maryland.

One cannot speak of the evolution of wine in this country without mentioning Philip Wagner of Riderwood, Maryland, former publisher of the *Baltimore Sun*. Wagner was a wine hobbyist and home winemaker in the 1930s. His source of California grapes disappeared following repeal of Prohibition, so he tried making wines from native labruscas but disliked the grapey flavors. When he happened upon some material about French hybrids, he ordered a batch and was delighted with the wines he made. In 1945 Wagner and his wife, Jocelyn—an indispensable partner in the venture—built a winery and sold their wines under the Boordy Vineyards label in Maryland, Washington, D.C., and New York. One of the seminal figures in eastern winemaking, Wagner is sometimes called the "Johnny Appleseed" of vineyards in tribute to the way he has dispensed vine cuttings of hybrids to help new growers get started. His book, *Grapes into Wine*, stands on the library shelf of every winery east of the Mississippi, and a fair number of those west of it. The Wagners retired from winegrowing in 1980 and sold Boordy to long-time friends, the Robert Deford family of Hydes, north of Riderwood, who continue to make wines under the Boordy label.

G. Hamilton Mowbray of Montbray Wine Cellars in Westminster is Maryland's modern pioneer with vinifera. Mowbray has grown Chardonnay for twenty-two years but believes it is only marginally viable in Maryland. "It's okay if you want to go through the pain and strain of losing it one out of every four or five years," he says, "but, properly handled, Seyval Blanc makes a better wine here than Chardonnay. It has more fruit and better balance." Seyval Blanc is currently the largest planting in Mowbray's twenty-eight acres.

Mowbray is most pleased, however, with the performance of Cabernet Sauvignon and Cabernet Franc, particularly the latter. He makes it as a varietal on its own, similar in style to Chinon and Bourgueil, two reds from the Loire Valley made entirely of Cabernet Franc. The Cabernet varieties have proved less susceptible to winterkill than Chardonnay, so Mowbray plans to plant more of both. An added advantage with Cabernet Franc is that it matures fairly quickly and is ready to drink within a year or so of the harvest—a boon in terms of cash flow.

Maryland's winegrowers, including such up-and-coming wineries as Byrd Vineyards and Catoctin Vineyards, have found that a mix of hybrids and vinifera are the wisest course at the moment, though vinifera plantings appear to be increasing.

THE CAROLINAS

North and South Carolina are making limited but significant forays into the world of winegrowing. The most promising enterprise is at the Biltmore estate near Asheville, North Carolina. The palatial Biltmore House was built in the foothills of the Blue Ridge Mountains by George Washington Vanderbilt around the turn of the century. In addition to drawing huge numbers of tourists, Biltmore House is now becoming known for its winery and 125-acre vineyard planted with vinifera grapes like Merlot, Pinot Noir, Chardonnay, Riesling and Cabernet Sauvignon. The Biltmore Estate Wine Company is the creation of William Van-

derbilt Cecil, grandson of George Vanderbilt. Cecil recognized the estate's unique microclimate and founded the winery in 1977. The soil contains iron and clay, components that, if not too dense, are highly desirable for certain varieties, particularly Merlot and Pinot Noir. Elevations around 2,500 feet, above the frost line, afford the vineyards protection from the killing spring frosts that commonly occur in the Southeast but also moderate summer temperatures. Pinot Noir is doing especially well here. French winemaker Philippe Jourdain has been particularly successful with estate-grown Pinot Noir, turning out a smooth, flavorful wine with a nice touch of oak. The estate is also gaining a reputation for well-made Riesling and sparkling wines. Biltmore imports some California wine for blending purposes, but only estate-grown grapes are used for the Chateau Biltmore label.

South Carolina's only premium winegrower is Dr. Jim Truluck, who established Truluck Vineyards near Lake City in 1976. The 120-acre vineyard, now managed by Dr. Tru-

luck's sons, includes vinifera like Cabernet Sauvignon and Riesling, as well as French hybrids and a rare native hybrid known as Ellen Scott, from which the Trulucks make sparkling wine. Jim Truluck was instrumental in getting the state to pass a farm winery law in 1980, which encouraged other small growers to start wineries.

Varieties from the native Muscadine species, among them Scuppernong, are widely grown in the Carolinas, and much of the juice is sold to large companies in New York and elsewhere. Although Sir Walter Raleigh is credited with "discovering" the Scuppernong—a giant vine on Roanoke Island reported to be over three hundred years old was named for him—it was the Italian explorer Giovanni da Verrazano who first sighted Muscadines growing along the North Carolina coast in 1524, according to Leon Adams. The first wine ever made in America was Scuppernong, made by French Huguenots who found the grapes along the Atlantic coast of Florida, near Jacksonville.

Muscadine vines differ from other wine grapes in that the berries are twice the size of other grapes and grow in clusters of three or four instead of in bunches. The vines have incredible vigor and thrive in the humid climate of the Southeast. The grapes are used not only for wine, but also for juice, jams and jellies. Scuppernong has a unique aroma and flavor, as anyone who has ever tasted wine or jam made from these grapes knows. The flavor is difficult to describe—an exotic spiciness mingled with hints of tropical fruit, honeysuckle blossoms and muscat. As a sweet wine, it can be quite delicious and is marvelous for sipping, but it is not really appropriate as a table wine. Several new hybrid varieties of Muscadine—Carlos, Magnolia and Noble—were developed recently by grape scientists at North Carolina State University in Raleigh. These varieties produce wines that are more palatable with food, though still a little curious when first tasted.

These new varieties, along with Scuppernong and other Muscadines, are increasingly planted in vineyards of the Deep South because

Muscadine grapes at Lafayette Vineyards near Tallahassee: at top, *the white variety known as Stover;* below, *Carlos.*

they are both easy to grow and prolific. Almost totally resistant to fungus, black rot, phylloxera and other pests, some of them also yield prodigious quantities of juice. As more Muscadine wines are produced, the audience for them seems to be growing.

A great deal of work has been done with Muscadine varieties in Florida. The Agricultural Research Station at Leesburg has developed several new grape varieties with names like Stover (named for grape breeder Loren Stover), Suwannee and Conquistador. Jeanne Burgess, trained in winemaking at Mississippi State University in Starkville, where considerable work is being done in viticulture, is now winemaker at Lafayette Vineyards near Tallahassee, where she produces a very good white from Stover that is crisp and lightly sweet. She also finds the Suwannee grape promising.

Florida growers are most enthusiastic about a new white variety called Blanc du Bois, developed by Dr. John Mortensen at Leesburg. Its spicy fruit flavors and Muscat-like aromas lead some to think it will become Florida's leading white wine grape. Another new product from Leesburg is Orlando Seedless, a bunch grape produced from Florida varieties and some vinifera. This prolific variety holds promise as a blending grape for white wine, as well as for table use. It has none of the native grape flavor and is resistant to rot and mildew.

THE DEEP SOUTH

It is remarkable that vinifera grapes are now being grown successfully in parts of the Deep South. Chateau Elan in Georgia, northwest of Atlanta at Hoschton, has 250 acres of vinifera and aims to produce several hundred thousand cases of wine. The short growing season—from early March to mid-July or August—makes the ability to develop definitive varietal character somewhat questionable as yet. For the moment, Chateau Elan blends Georgia grapes with those from California and may continue to do so even when the Georgia vineyards are fully bearing. Owner Donald Panoz sends his French wine-

maker to California at harvest each year to select the grapes, which are then shipped to Georgia in refrigerated trucks.

Impeccable techniques and equipment have produced clean, reasonably well balanced wines from Georgia vineyards, but they are a little shy in flavor. Interestingly, grapevines thrive in the severe drought conditions that prove catastrophic to other southern crops. Farmers suffered disastrous losses in the summer of 1986 because of prolonged drought, but Chateau Elan's vineyards were healthy and produced an excellent crop. Irrigation supplied the vines with the water they needed, and the drought staved off the usual attacks of mildew and rot, so little spraying was needed that year.

Georgia's wine industry, on the other hand, has faced considerable resistance to making wine from a different power: members of the state government. This is the heart of the Bible Belt, and some of those who would never question a word of the Holy Bible are nonplussed by the Good Book's numerous positive references to wine. One Georgia grower who applied for a license to make wine used the example of Christ turning water into wine at the wedding feast of Cana as part of his testimony. "I can't understand why Jesus did that," one of the commissioners was heard to remark. "It's been an embarrassment to me all my life." The grower eventually got his license, but in an adjacent, nondry county.

The fact that the Mississippi Delta is now an officially designated viticultural area came as something of a shock to me. Having grown up near the Delta, I knew it to be stifling with heat and humidity in summer. How could wine grapes possibly survive, much less make drinkable wine?

One usually thinks of Delta country as the flat fan-shaped plain at the river's mouth where the river pours into the ocean. But, though several hundred miles above the mouth of the Mississippi, the flat alluvial plain stretching south of the bluffs at Memphis has been called "the Delta" since antebellum days.

This is river-bottom land: deep, rich, fertile black earth planted with cotton, soybeans, corn and sunflowers. On their way to the Mississippi or one of the rivers that feed it, languid bayous lace their way among cypress trees hung with Spanish moss. The sun bakes down in summer, making it ninety degrees in the shade in June. The heat, coupled with lowland humidity, may be wiltingly oppressive for people, but wine grapes, both native Muscadine and European varieties, are able to prosper.

Although bourbon has long been the preferred drink in this part of the South, wine was not an unknown commodity. The dining room sideboard or a small table in the parlor of many a genteel home traditionally kept a crystal decanter of sherry or port, ringed with delicate stemware, for late-afternoon or after-dinner sipping. Mississippi has been home to at least one famous wine lover—William Faulkner—though his status as an oenophile is not as well known as his love for whiskey. Rows of empty wine bottles are lined up along a mantel in the dining room at Rowan Oak, his stately home in Oxford. The labels show how well he drank— Richebourg, Gevry-Chambertin, Château Haut-Brion, Château d'Yquem.

The Delta's pioneer with vinifera grapes is Claiborne Barnwell, who planted a small vineyard in 1982 at Indianola, about thirty miles east of the Mississippi River on Highway 82. Claiborne Vineyards is easy to miss. A little building near the road that looks like an old country store, complete with its faded red gas pump out front—vintage 1940s —is the unlikely exterior. Inside, however, is a charming tasting room with peach-colored wicker sofa and chairs. Stainless steel fermenting tanks stand in the back corners behind the tasting bar.

Claiborne Barnwell is enormously enthusiastic about what he is doing. Since the operation is still so small, Barnwell does not speak in terms of acres or cases, but of vines and bottles. He planted a thousand vines in 1982, mostly

French hybrids like Seyval Blanc, Vidal Blanc, Maréchal Foch, Baco Noir. In 1984 he planted one hundred Cabernet Sauvignon vines, and made thirty bottles from the first crop. Now he is also growing Sauvignon Blanc, Sémillon, Chenin Blanc and Pinot Noir. The wines are quite good, all dry, and made to go with food. The whites, like Vidal Blanc and Seyval, are crisp and clean, attractively fruity but bone dry.

Barnwell, whose uncle is the well-known food writer Craig Claiborne, was an engineer who also farmed cotton and soybeans. He taught himself winemaking with a book, but he obviously has an intuitive sense for it.

"The soil here is rich clay cropland, what they call alligator clay," Barnwell told me, "not as heavy as the black gumbo soil of other parts of the Delta." He gets good yields without too much vigor, which can be a problem with rich soils that produce more green foliage than fruit. He is especially pleased with the Chenin Blanc and Cabernet Sauvignon, and has reason to be. The 1985 Cabernet, for instance, had excellent color for a wine from two-year-old vines; it was rather light in flavor, which is to be expected from such young vines, but it had the cedary, herby aromas typical of good Cabernet. Barnwell justifiably has high hopes for Cabernets to come. "I guess the serious goal of anyone growing grapes these days," he says, "is to make a Cabernet that can stand with the best."

There is reason to believe he may do so, if the robins don't make away with all his fruit. Birds are a problem in this wooded country, especially for Cabernet Sauvignon and Baco Noir. One of the advantages of a small vineyard, however, is that situations like this are more easily solved. The Barnwells drape black netting over the vine rows, which, since it is both expensive and laborious, is prohibitive in larger vineyards. The robins are smart about getting to any exposed fruit, so the netting must be tucked securely around the lower trunk of the vines to keep them out.

Barnwell's most delightful wine is Bayou Rouge, named for Bayou Indianola, which runs behind the Barnwells' house in town, a couple of miles away. The bayou's namesake is a fruity, gutsy little red blended from seven or eight varieties, rather like Côtes du Rhone in style. If America's small regional wineries can produce wines as lively, clean and well made as these, then the future for winegrowing in this country is bright indeed.

Elsewhere in Mississippi the emphasis is on the native Muscadine. In Merigold, another Delta community, The Winery Rushing, Mississippi's first winery since Prohibition, was bonded in 1977. Owners Sam and Diane Rushing grow only Muscadine varieties—including Carlos, Magnolia and Noble—derivatives of the same wild grapes that flourish in the southern backwoods. The winery is a popular local tourist spot, becoming especially so in 1982 when the Rushings added a congenial meeting place called Top of the Cellar Tea Room, where Rushing wines are served with light lunches, snacks and desserts. Diane Rushing's wine muffins, flavored with Muscadine, are a specialty of the house and are so popular that she has patented the recipe and sells her muffin mix nationwide in gourmet food stores.

Mississippi's budding wine industry gets important support from the department of oenology and viticulture at Mississippi State University in Starkville. The agricultural research station, a joint enterprise with the United States Department of Agriculture, conducts research on adapting the vine to Southeastern growing conditions. Dr. Richard P. Vine, director of the university's viticultural program and oenology laboratory, is at present involved in several projects that will aid existing winegrowers and possibly encourage new ones. Dr. Vine likes to remind people that before Prohibition, the South produced enormous quantities of wine. "There were something like a hundred wineries in Mississippi; Georgia was producing a million gallons," he says. "There's a great future in the South once we get the industry back on its feet."

Tennessee is progressing fairly rapidly with wine grapes. The state now has ten wineries (there were none prior to 1980), including one right in the middle of Memphis. Many small growers scattered around the state make wine, but not on a commercial basis. One reason for the recent flurry of activity is an organization known as the Tennessee Viticultural and Oenological Society, a group of amateur growers who meet regularly to exchange information, frequently inviting experienced oenologists and viticulturists from around the country to share their expertise. The organization now has about two hundred members, including several from other states, all of whom grow grapes and make their own wine.

Most Tennessee vineyards grow all three species: French hybrid, native and vinifera. Ray Skinner, for example, owner of Laurel Hill Vineyards in Lawrence County, an important growing area in central Tennessee, owns just under eight acres planted in French hybrids like Seyval Blanc and Chambourcin, native grapes such as Lenoir, as well as a little Chardonnay and Cabernet Sauvignon. Skinner is very optimistic about the Cabernet. Although it is more cold-tender than Chardonnay here, it buds out later and thus is protected against early spring frosts. The growing season is long enough to ripen it by September, and rain during harvest is less of a problem here than farther east in Virginia and the Carolinas, which suffer from ocean storms.

Vinifera as yet are grown on a very limited basis in Tennessee. Skinner, like most growers, makes blends of native and hybrid grapes labeled with proprietary names. His Central Gardens Red is a dry, attractively fruity red wine blended from several varieties. He occasionally makes Mississippi Cousin, a red made with grapes purchased from Mississippi vineyards. Skinner harvests his grapes, crushes them in the field and trucks the must, or juice, to his winery in the heart of Memphis, an old stone residence that he converted to a winery in 1985. Skinner's goal is to plant more acreage, probably vinifera, and increase production to about 2,000 cases, all of which will be sold at the winery. If he gets any larger, marketing will become more expensive. As is the case in many states, Tennessee laws do not permit wineries to sell directly to stores or restaurants. They must go through a wholesaler, which adds considerably to the mark-up. The growers' society is currently working toward legislation more favorable to the small grower.

What is most encouraging regarding Southern vineyards is the recent experience with varieties that are new to the South—vinifera as well as newly developed grapes that will play a much greater part in Southern winemaking over the next decade. Several states now produce wines that could well become prototypes for future winemakers, wines like Chateau Biltmore Pinot Noir; Montbray Cabernet Franc; Cabernet Sauvignon, Merlot and Chardonnay from several spots in Virginia; Stover from Lafayette in Florida and blended reds from Tennessee. As the South's young vineyards mature and the lack of experienced winemaking gives way to greater expertise, the Southern renaissance in winegrowing is likely to spread, particularly if the demand for wine continues to grow as it has in the last decade. Wine consumption south of the Mason-Dixon had nowhere to go but up, some Southern states being the lowest in the country. The numbers are expanding gradually but steadily. A good portion of the increase is the result of the growing number of good Southern wines and new wineries, which in many cases are introducing wine to people who have never tasted it before.

CHAPTER THREE

VINEYARDS OF THE HEARTLAND

THE COUNTRY'S MIDSECTION EMBRACES A broad geographical area that extends across America's grain belt from Ohio to Minnesota and south to Missouri. Of all the states in this area, Ohio, Michigan and Missouri have the largest number of wineries and produce the greatest volume of wine in the region. Michigan and Ohio are the only two with sizable wine industries, both having large wineries producing 2 or 3 million gallons of wine annually, such as Meier's Wine Cellars in Ohio and Michigan's St. Julian Wine Company. Most of the Heartland wineries, however, are small family operations that make from 5,000 to 20,000 or 30,000 gallons annually (between 2,000 and 12,000 cases). For the most part, they farm their own vineyards, which range in size from as little as 5 acres to 100 or so.

Perhaps more than in any other region of the country, these winegrowers are modern-day pioneers, true perpetuators of the legacy of the early pioneers. They have had to start from scratch, working with new varieties in untried areas, determining through trial and error what varieties would work where. "It was really hit-and-miss here for a long time," one young Michigan vintner told me. "We had no one to turn to. The University of Michigan is a font of information today, but in the early seventies when we started they had only just begun viticultural research. California had all the expertise, but they don't see temperatures of zero or ten below out there. If I had gone to California they'd have told me I was crazy and not to bother."

Of course, inhabitants of the Heartland have a long heritage of facing formidable odds—and surmounting them. The Midwest was settled by people with grit and determination who forged homes and livelihoods out of the wilderness. Their story is one of the most colorful in American history. In 1767 the first pioneers came through the Cumberland Gap with Daniel Boone and settled the river valleys in Ohio, Kentucky and Tennessee, paving the way for the second decade of the nineteenth century, which brought an enormous surge of migration into the Heartland.

The westward movement was intensified when the Northeast was plunged into an economic crisis of sorts by the peace that followed the War of 1812. The restriction on imports during the conflict had given a great boost to commercial, manufacturing and industrial interests, which, as a result, had devoted their energies to producing goods of the highest quality. Many prospered mightily during the war, when demand was high, but once the Treaty of Ghent was signed and the ports reopened, foreign producers flooded the country with cheaper goods, bringing about the ruin of many businesses. That blow, coupled with the disastrous crop failures of 1816 and 1817 in the Atlantic states, prompted many to look west.

The lure of the frontier with its new land, open spaces and brighter prospects had increased steadily since Lewis and Clark had opened up the area with their explorations for a Northwest Passage from 1804 to 1806. As people migrated farther west to southern Michigan, Illinois and Missouri, their letters home told of fertile valleys and plains that could grow almost anything, rivers and lakes full of fish and waterfowl, and forests teeming with game and

The stone-lined route to the underground cellars of Stone Hill Winery at Hermann, Missouri.

fur-bearing animals. They also told of the hardships of settling the new land and of fearful encounters with hostile Indians. The negative prospects seemed to provide little deterrent to the droves of people who moved into the territory, more than willing to face the challenges. By 1820 the banks of the wide Missouri had become the young country's new frontier. A youthful sodbuster—as the first Midwestern farmers were called—wrote back to his home in the East, "Ma, you can see as far as you please here and almost every foot in sight can be plowed."

One young man who ventured into the Ohio River Valley was Nicholas Longworth, who became one of the earliest American wine entrepreneurs. Making his way west from Newark, New Jersey, Longworth settled in Cincinnati in 1803. Ohio had just become a state and Longworth's law practice and land acquisitions soon made him a wealthy man. Within a few years he had taken up grapegrowing as a hobby and, by 1823, had planted vineyards along the steep banks of the Ohio River outside Cincinnati. In 1825, he acquired cuttings of a new variety, the pink Catawba, developed by Maryland grape breeder John Adlum. So pleased was he with the wine he made from this grape, he quit his law practice to devote full time to winemaking. Ohio Catawba wines soon became famous, aided in part by America's best-known poet of the day, Henry Wadsworth Longfellow. In 1854, Longfellow's experience of a bottle of Longworth's sparkling Catawba prompted the poet to pen his appreciation with an "Ode to Catawba." The eleven-stanza ode served to immortalize the wine and the grape with these familiar lines:

> Very good in its way
> Is the Verzenay,
> Or the Sillery soft and creamy,
> But Catawba wine
> Has a taste more divine,
> More dulcet, delicious and dreamy.

OHIO

By 1859 the banks of the Ohio River were being referred to as "America's Rhineland," and as early as 1836 Ohio, whose vineyards also extended along the shores of Lake Erie, was the wine center of the United States. The state was producing over half a million gallons, far more than any other wine region of the day. The 1850s saw the heyday of river traffic; this was the era of the keelboat and the steamboat. The Ohio River was a major waterway and barrels and bottles of wine made up a fair portion of the cargo on these vessels. Wine was shipped from the port of Cincinnati to New Orleans, New York and abroad. The triumph was short lived, however. Black rot and powdery mildew scourged the vineyards in 1859, destroying some 10,000 acres of vineyard in the southwestern part of the state within a few years. Longworth's magnificent dream ended in failure; in 1863 he died and the vineyards, dispersed among his heirs, were abandoned shortly thereafter.

Ohio is experiencing a resurgence in winemaking. After the vines in the southern part of the state were wiped out, the bulk of the Ohio wine industry shifted to the shores of Lake Erie, where today vineyards stretch from Toledo to Cleveland and beyond, across Pennsylvania into New York. The lake tempers winter temperatures enough to permit the flourishing of wine grapes, even the cold-sensitive vinifera, and lake breezes help reduce the threat from insects in summer. Ohio has more than thirty wineries, most of which are small operations. The state's largest winery is Meier's Wine Cellars, which owns vineyards on Isle St. George in Lake Erie, and others near Sandusky. Meier's produces some 3 million gallons (about 1.3 million cases) of wine annually—from native grapes, French hybrids and vinifera (Chardonnay and Riesling)—under several labels, including Lonz, Mon Ami and Isle St. George.

It is, however, the small young wineries of Ohio that are producing the most interesting wines. Markko Vineyard at Conneaut near the

Pennsylvania border, just inland from Lake Erie, produces excellent Chardonnay, a wine that is about as near as one comes to French Chablis in this country. Owner Arnulf Esterer was inspired to grow Chardonnay, Cabernet Sauvignon and Riesling by Dr. Konstantin Frank of New York, and Markko's success has encouraged others in the state to plant vinifera.

Other bright spots on Ohio's wine horizon include growing operations like Chalet Debonné, Breitenbach Wine Cellars and Grand River Wine Company, which grow hybrids and some vinifera. Grand River, east of Cleveland, is doing quite well with Merlot, a useful development, since Cabernet Sauvignon will not always ripen here because the growing season is too short. Merlot ripens earlier, however, and Grand River has produced wines of rich color and good body. The winery also grows limited quantities of Chardonnay, Gewürztraminer and Sauvignon Blanc, all of which require hilling up in winter. Grand River's most popular wine is Vignoles, a white French hybrid made in both dry and sweet styles.

MICHIGAN

Wine grapes were first planted in Michigan in the mid-1800s, but more of them went into juice than into wine, even before Prohibition. Today Michigan is the fifth-largest wine region in the country, but success with wine grapes will come as little surprise to anyone who knows of the state's cornucopia of gastronomic delicacies. Michigan is second only to California in the variety of foodstuffs—both wild and cultivated—that grow in its fields, forests, rivers and, of course, Lake Michigan.

Skepticism on the part of consumers and their own lack of experience are the biggest hurdles modern winegrowers have had to surmount in Michigan, especially those who wanted to grow species other than the tried-and-true, cold-hardy labrusca, including Catawba. Most of the 1960s and 1970s generation of winegrowers have wanted to make wines that people could drink with food, rather than the types

that have traditionally been produced here, like Concord, Catawba, Cold Duck and fortified wines. Tabor Hill Vineyard, founded in 1970, was the first to concentrate on premium grapes like French hybrids and, later, Chardonnay and Riesling.

Fenn Valley Vineyards is typical of the small, family-owned vineyards of the Heartland. Owned by the Welsch family, it is situated about four and a half miles east of Lake Michigan, halfway between Grand Rapids and Kalamazoo, and produces some 10,000 to 12,000 cases of wine a year. On the wet spring day that I visited the winery, Doug Welsch, son of the founder, was in the winery laboratory testing a Seyval Blanc to be sure it was stable for shipping. Placing a beaker over a blue gas flame, he explained that the winery doesn't use any preservatives in its wines, so the wine must be sterile before it is shipped.

Welsch performs this operation for every wine that Fenn Valley makes. It is one of many painstaking tasks required by the labor-intensive pursuit of making wine—hardly what he had envisioned a decade ago when he gave up teaching high school science to become a winemaker. "By and large, wineries of this size are family operations that got into the wine business—and I can honestly say this in every case—for the romance of it," he said.

The hilltop farm that Welsch's father purchased at Fennville in 1972 was well suited to grapegrowing. The farm is on top of a large dune glacial deposit with deep, sandy soil. The climate had already proved suitable for such fragile, cold-sensitive crops as peaches and cherries. Because cherries are particularly susceptible to spring frost, as peaches are to winter cold, the presence of the two crops indicated that the land was also suitable for grapes.

Doug Welsch had just graduated from college, where he had been trained as a teacher. Discovering that he didn't like teaching, he got the job of clearing his family's land and planting the vineyard. By the third year, Welsch had planted fifty acres of vines, but like many of the young winegrowers in the region, he was oper-

ating in the dark to a large extent. "We didn't really know what we were doing," said Welsch. "It wasn't until six or seven years later that I discovered many of these varieties we had planted weren't appropriate for our region. Either they couldn't be grown economically or they didn't make good wine." Cascade (a French hybrid), for instance, should grow here according to the experts—it makes a beautiful rosé in the East—but in Michigan it produced such a feeble crop it was abandoned. Other grapes that grew well in the Niagara Peninsula and elsewhere in New York failed as well.

Fenn Valley at present grows mostly French hybrids that include white varieties such as Seyval Blanc, Vidal Blanc and Vignoles, and reds like Chancellor and Chambourcin, along with Chardonnay, Riesling and other vinifera varieties. They are also trying some Pinot Noir, Gamay and different kinds of Muscat. "Some wineries are going exclusively for vinifera," said Welsch. "That's fine, but I don't see how they're going to make out economically here, because the grapes are low yield. Look at it this way—if it costs me $1,200 an acre to take care of Riesling, and I get only 2 or 3 tons of grapes, I've got to get at least $800 or $900 a ton out of it. That translates to $7 or $8 a bottle. On the other hand I can take Seyval or Vidal, put in $500 to $600 worth of labor, get back 4 to 6 tons an acre, and charge only $3.50 to $4.50 per bottle. We want to produce some of the premium wines like Chardonnay and Riesling, but we pay the light bill with the less expensive wines."

Labor is the key word here. In regions where vinifera can die from the cold, what vineyardists call "winterkill," the extra care the vines require—hilling up before the first freeze, unhilling in spring, replanting vines that do not survive—is costly in terms of labor. The yield is often significantly lower than with hybrid varieties, and consequently less wine can be produced. These factors mean the wine will cost more, and here, as in many parts of the country, young wineries struggle to market their wines against stiff competition from the established

names in imported and California wines. Little by little, they are gaining more acceptance locally, but the pace until recently has been agonizingly slow.

Down in the cellar we tasted Fenn Valley wines from barrel, starting with the 1985 Chardonnay. The wine was dry, lean and austere, with a little extra flavor and roundness picked up from aging in Limousin oak barrels, the same type used for many white Burgundies and California Chardonnays. It had good acidity and probably enough fruit to blossom with time, though it was a little shy on what is called varietal character, the essence of fruit character that distinguishes each variety. Varietal character varies somewhat, depending on where the grapes are grown and the style of wine for which the winemaker aims. "We're still working out our oenological style here in the cellar, just like we experiment in the vineyard," said Welsch. "I'm going to try something different with Chardonnay next year. We had a winemaker here from California last week and he suggested

VINEYARDS
OF THE
HEARTLAND

All Fenn Valley
wines are fermented
in stainless steel vats
before the reds, like
Chancellor, go on to
be aged in American
oak.

that I try giving it more contact with the lees
[spent yeast cells and other sediment that sink
to the bottom of the vat or cask after fermenta-
tion]. It will be creamier with about thirty days
on the lees."

Welsch uses a combination of techniques
employed in the Beaujolais and Bordeaux regions with his principal red, the French hybrid
called Chancellor. About 30 percent whole
clusters go into the fermenter to develop the
fruitiness of Beaujolais. The remainder of the
grapes are destemmed and crushed in the traditional Bordeaux manner, the skins and juice
macerated to extract the necessary tannin and
astringency for aging. The Chancellor was a
good solid red, flavorful and fruity, with cher-
rylike aromas. It had what winetasters refer to as
"backbone," an underlying structure of acidity
and tannin that holds it together nicely and
gives it some potential for aging. I could see it
as an excellent match for roast beef or grilled
steak in a few years. Fenn also produces a Rasp-
berry Wine, made from Michigan red raspber-

ries, which makes a delicious substitute for *crème
de cassis* in Kir Royale.

Like all small winegrowers, the Welsches
discovered that the hard work as well as the
problems that crop up constantly had a sobering
effect on the dream aspect of growing grapes
and making wine. As Doug Welsch remarked,
"With all the problems of growing grapes, production and marketing, it's not so much living
a dream as living a nightmare." But he laughed
as he said it.

"Reality finally comes into play," said
Welsch's father, Bill. "If our goal was to make
money then we've made a gigantic mistake. But
the fact that it offers such an attractive way of
life is still an important part of why we're here.
The contacts you make in this business are far
more interesting than what you find in ordinary
commerce. And there is a certain romance about
it even when it's tough. So much of you is tied
up in this. [We're] not just selling a bottle of
wine, it's something we grew and made and
watched over ourselves. There's an aura about it

and a future maybe."

Michigan does indeed have a future in wine, not only in the fruit belt of the southwest, but in other parts of the state, where families like the Welsches own small vineyards and wineries. Some of the state's best wines in recent years have come from the northern Leelanau Peninsula, which juts into the northern end of Lake Michigan. The lake's strong moderating influence on winter and summer temperatures makes it highly suitable for growing fruit, especially cherries. Quite a cluster of wineries are now situated here, including L. Mawby Vineyard, Good Harbor Vineyards, Leelanau Wine Cellars, Boskydel Vineyard and the area's largest, Grand Traverse Vineyards near Traverse City. Edward O'Keefe, who founded Grand Traverse in 1976, began making wine with grape juice imported from California until his own vineyards came into bearing. Though he still uses California juice for nonvintage blends, wines under the Chateau Grand Traverse label are all estate grown and include Chardonnay,

Riesling, Gamay, Merlot and Scheurebe (a German vinifera cross used for sweet late-harvest wines).

Other cold-climate states of the northern Midwest, such as Wisconsin and Minnesota, have a few daring souls. The Alexis Bailly Vineyard southeast of Minneapolis produces surprisingly flavorful red wines from hybrids like Maréchal Foch and Léon Millot. The Wollersheim family in Prairie du Sac, Wisconsin, makes an excellent German-style Riesling that has bested its counterparts from California in several competitions.

MISSOURI

Along the banks of the Missouri River at historic little towns like Augusta and Hermann, as well as south of the river on the Ozark Highlands, growing conditions for wine grapes are somewhat different. Winters are not quite as long or severe as those in the northern sections

of the Heartland, though occasionally a fierce arctic storm sweeps through, like the one in the winter of 1985. Known locally as the "Alberta Clipper" (it took shape on the plains of the Canadian province of Alberta and swept as far south as Tennessee), the storm exacted a heavy toll on the less hardy species in Missouri, particularly vinifera like Chardonnay and Riesling, many vines succumbing to winterkill. This was disheartening to growers like Larry Carver in Rolla, who had come back home to Missouri from California with the express desire to succeed with vinifera.

Carver started out in 1977 with five acres in the viticultural area known as the Ozark Highlands, a region of deeply eroded hills with prairie plateaus north of the Ozark mountains. Limestone caves and caverns crisscross the area, and mountain springs feed a network of rivers, underground streams and hidden lakes. It was a great place to hide out if you needed to, as did the infamous James brothers, Jesse and Frank, whose escapades are recounted in many local

legends. Droves of tourists visit Meramec Caverns, where the Jameses supposedly took refuge. Today the area is mainly a recreational playground for spelunkers, canoeists and other outdoor enthusiasts.

Larry Carver's vinifera vines were not exactly thriving in the cold Missouri winters. But he—and the vines—hung on until the Alberta Clipper sailed through, dealing the vineyard its final blow, killing most of the vines. But Carver was philosophical about his loss and took it in stride. He has since shifted away from vinifera, maintaining only about an acre and a half, planted primarily with Chardonnay and a few vines each of Riesling, Cabernet, Gewürztraminer and Gamay. It's simply more profitable to grow hybrids here, so he switched to varieties like Seyval Blanc, Vidal Blanc and Chancellor, although he will persevere with the little plot of vinifera. His best wine, in fact, is Chardonnay. The 1985, of which he made a single barrel, had a crisp appley flavor, nicely rounded fruit and a touch of oak that promised an excellent future.

Venison sausage, homemade bread and native Missouri wines are featured fare at Stone Hill's restaurant, Vintage 1847. (PAGES 90–91): Stone Hill is Missouri's oldest winery, founded in 1847. During Prohibition, their underground cellars (PAGES 92–93) were used for growing mushrooms. Now that the winery has been recently restored, the cellars once again host barrels of wine.

"Nearly every grapegrower in the state grows vinifera," said Jim Held of Stone Hill in Hermann, "we just don't grow them very long. You always hear about it when it's planted. You just hardly ever hear about harvests."

Stone Hill, on a high knoll in the town of Hermann, is Missouri's oldest winery and its largest, producing about 35,000 cases a year. It was founded over a century ago, in 1847, shortly after Hermann was settled by a group of German immigrants from Philadelphia. The winery was enormously successful: By the turn of the century it was the third-largest winery in the world, producing over a million gallons of wine a year and winning numerous medals in international competitions. The handsome redbrick winery has underground tunnels that lead to cellars carved into the hillside. When Prohibition halted the production of wine, the cellars were turned over to the growing of mushrooms.

James and Betty Ann Held were local farmers near Hermann, growing typical Missouri crops—corn, soybeans, vegetables and fruits, including grapes. One day they got a call from a St. Louis doctor, who invited them to a meeting at Stone Hill. The doctor's wife had a relative in Germany who was a winemaker and the two men had decided to go into partnership and buy the winery from the mushroom grower. "To make a long story short," Jim Held recounted, "it turned out that the doctor didn't have as much money as the German winemaker thought he had, and the German winemaker didn't have as much money as the doctor thought, so they parted company. But it started us thinking about how we could buy it and start up in a small way. So in 1965 we did."

The Helds were not fully aware of the dramatic step they had taken at the time. "We really didn't know what we were doing," said Betty Ann. "We were young and knew so little that we weren't afraid." Jim laughed. "We started with $1,500; last week our payroll was a little over $12,000. We have twenty-five full-time employees now." Their two sons are among them. Jonathan is vineyard manager at Stone

Hill, and the younger son, Thomas, is in charge of the family's new operation at Branson in the Ozarks, which specializes in fruit and sparkling wines. The Helds' oldest daughter, Patricia, is a winemaker in New York State. Clearly, the move in 1965 affected the destiny of the entire family.

In the first year the Helds made 1,500 gallons of wine, aging it in used whiskey barrels. "It was pretty awful," said Held, "but the next year we bought some used oak ovals from a liquor distributor in St. Louis who brought in bulk wine from California and bottled it himself. Each year we learned a little more, but finally in 1976 I went out to the University of California at Davis and hired a winemaker. We didn't get the top of the class, but at least he knew more than we did. Two years later we hired our present winemaker, David Johnson, and that was a great step forward for us." Stone Hill now produces 85,000 gallons annually. In 1986, about 38 percent of Missouri wine sold in the state was from Stone Hill.

To Jim Held and other local vintners, the failure of vinifera varieties is no real disappointment. They feel that the key is to be sufficiently open-minded to find out what grows best in Missouri and which varieties make the best wine, and in some cases this means retracing paths ventured upon seventy or eighty years ago.

The most intriguing wine I discovered in Missouri is a red made from a native American grape variety known by various names: Norton, Virginia Seedling, Cynthiana. Stone Hill's 1981 Norton is solid, meaty wine that can easily stand with some of the world's better reds. Sturdy and well balanced, this deep red wine has complex aromas reminiscent of Bordeaux and California Cabernet but a taste all its own. The grape has been grown in the Midwest since the mid-1800s—Frederick Muench, who wrote a treatise on viticulture in 1865, praised it:

The Virginia Seedling as yet far surpasses any other variety. A Mr. Norton in Virgina, raised a bastard seedling,
which was afterward brought to Cincinnati...Almost
twenty years ago a Mr. Widersprecher brought a sprig of
it from there to Hermann, Missouri, little thinking that
in doing so he was presenting the State with a gift worth
millions.

No one in Missouri has made millions
from the Virginia Seedling as yet, but some believe that day may come. According to Jim
Held, Norton wine won gold medals in New
York, Vienna and Paris before Prohibition.
Stone Hill sold it as Red Label Burgundy, but
there is still some confusion over the name used
for the wine today. "We call it Norton because
I'm convinced that's the right name," said
Held. In Hedrick's *Grapes of New York*, printed
in the early 1900s, it is listed as Virginia Seedling and Norton Seedling. At Montelle Vineyard in Augusta, the name for the wine is
Cynthiana, certainly a more euphonious designation than Norton.

Regardless of how this is ultimately re-
solved, the variety deserves to be better known
and more widely planted. It is one of the few
native varieties with none of the grapiness so
objectionable in other American grapes. Norton is the easiest to grow in Missouri, and it
withstands winter cold and temperature fluctu-
ations better than any other variety. The Helds
and other producers are constantly experimenting with the grape, aging the wine in different
types of oak, for example. They experiment in
the vineyard as well. It is tremendously vigorous in terms of foliage. In an attempt to divert
some of that vigor toward the production of
more fruit, Jonathan Held is trying closer vine
spacing. "We're hanging a lot on this one," said
Jim Held about the Norton variety. "This is the
one we want to be known for."

In terms of white varieties, Held believes
that Ravat, a French hybrid, is the white grape
of Missouri's future. "It has better balance,
more character and flavor interest than Seyval or
Vidal," he said. "I think it will be the leading
variety planted twenty years from now." Ravat
is not widely planted at the moment. The lead-

ing white varieties in Missouri are Seyval Blanc
and Vidal, with Chardonnay retaining some interest as more people work with it.

Montelle Vineyards, whose name means
"Little Mountain," is set on a steep hill overlooking bottomland along the Missouri River.
Started in 1970 by Clayton Byers, a St. Louis
newspaperman, Montelle is now owned by a
partnership that includes Bob and Judith Slifer
and Bill and Joanne Fitch. Montelle produces
some very attractive French hybrid varietals,
such as Villard Blanc, de Chaunac and a Baco
Noir labeled Mayfair Reserve, as well as blended wines in sweet and dry styles. The winery's
most interesting wine is Cynthiana, made in a
claretlike style that is firm and moderately concentrated. It sells out within months at Montelle (which sells all its wines right from the
winery); one enthusiastic customer comes out
every week while the supply lasts, buys a bottle
and drinks it out in the rose garden. A bit of
cheese, some good bread, and Missouri Cynthiana—conceivably, a most congenial way to
while away an afternoon.

Arkansas

Since the greater part of Arkansas's 4,500 acres of vineyard are located in the Ozarks, it is most fitting to treat this state as part of the Heartland, even though it is perhaps more usually thought of geographically as part of the South. Arkansas vineyards are situated in the mountains and foothills around such towns as Springdale, Altus, Paris, Morrilton, Harrisburg and Wynne, and small vineyards have also been planted in the southwest near Hope.

The state's largest and most important winery is Wiederkehr Wine Cellars, founded in the 1880s by Swiss immigrant Johann Andreas Wiederkehr. Producer of about one million gallons annually, Wiederkehr's repertoire includes a broad range of table wines, sparkling wines, dessert and fortified wines. Under the direction of the founder's grandson, Alcuin Wiederkehr, the winery has come a long way since the 1950s, when most of the wines were made from labrusca varieties. Al Wiederkehr, who studied oenology and viticulture at the University of California at Davis, has steadily increased plantings of vinifera varieties, and they now make up nearly 70 percent of the vineyard.

The vineyards in this area fall under the Arkansas Mountain appellation, and they share what may be a uniquely favorable situation for vinifera east of the Rockies. Sheltered by the Boston Mountains of the southern Ozarks, they are protected from the severe winter cold that strikes Missouri vineyards. Plantings on the south slopes of Mount St. Mary benefit from a thermal inversion (a climatic phenomenon in which warm air is trapped in the lower atmosphere) that develops over the Arkansas River Valley and the Ouachita mountain range south of it. "We have never had a vineyard killed to the ground like they have in Missouri," says Wiederkehr. There are rare occurrences of problem weather, nonetheless, like the early winter thaw in 1984 that prompted a false spring, followed by temperatures of six degrees below zero. A drought in 1980—the driest summer in

Arkansas history—crippled the industry briefly, destroying vines that had no irrigation. The Wiederkehr vineyard, which has its own reservoir, survived with only minor damage.

Wiederkehr continues to expand the vineyard, now about 255 acres, planting more vinifera but also maintaining certain native varieties like Cynthiana and Niagara, both made in a lightly sweet style that pleases customers. The white French hybrid Verdelet, crisp and off-dry, also sells briskly.

Wiederkehr's most notable successes have been with Riesling, Cabernet Sauvignon and Muscat. He also grows Chardonnay, Chenin Blanc, French Colombard, Merlot and Cabernet Franc. His biggest problem, in fact, stems from the number of varieties he is juggling and he is therefore trying to focus on those that seem to have the greatest potential, in both the vineyard and the marketplace. The winery still produces large quantities of labrusca wines like Concord, as well as various inexpensive fortified wines, since they are important for cash flow at the

moment, but the plan is to phase them out gradually. "I would rather sell one case of Chardonnay," says Al, "than ten cases of white port."

Arkansas's other wineries mostly produce wines from native species and French hybrids. The Post family, also at Altus, produces half a million gallons annually, primarily from native species including Cynthiana and Muscadine. Smaller wineries like Cowie Wine Cellars, Mount Bethel Winery and Mt. Kessler Winery are also capitalizing on the state's increasing enthusiasm for the wine grape.

Elsewhere in the Heartland region, there are wineries and vineyards in Iowa, Illinois, Wisconsin, Minnesota and Kansas, though on a limited scale. According to Marian Russell, a frequent traveler along the Santa Fe Trail in the 1850s, Kansas once was considered prime land for grapes. Rumor flew that the entire state was to be turned into a massive vineyard, so mild and genial was the climate. The problem in Kansas was twofold: Prohibitionists sought to keep the state dry and effectively scotched the budding industry in 1880, and during the revival of grapegrowing in the 1960s and 1970s, wheat farmers' use of the herbicide 2,4-D fatally damaged the grapes of amateur growers during flowering. Nevertheless, recent experimental work at Kansas State University may ultimately revive winegrowing on a commercial scale.

Charles Sax hoses down his 1920s wine press (LEFT). From vines planted in the 1880s near Altus, Sax makes a sweet Cynthiana aged in used whiskey barrels. (BELOW): Swiss-style carvings enhance the alpine atmosphere at Wiederkehr.

CHAPTER FOUR

VINEYARDS OF THE SOUTHWEST

"AT LAST, I HAVE FOUND MY GRAPE PARADISE! Surely, now, I thought, this is the place for experimentation with grapes." Driving through Texas twenty years ago, who would have imagined anyone uttering such a statement? Texas is cotton country, cattle country, oil country. But wine grapes? Preposterous! Yet, this ardent assertion was indeed uttered—over a hundred years ago, in 1876—by one Thomas Volney Munson, who was prompted to such enthusiasm by the proliferation of wild grapes that he saw everywhere he went in Texas.

Though few are aware of it, this plant hunter and grape breeder is one of the heroes of American viticulture. It was Munson's strongly held conviction that "the grape is the most beautiful, most wholesome and nutritious, most certain and profitable fruit that can be grown." With this outlook, he embarked on a search that took him on a journey of some 75,000 miles, crisscrossing the United States through all but six states, even dipping into Mexico. His life's work was devoted to the hybridization of new grape varieties that could be grown in Texas and the Midwest; varieties that were resistant to local pests and diseases; that were both cold-hardy and able to flourish in dry or humid areas. Munson developed over three hundred new varieties, many of which, unfortunately, disappeared after his death in 1913.

Munson's greatest achievement, however, was saving the vineyards of France in the 1880s, when they were nearly destroyed by the parasite known as phylloxera. Native American vine species were resistant to the little bug, so Munson and Hermann Jaeger, a grape breeder in Missouri, shipped thousands of American root-

stocks to grateful winegrowers in France. In 1888 Munson and Jaeger were awarded the Légion d'Honneur de Mérite Agricole by the French government.

Winemaking in Texas, however, predated the Munson era by some 250 years. This, too, is a surprise to most people, who consider the birthplace of American wine to be either California or New York; but in fact, the earliest American wine was made from Scuppernong by Huguenots in Florida, and Texas can claim credit for the earliest American efforts with European species. In 1662, a full hundred years before the planting of California's first vines, Franciscan fathers came up from Mexico into the El Paso Valley, where they established the San Ysleta Mission. Strapped to the backs of their pack mules were vines of the Spanish Mission grape from which they made wine to celebrate the Eucharist. Vineyards undoubtedly went in elsewhere in the territory as well. The Spanish inhabited the southern half of Texas and other parts of the Southwest for two centuries after the arrival of Coronado and Cabeza de Vaca in the mid-1500s. Missions were started in various places, but they were frequently abandoned because of insurrection, Indian attacks and encroachment by the French and English who were also trying to claim the region. The abandoned mission vineyards died off, but wild grapes grew in abundance throughout the territory.

When Mexico gained independence from Spain in 1821, Texas was part of Mexican territory. For the next fifty years Texas, especially west Texas, was a wild and woolly place that belonged mostly to the Comanches, the

Thistle blooms at the end of vine rows at Sonoita Vineyards in southeastern Arizona.

Apaches and the buffalo. These were the lords of the plain, and it was a dangerous place for anyone else. Even after Texas became part of the Union in 1836, settlers who pressed westward stopped short of the *llano estacado*, the "staked plain" that lay some three hundred miles to the west of Fort Worth.

What is often thought to divide east Texas from west Texas today is the string of cities that begins at Fort Worth and winds south through Waco, Austin, San Antonio and Corpus Christi. East of here, Texas is green and rolling, much of it supporting rich and fertile land planted with cotton, corn, soybeans, fruit trees and other crops; but it is not considered suitable for wine grapes because it is so humid. Nevertheless, two modern vineyards are situated here: Messina Hof Wine Cellars, near Bryan, and Chateau Texas, at Driftwood. Most of the vineyards in Texas, however, are west of the dividing line, in the rugged hill country west of Austin, out on the *llano estacado* around Lubbock and in mesa country south of Midland–Odessa; a handful of vineyards also dot the vicinity around Fort Worth.

As you head west toward Fort Stockton on Interstate 10, the relentless bleakness of the landscape is almost oppressive. The gray plains, devoid of life except for the tough and wiry sage and creosote bushes and an occasional long-eared jackrabbit, stretch for miles as far as you can see in every direction, for the most part flat though slightly undulating in spots. A lone mesa breaks the monotony now and then. The main drama out here is the weather. There's a saying in Texas: "If you don't like the scenery, drive a few miles; if you don't like the weather, wait a few minutes." The weather all over Texas can change in a flash, bringing horrendous storms with barely enough rain to settle the fine, powdery dust continually kicked up by whirlwinds.

People do live out here, but why, one wonders, would a person have settled on land that appears so harsh and desolate? Buffalo had a lot to do with it. The first white settlers saw herds by the thousands thriving on the thick grasses that grew here, and all they could think of was getting rich by running cattle. What they did not see was everything else that went with it—the sandstorms; the droughts that starved the cattle in summer (buffalo simply migrated north when things got tough); the blue northers that broke across the plains in winter, bringing blinding snow, some years freezing the cattle in their tracks; the tornadoes and crackling thunderstorms that could run a herd to destruction in the stagnant heat of a summer night. But the cattlemen came, irresistibly drawn to the limitless space that could be had for the asking, or taking. As Indians became less of a threat, the ranchers moved onto the range and a new kind of hero emerged, that American original, the cowboy. Our image of the cowboy, fostered by fiction and film, is as hero, but more usually he was a fairly simple fellow not much given to talk or heroics, happiest and most comfortable astride a horse herding the Texas Longhorn.

It is estimated that some 10 million cattle moved out of Texas between 1866 and 1890, on long cattle drives northward to markets like Abilene, Kansas, or to richer grasslands in Nebraska, Wyoming and Montana. One cannot speak about this country without mention of the Longhorn and the buffalo. The land was theirs to roam and graze to begin with, back when a sea of grass covered the prairie. The grass could be so tall in some places, in fact, that it easily concealed a man on horseback. It is said that the *llano estacado* was so named when Coronado marched across what is now Texas in search of the legendary Seven Cities of Cíbola, marking his route by driving in tall wooden stakes that could be seen above this grass.

By 1870 the buffalo had been almost annihilated, and the Longhorn too was soon almost extinguished as range barons turned to other breeds. Within forty years the grasslands had been practically grazed out. Today, a cow and a calf require fifty acres to nourish them, and when you're grazing several hundred head—or several thousand—that calls for vast amounts of territory. The land area per se is no problem: There is plenty of it in west Texas. But the waning demand for beef seen in recent years has lowered beef prices, thus bringing poor return on the land, both for cattlemen and for the landowners who leased out the land.

This situation presented a challenge to the University of Texas, the largest landholder in the western part of the state with its endowment of over 2 million acres that currently seem to be punctuated with as many oil derricks as head of cattle. Oil can run out, however, and the prospect for beef prices rising significantly seemed remote, so in the early 1970s the university began to investigate other ways to utilize the land. Several crops were considered: cotton, which already grew on the northern plain around Lubbock, fruit trees, almonds and, among other crops, grapes—both wine and table varieties.

A preliminary study indicated that wine grapes were the most feasible as well as the most likely to bring a good return on investment per acre. Limited water was a key factor and one that worked in the grape's favor. With modern irrigation techniques such as the drip method (a system that waters each vine individually), grapevines need only twenty to twenty-four acre inches of water a year; cotton requires thirty-six to forty-eight. So, in 1975, the university team planted an experimental vineyard near Bakersfield on Interstate 10.

About this time others were becoming interested in the possibility of winegrowing in Texas as well. The California wine boom was just taking off and Texans, like other Americans, were beginning to learn that wine was a different substance from other alcoholic drinks. They not only wanted to know more about it, many wanted to grow it and make it themselves. Bobby Smith, an osteopath in Arlington, started La Buena Vida in 1974; Ed and Susan Auler, who had traveled to Burgundy in 1973 and had come back eager to start a vineyard, did so in the hill country west of Austin in 1975. Cypress Valley Winery and Messina Hof Wine Cellars began in 1977. Today there are eighteen wineries in Texas with others undoubtedly in the offing. A single winery survives from the last century: Valverde, down on the Rio Grande at Del Rio on the Mexican border. Founded in 1883 by Frank Qualia, an immigrant from Milan, Valverde produces wines made from sturdy native grapes like Lenoir and Herbemont. The winery in fact survived during Prohibition by selling these and other varieties as table grapes.

It takes six or seven years to know for sure what a vineyard is capable of producing, though eager beginners will make wine off third leaf (the grower's term for a three-year-old vine). By 1981 the team at the university, supported by additional research from horticulturists at Texas A & M, were convinced that vineyards offered a viable future for west Texas. The University of Texas was interested in growing grapes but not in making wine. This was, after all, the western arc of the Bible Belt, and it was felt that wine production should be undertaken by a separate organization. The university's 1,000-acre vineyard was leased to a corporation known as S.G.R.C., a partnership between two French concerns and a couple of Texas investors that founded Ste. Genevieve Vineyards.

The vineyard is the patch of vibrant green that suddenly appears along Interstate 10, a few miles east of Fort Stockton. Anywhere else, a 1,000-acre vineyard would be considered vast; here it is merely a bright spot on the landscape, dwarfed by the vast monochromatic countryside surrounding it. The vine rows run two miles in length to the foot of a giant mesa—a landmark that University of Texas scientists have christened Skyscraper Peak—and it is this striking setting that is captured on the Ste. Genevieve wine label. Ste. Genevieve was the patroness of Paris, and S.G.R.C. chose the name to reflect the French connection in the partnership.

The first wines under the Ste. Genevieve label were from the 1984 vintage and made at Llano Estacado Winery near Lubbock, since S.G.R.C.'s $15 million winery was yet to be built. The mammoth white structure, completed in 1985, looms like a monolith out of the plain about a mile west of the vineyard and has the look of a fortress, or a giant grain dryer. It has none of the visually appealing design fea-

tures that attract visitors, but the site was not chosen for its tourist appeal, though I-10 is a major artery linking Los Angeles to Florida via Tucson, El Paso, San Antonio and New Orleans. It was positioned to be close to the vineyard, enabling the winemakers to get the grapes to the crusher in the shortest possible time. The interior gleams with the high-tech sheen given off by rows of 30,000-gallon stainless steel tanks, which accommodate a fermenting capacity of 1.5 million gallons.

S.G.R.C. was dissolved in the fall of 1986, leaving Ste. Genevieve's future somewhat in question. An enormous investment was made here—in time, in effort, and in huge amounts of money. Control of the vineyard has reverted to the University of Texas, which plans to maintain the vineyard and bring in consultants from California to operate the winery until new owners can be found. Meanwhile, wines continue to be produced under the Ste. Genevieve label.

The university has retained Ste. Gene-

vieve's vineyard manager, Tom Childs, who spent years as a viticulturist in California's San Joaquin Valley. Growing grapes here is an entirely different proposition than in California. For one thing, the constant breezes that sweep across Texas—averaging ten miles per hour, and often moving at fifteen or sixteen miles an hour—create good air circulation through the vineyard, reducing the humidity that would promote rot and moving cold air along when frost threatens. They are also helpful against some insects, although leafhoppers and flea beetles are still problems at times.

Sunburn can be a problem, too, both for the vines and the grape clusters, so Childs encourages the creation of a vigorous leaf canopy and he trains the vines so that the canes and fruit are well shaded. Although the mercury climbs to over one hundred degrees on some days, temperatures during the growing season generally range from seventy-five to ninety, and drop twenty or thirty degrees at night. Under the University of California climatic classifications

(see page 130), west Texas is a warm Region III, but the wind is still a factor, as are mild winters when the vines do not go fully dormant. If temperatures drop suddenly, the vines suffer winterkill.

Rainfall is scant here, ten or eleven inches annually, but drip irrigation provides precisely the amount of water and nutrients the vines need. Although iron and zinc are in the soil, for example, they are bound up in a way that makes them inaccessible to the vine roots, so these and other nutrients are fed through the drip system to each vine.

Only vinifera varieties are planted; and the white wines from these young vines are more attractive than the reds, thus far, although more time is required to fairly evaluate their potential here. The Barbera, for instance, is rather light in character now but may develop more interesting flavor as the vines mature. The whites, especially Sauvignon Blanc and Chenin Blanc, have fresh crisp fruit and are light in body. Ste. Genevieve's styles of wine are dictated by the marketplace. The 1984 Sauvignon Blanc, for example, was dry, but the 1985 was rather sweet, which the marketers felt was more what wine drinkers preferred. "If consumers want sweet Sauvignon Blanc, we'll sweeten it," stated the winery's manager. Such shifting of style could result in some confusion among consumers, however, and it is not always easy to keep pace with swings in the public taste.

Ste. Genevieve embodies the corporate approach to Texas winemaking, but most Texas wineries are small, family-owned operations that were started for very different reasons. Ed Auler, a successful young lawyer and cattle rancher in Austin, had little notion in 1973 that in ten years he would be selling all the wine he could make from his own vineyard. At that time he and his wife, Susan, knew very little about wine. Twenty days in France changed their lives. Going to France to learn more about French cattle breeds, they also visited vineyards in Burgundy, Bordeaux and other wine regions. As they acquired an appreciation for some of France's fine wines, Auler noticed that certain areas of France were similar in soil, topography and climate to the hill country west of Austin where, as a boy, he spent summers on the family ranch. The limestone outcroppings in Burgundy reminded him of stony ground at Fall Creek Ranch, causing him to wonder why grape growing had not been tried in Texas.

As Auler soon learned after returning from France, experimentation was well underway at the University of Texas, Texas Tech and Texas A & M. A handful of hobbyists had also started vineyards of their own, so it seemed an idea worth pursuing. Urging things along was the devastating nosedive taken by the cattle market in 1974, so that year the Aulers planted a quarter-acre test plot, working with plant scientists at Texas A & M. As with any new and untried region, the experts always say it cannot be done. You can grow native grapes, and you *might* grow hybrids, but certainly not vinifera.

Auler started with a mix of hybrids—Aurora, Baco Noir, Villard Blanc and vinifera crosses like Ruby Cabernet, Emerald Riesling and Carnelian. All the vines, vinifera and hybrid, exceeded everyone's expectations, growing with a vigor heretofore inconceivable. They expanded the vineyard and were doing exceptionally well, selling out their first few vintages of wine. In 1980, catastrophe struck—or so it appeared at first. Cottonroot fungus attacked the vineyard, destroying most of the vines. Auler had to replant the vineyard on different rootstock, starting over almost from scratch. "It turned out to be the best thing that ever happened to us," he recalls today. "The vinifera

Comanches once roamed the country around Fall Creek, which tumbles over a thirty-foot bluff into Lake Buchanan. (OPPOSITE).

*Catfish, hush pup-
pies, and Fall Creek
Sauvignon Blanc—
a felicitous combi-
nation.*

crossings were even more successful than hybrids, so we were able to phase the hybrids out
gradually and graft over to true vinifera like
Chardonnay, Sauvignon Blanc, Chenin Blanc
and French Colombard.''

The hill country is a rocky escarpment
known as the Edwards Plateau, part of the Bal-
cones Fault that runs from Hudson Bay to the
Sierra Madre range in Mexico. It is rugged
country, littered with broken granite and jag-
ged promontories. The Spanish called this
brush country *la brasada*, dotted as it is with
mesquite, juniper, prickly pear and other
thorny growths, but wild grapes grow here too,
and the sandy loam topsoil of the meadows supports grasses rich in the protein and minerals
that are ideal for cattle.

Fall Creek Vineyard is planted on a deep,
well-drained plot that abuts Lake Buchanan (lo-
cals put the emphasis on the first syllable and
pronounce it *buck*-an-an), a huge manmade lake
created by a dam on the Colorado River.

The best view of the setting is from a high
plateau above the ranch along Fall Creek, and
from this vantage point the lake's effect on the
vineyards can be seen clearly. Large bodies of
water always moderate the shoreline climate,
and the 23,000-acre, 32-mile-long Lake Buchanan is large enough to have an important effect on the vineyard's microclimate. The
Edwards Plateau is also affected by air currents
from two directions. The southeastern wind,
from the direction of Austin and, beyond it, the
Gulf of Mexico, is warm and humid. The prevailing winds are westerly, however, blowing
up from Mexico's Chihuahuan Desert cool and
dry in the morning, but heating up considerably in the afternoons. This is where the lake
helps. The hot air cools down as it moves across
the lake. It gets very warm even so—ninety to
one hundred degrees during the day—though
the vineyard cools off quickly at night, to sixty
or seventy degrees. "Our poorer vintages," says
Auler, "are in years when the humid winds from
the gulf override the dry winds from the southwest. Then we'll get rot or mildew or rain dur-

ing the harvest." Fortunately, it does not happen often.

Fall Creek's most popular wines are Chenin Blanc and Emerald Riesling, crisp white wines that are lightly sweet and well balanced, easy to like. Close on their heels is the fruity red Carnelian, made in Beaujolais style that emphasizes ruby-red fruit reminiscent of raspberries and cherries. The dry Sauvignon Blanc, blended with Sémillon and aged in Limousin oak in the manner of fine white Graves from Bordeaux, is quite good. Auler is very pleased with his Sémillon, which has begun to develop a figlike character typical of the variety in Bordeaux. Fall Creek Chardonnay and Cabernet Sauvignon demonstrate promise as well, though the young vines need a few more years to show their true character.

The Aulers built a new winery in 1984, with handsomely appointed living quarters where they planned to spend weekends and entertain friends. But they are spending more and more time there. Ed basically has given up practicing law and breeding cattle. "Winemaking is the perfect work for me," he says, "because I like to work with my mind and I like to work with my hands, but I never could do either one full-time. The vineyard and winery allow me to do both." Susan strongly supports this and is fully involved. She does a lot of traveling to conduct tastings, appear at wine events and meet a public that seems increasingly receptive to Fall Creek wines.

There are other success stories in Texas, notably in Lubbock County, heart of the *llano estacado*. Pheasant Ridge Winery—named for the ring-necked pheasants that populate the area—was founded in 1982. The vineyard was first planted in 1978 by Charles Robert Cox III, who has concentrated primarily on proving that good Cabernet can be grown on the High Plains. Pheasant Ridge's first Cabernet won immediate recognition for its fine character and balance in 1982. Other Pheasant Ridge wines—Chardonnay, Sauvignon Blanc, Chenin Blanc and Bar-

bera—have also been well received by consumers and wine critics.

Cox maintains that closer spacing is essential for good fruit and healthy vines. With the vines planted four feet apart, with six feet between rows (eight by twelve is the traditional spacing in California), the vines' roots are forced to grow more deeply into the soil. Competing for nutrients in the closer spacing also stresses the vines to some extent, limiting new growth and sending more energy into the fruit. This results in wines of better balance and more concentration. The Lubbock area has a shorter growing season than California, but Cox says this is offset by the fact that they get maturity in the grapes at lower sugars.

Expanding his work with Cabernet, Cox is planting new vineyards in separate parcels as a hedge against the region's worst danger to grapevines—hail. Lubbock is on the edge of the Midwest's "tornado alley," which suffers sudden changes in temperature and the constant threat of hail. Vineyards concentrated in a sin-

gle area could be wiped out in the space of minutes by a storm that brings hailstones the size of golf balls, which can do enormous damage by tearing leaves, destroying flowers or bruising fruit. The same problem exists in the French Beaujolais and Burgundy regions. Various things have been tried to combat the problem —shooting hail rockets to break up the ice balls with silver iodide, or laying hail nets over the vines to shield them—but these methods are costly and do not always work. "We pray a lot and watch the clouds," says Cox.

Near Pheasant Ridge, another important Texas winery is Llano Estacado Winery. Founded in 1976 by a chemist, Dr. Clinton McPherson, and a horticulturist, Professor Robert Reed, Llano Estacado grows only vinifera varieties, producing about 40,000 cases of wine annually. The winery, which has the largest distribution outside the state, concentrates primarily on white wines such as Chardonnay, Chenin Blanc and Riesling, all of which are notable for their crisp character and clean varietal fruit. Llano also grows Cabernet Sauvignon, making a red varietal as well as a rosé of Cabernet.

One of the selling points for Texas wines is the very *idea* of wine from Texas. People are immediately intrigued when they hear about it— they want to know more; they want to taste it. Such interest has surfaced in New York, California and many other places, and can be a tremendous encouragement to a young industry, as well as a boon in terms of cash flow. The wine, however, has to be good—otherwise people can quickly be turned off and may be reluctant to try other wines. Response to many of the newer Texas wines, both inside the state and elsewhere, has been positive on the whole.

It seems quite likely that Texas will eventually become a significant presence on the American wine scene. Although the industry is basically still in its infancy, achievements so far indicate that wines of sound and attractive quality can be made here on a fairly large scale, and

with some consistency. In years when climate conditions are more favorable, even better wines are possible, particularly among top varietals like Chardonnay, Cabernet Sauvignon and Sauvignon Blanc. Growth has already come fairly quickly. Prior to 1975, Texas had one bonded winery; today there are eighteen. In 1982, Texas wineries produced 50,000 gallons of wine; by 1986, quantity had jumped to over half a million gallons.

New Mexico

In the late nineteenth century, about 1880, New Mexico was producing a million gallons of wine annually, ranking fifth in U.S. wine production. None of its wineries survived Prohibition, but in recent years the state has made an astonishing comeback. Today there are some eighteen wineries in New Mexico, large ones like St. Clair Vineyards in Deming, farm wineries like La Chiripada Winery north of Santa Fe, and others of various size in between.

Winter snow is common in the vineyards hosted by the high desert plateaus of New Mexico.

La Chiripada has the distinction of being at the highest elevation of any commercial winery in the country: six thousand feet above sea level. Situated halfway between Santa Fe and Taos, it is a quaint white adobe structure built by two brothers, Michael and Patrick Johnson. The Johnson brothers were both monks who left their respective orders in 1968 and resettled where they had grown up. Patrick is a talented potter and his pottery is on display and sold, along with the wines, in La Chiripada's tasting room. Michael, a former Jesuit, worked for a time in the winery at the Novitiate of Los Gatos in California.

La Chiripada is in the Española Valley in the foothills of the Sangre de Cristo mountain range. The region depends a lot on mountain snowmelt for its water. Fed by the Embudo River, which rushes west and joins the Rio Grande within three miles of the vineyard, the valley becomes green and lush during the growing season.

Even small wineries today use technologi-cally sophisticated equipment, and it is there-fore surprising to see the small basket press on the concrete platform where the grapes are crushed at La Chiripada. The Johnson brothers make only two thousand cases a year, mostly from French hybrids like Cayuga, Aurora, Ro-sette, Léon Millot, Chancellor and Foch, all of which can withstand the winter cold and frosts that can come as late as May. They also grow small amounts of Riesling and Pinot Noir.

The Johnsons use proprietary names in-stead of varietal grape names, which gives the wines more of their own identity. They are pleasantly attractive wines, simple for the most part but clean and fresh, just what you want for everyday drinking, a picnic or a cookout. One of the most appealing wines is Vino Sonrojo—*son-rojo* being Spanish for "blush"—a pale pink wine that is delicately sweet and very enjoyable. Primavera is a blend of white grapes, fragrant and fresh, light bodied and fruity. What Pat-rick calls "our robust red" is Rojo Grande, made from Chancellor and Carignane. It is sturdy and

full bodied, aged in French oak for about eighteen months.

The Johnsons have reserve wines, too, a Reserve Riesling made from grapes purchased from Rio Valley Vineyards, in Belén to the south, and a Vinter's Special Reserve Red, made from selected lots of red wines in certain years.

La Chiripada wines are sold mostly from the winery. The sign on the highway between Santa Fe and Taos gives directions to the winery and advertises the wine and pottery, an unusual combination that lures tourists. There is also a small tasting room in Taos, extending the winery's reputation further. The Johnsons receive an increasing number of requests for their wines from other parts of the state, and they are already making plans for expansion that include planting more vinifera vineyards.

At the opposite end of the scale—and the state—is St. Clair, an ambitious operation in the Mimbres Valley west of Las Cruces. St. Clair is owned by a family of Swiss winegrowers and a group of investors. Vincent and Noël Vuignier looked at various regions in America in 1982, including California, Texas and Arizona, before settling on southern New Mexico in what was once known as the Uvas Valley. "I believe in old names," said Vincent Vuignier. "*Uvas* means 'grapes' in Spanish and there must have been a reason for that." Underground water is abundant here, and plenty is needed for the six hundred acres of vines surrounding the large winery. The Vuigniers liked the climate in Deming, with its warm days for ripening followed by cool nights. This is high desert, 4,350 feet above sea level, but warm enough, the Vuigniers believe, to ripen vinifera. The vineyards were planted in 1983, 1984 and 1985, and are therefore too young for one to judge the quality of the wines they will yield. The first vintages seemed rather thin and lacking in fruit, especially the Chardonnay, though a light fruity Muscat was more appealing. The red wines, Barbera and Cabernet Sauvignon, also tasted green and not entirely ripe, though the color was good. At present more time is needed to see what sort of character they are capable of developing.

Efforts elsewhere in New Mexico offer further encouragement. One of the best New Mexico wines I have tasted is a red wine made from a little-known French hybrid called Lucie Kuhlmann. In 1983, amateur winemaker Richard Jones planted a quarter-acre experimental vineyard in the Sangre de Cristo Mountains a thousand feet above La Chiripada. The Lucie Kuhlmann, of which there were a mere thirty cases, is a dark, richly complex red, packed with more flavor, tannin and extract than any red wine of my experience from the Southwest. It is a wine I hope we see more of in the future.

South of Las Cruces, Dr. Clarence Cooper, a former physics professor, has a small vineyard and winery called La Vina Winery. Dr. Cooper's Cabernet Sauvignon, very highly regarded for its sound varietal character and balance, is an indication of the potential for reds in the southern part of the state. To the west, toward Arizona, Blue Teal Vineyards produces fresh, attractive wines from a three-hundred-acre vineyard about ten miles north of Lordsburg. Blue Teal makes white Zinfandel, a generic Blanc de Blancs and a fine dry Riesling and will also produce Chardonnay. A siege of locusts damaged the Blue Teal vineyard in 1986, consuming the leaves and effectively shutting down the vines, but this is not a common occurrence. It does show once again, however, what growers can find themselves up against in this part of the country.

ARIZONA

Some of the best wines in the Southwest come from a small vineyard in the hills southeast of Tucson, Arizona: Sonoita Vineyards, started in 1978 by Dr. Gordon Dutt, a professor of agriculture at the University of Arizona. Dr. Dutt is a soil scientist who became excited about grape-growing when he worked on a project in Arizona that investigated growing fruits and other

A vine on the verge of flowering (TOP). *Gordon Dutt* (BOTTOM), *founder of Sonoita Vineyards in the hills southeast of Tucson.*

crops without irrigation. Among those that thrived were wine grapes. Dutt taught himself to make wine in an unused building owned by the university. Pleased at the outcome, he immediately purchased vineyard land on part of the Babocamari Ranch near Elgin, one of the legendary ranches of the nineteenth-century Southwest. What brought the professor to Sonoita Vineyards is the soil. "Soil makes the difference in making exceptional wine," he declares. "They know this in Europe. In California all you hear about is climate, but soil makes the wine." Professor Dutt expounds on this thesis, explaining the geological phenomenon known as *terra rosa*, or red earth, that is frequently found in some of the world's greatest wine regions, notably Burgundy. Soils of the Côte d'Or, where the great red and white Burgundies are grown, contain a sublayer of red clay with an underlying layer of limestone, which are thought to give the wines their distinctive character. Since the soil of southeastern Arizona has a similar makeup, the professor believes that the state, and specifically Sonoita, may produce America's best Pinot Noir.

Perhaps it will, or he will. Professor Dutt has already produced the most interesting and complex wines to come out of the Southwest, including Texas. His dry Chenin Blanc has the aroma and flavor of good Vouvray. His Fumé Blanc is crisp, tart but flinty, and slightly austere, much like a good Sancerre. Sonoita's 1984 Cabernet Sauvignon is superb, unlike any that I have tasted from American wineries. It is lean structured, but deeply colored, intensely flavored and complex, all one would expect from good Bordeaux. It will be interesting to taste it fully developed about ten years down the road. Sonoita is leading Arizona winemaking.

Professor Dutt has coined his own term for the area that runs through southeastern Arizona, New Mexico and west Texas not far from the Mexican border. He calls it the Border Wine Belt and believes that it will someday be one of the important winegrowing regions. High elevations ranging from 2,500 to 5,000 feet above sea level moderate the desertlike conditions. The soil composition indicates that development of varietal character—the essential aroma and flavor of the grape—is highly promising.

Other Arizona growers support this view. R.W. Webb built a large winery on the outskirts of Tucson in 1986. He owns an eight-acre vineyard but also buys grapes from the Roberts Vineyard, a sizable operation a few miles east at Bowie, Arizona. The R.W. Webb winery produces good Chenin Blanc, French Colombard and a Reserve Cabernet Sauvignon. Additional vineyards are reportedly starting up and the Arizona farm winery bill passed in 1982 will undoubtedly encourage others.

As for the remaining states of the Southwest, Nevada and Utah have a few small, hobbyist-owned vineyards. The sole commercial operation at the moment is Summum in Salt Lake City, a winery that purchases grapes from California and makes only sacramental wines. Colorado, somewhat peripheral to the Southwest, has about fifteen small growers and three wineries, two of which purchase California grapes. Pike's Peak Vineyards at Colorado Springs grows its own, a mix of French hybrids and a small amount of Chardonnay and Riesling. New vinifera planted in the western part of the state around Grand Junction show possibilities for grapes like Merlot, Sauvignon Blanc and Chardonnay.

Texas, with the most wineries and the broadest visibility for its wines nationwide, has taken the lead in the Southwest. As New Mexico gains in vineyard acreage and production and Arizona increases its stylish output, the Southwest may ultimately emerge as a major force on the American wine scene.

Sonoita Vineyard occupies a high plateau southeast of Tucson.

CHAPTER FIVE

VINEYARDS OF CALIFORNIA

CALIFORNIA IS REGARDED AS A PARADISE FOR the vine—stick anything into its fertile earth and it grows—and when seen in light of the difficulties inherent in winegrowing in other regions, the reason for California's eminence becomes clear.

What sets California wines apart from all others on the continent is sheer power; all that sunshine translates into a richness of flavor and of body that makes for a commanding presence. Of course it can be overdone. Sometimes overpowering to the point of coarseness, California wines have been known to be overripe, overly alcoholic or so intensely concentrated that they nearly knock you over.

These wines weren't always that way, and they are far less apt to be today, but many of the winemakers who emerged in the 1960s and 1970s underwent a period during which they were mesmerized by just that power. The watchword was *extract*. "We want to extract everything there is in that grape," one young winemaker told me in 1979, during a tasting of his 1977 Cabernet Sauvignon, a sample drawn from the oak barrel. It had everything, all right—and too much of all of it. Big, brawny wines in the 1970s impressed a lot of people, including the critics, who frequently praised the blockbusters that assaulted the palate with tannin, alcohol and *extract*. But in the hands of a gifted winemaker, that raw power is harnessed, sculpted into the refined structure, elegance and harmony that have increasingly become the hallmarks of California's best wines.

California is the only place where *Vitis vinifera* has thrived vintage after vintage from the very beginning, a beginning that goes back over two hundred years to 1769, when Spanish padres moved from Mexico into Alta California. The missions established by these Franciscans had the aim of making Christians of the native tribes and instructing them in their ways of civilization. The Spanish government set a timetable of ten years in which each of the missions was to accomplish this task, after which they were to be secularized and turned over to the Indians to be managed as permanent communities. Twenty-one missions were built—from San Diego in the south, to Sonoma, north of San Francisco—over the ensuing fifty years.

Father Junípero Serra, who was in charge of the earliest missions, is known as the "father of California wine." Historians have not been able to verify whether or not he actually brought vines with him on the overland trek from Mexico. It may have been some years later, by ship, that the Spanish vinifera vine that came to be known as the Mission grape arrived. Wine was needed immediately for the Sacrament, however, and it is surmised that the fathers at first made this from the abundant wild grapes. These were soon abandoned because the wine was not good. Once the Spanish vines arrived and were planted, the Indians were taught to tend the vines and make wine. According to Ruth Teiser and Catherine Harroun's detailed history, *Winemaking in California,* whole families of Indians took part in the grape harvest and trod the grapes in the mission wineries. We can assume that the early wines were sweet and fairly potent, since the Mission grape ripens to high sugars. Mission grapes have traditionally been used for fortified dessert wines, which vines that survive continue to produce today.

The bells of Mission Santa Inés, which was founded in 1804 by Spanish padres—who were the first to plant vines in California. (PAGES 124–125): Neatly pruned Zinfandel vines stand amid rows of wild mustard along the Silverado Trail. Mustard is grown between vine rows as a cover crop.

After the missions were secularized in the 1830s, winegrowing began to spread, first to the pueblo of Los Angeles, then north to Sonoma, gradually expanding into the fertile valleys surrounding San Francisco Bay. As the population of California increased, so did the demand for wine. By the second half of the nineteenth century, winegrowing had become a thriving industry in several areas of the state. A succession of dynamic people were instrumental in the process, beginning in the 1830s. Jean-Louis Vignes, a Frenchman from Bordeaux, established a large vineyard at Los Angeles—right in the heart of today's downtown—with cuttings he imported from France. These were the first vinifera vines other than Mission to be planted in California. In the north, Colonel Agostón Haraszthy, a Hungarian immigrant who came to be known as the "father of California viticulture," distributed cuttings he had gathered on a lengthy foray through Europe's leading vineyards. General Mariano G. Vallejo, governor of Alta California, established his headquarters in Sonoma and became the first significant winegrower in the north. Impressed by Vallejo's wines, Colonel Haraszthy purchased land from him to start his own vineyard. The colonel's two sons, Arpad and Attila, each married a daughter of Vallejo, uniting the two leading wine dynasties of the day.

Within another decade or so, more famous names were established: Jacob Schramm of Schramsberg, Charles Krug, the Beringer brothers, the Korbels. Gustave Niebaum, a Finnish sea captain, founded Inglenook Vineyards. In Santa Clara Valley at San Jose, French immigrants Etienne Thée and Charles LeFranc established Almadén; Paul Masson and the Mirassou brothers planted vineyards nearby. Wente Bros. was founded at Livermore in 1883.

Thanks to the favorable climate, the wine and grape industries of California prospered, but not entirely without ups and downs. Boom and bust periods alternated, success invariably following catastrophe: Phylloxera struck in the 1880s; a grape glut in the early 1900s caused prices to plunge; the earthquake of 1906 took a heavy toll of wine stored in cellars that caved in, from San Francisco as far north as Santa Rosa. The industry survived them all. The one thing it could not survive was Prohibition.

Most of the vintners never really believed it would come to pass, or at least that wine would be exempted if it did. All but a handful of wineries were closed down. Wineries that had special dispensation to produce sacramental wines remained in operation but were restricted to making sweet fortified altar wines. The rest of the wineries were padlocked. Wine sat in casks for years, eventually becoming moldy or acetic. Equipment rusted. Vineyards were abandoned.

Some growers fared better, however. Those who grew the tougher-skinned grapes like Zinfandel or Alicante Bouschet found a ready market in the home winemakers of the East. Soon grapes were being shipped by the carload to Boston, New York, New Jersey, largely to supply Italian immigrants with a means of making wine. The demand for home-made wines was a lifesaver for some California vineyards, and it explains why a few sixty-year-old Zinfandel vineyards still exist in scattered pockets, producing highly concentrated wines that are treasured and treated with reverence.

After Repeal in 1933, the industry basically had to start again. It was a sluggish effort at first; the Depression was on, so money was tight, but the seeds of a new era were being sown. In the San Joaquin Valley, the young Gallo brothers, Ernest and Julio, borrowed money to buy a grape crusher and a pair of redwood vats. Though their father had made wine, the boys knew little about the process, and they learned the rudiments of winemaking at the public library in Modesto. About this time Louis M. Martini, whose family had emigrated from Italy early in the twentieth century, came to Napa Valley, building a new winery there in 1933. A few years later Georges de Latour brought André Tchelistcheff over from France to be winemaker at Beaulieu Vineyards. Captain Niebaum's grandnephew, John Daniel, was in charge at Inglenook.

Gallo went on to become the world's largest winery, best known for fortified wines and quality jug wines. The other three, along with Wente in Livermore Valley, quietly produced some of California's best wines from the nobler grape varieties: Cabernet Sauvignon, Chardonnay, Riesling, Pinot Noir, Sauvignon Blanc, Sémillon. The market for wine was not very strong in this country through the 1940s and even the 1950s, but a few things were happening during those decades that would have far-reaching significance:

• Frank Schoonmaker, a knowledgeable importer and possessor of one of America's most discerning palates, had sought out California's best wines in the 1940s. He urged producers to stop using old generic names like "Burgundy" and "Chablis" and call the wines by varietal names of the grapes used to make them.

• A maverick winemaker named Martin Ray began producing extraordinary wines from his hilltop vineyards at Saratoga in the Santa Cruz range: Cabernet Sauvignon, Chardonnay, Pinot Noir and champagne. In the 1950s, Ray's wines garnered a following among those who were familiar with great French Burgundies and Bordeaux.

• In 1952 James Zellerbach, a wealthy businessman who had served as U.S. ambassador to Italy, established Hanzell, a Burgundian-style wine estate in Sonoma Valley. While living in Europe he had fallen in love with the great wines of Burgundy's Côte d'Or—Montrachet, Clos Vougeot, Romanée-Conti. Aiming to make wines of similar character, he planted hillside vineyards of the Burgundian varieties Pinot Noir and Chardonnay, and imported Burgundian oak in which to age them. He even built a miniature replica of the great Burgundian chateau, Clos de Vougeot. The wines' French style and flavor impressed wine lovers and experts alike.

By the mid-1960s a new breed of winemaker had appeared on the scene. These were people fired with the romantic notion of making fine wines that could equal those from Europe's greatest vineyards, and who were convinced it was possible because they had tasted great wines that had come out of California soil. In 1959 a group of Stanford professors founded Ridge Vineyards in the Santa Cruz mountains; in 1964 Joseph Heitz founded Heitz Cellars in Napa Valley. Robert Travers bought Mayacamas (in the mountain range of the same name, which separates Napa from Sonoma) in 1965, and that same year Jack Davies revived the old Schramsberg estate and began making champagne, while Richard Graff acquired Chalone Vineyards in Monterey. In 1966, Robert Mondavi left Charles Krug and started his own winery at Oakville. It was one of those periods when new forces are set in motion. As the social upheaval of the 1960s erupted throughout the country, new waves were making themselves felt in the wine industry. America was on the brink of the love affair with wine that would flower in the 1970s and 1980s.

Actually, it exploded. The number of California wineries in 1960 numbered under one hundred; today it is over seven hundred. In the 1970s California began to be recognized as one of the most technologically advanced and innovative wine regions in the world. The schools of oenology and viticulture at the University of California at Davis and Fresno State University drew winemakers and would-be winemakers from many points on the globe, including France, Italy and Australia. And, of course, California winemakers continued to make their fact-finding treks back to these countries to better understand the nuances of grapegrowing and winemaking.

Although nearly 80 percent of California wine comes from the sprawling inland valley of San Joaquin—a 230-mile stretch from Lodi to Bakersfield with more than half a million acres of grapes—most of it is produced in bulk and goes into jugs. These are not the wines that brought about the wine boom of the 1970s.

California's best wines come from the cool coastal regions: Napa, Sonoma, Mendocino and Lake counties in the north; Alameda and Santa Clara to the east and south of San Francisco; the Santa Cruz mountains; and Monterey County,

San Luis Obispo County and Santa Barbara County along the Central Coast. South of Santa Barbara there are a few isolated pockets suitable for fine wine grapes, like Temecula and Escondido, but most of southern California is too hot to grow quality grapes. Starting in the 1930s, professors at the University of California at Davis developed a system of climate regions ranging from the coolest, Region I (including Carneros and the Russian River Valley), to the warmest, Region V (including San Joaquin and southern California). Based on "degree days" (when the temperature is 50 degrees or above), the system defines regions in terms of heat summation. A mean temperature of 70 degrees, for instance, would equal 20 degree days (70 − 50 = 20). The number of degree days between April 1 and October 31 determines the region:

Region I: 2,500 (or fewer) degree days
Region II: 2,501 to 3,000 degree days
Region III: 3,001 to 3,500 degree days
Region IV: 3,501 to 4,000 degree days
Region V: 4,001 (or more) degree days

Winegrowing in California has been a serious business from the start, and it is the place that holds the longest American track record for quality and consistency. In California, grapegrowing is a profession of long standing, unlike in many regions of the country where owning a vineyard is apt to have started out as a hobby or weekend pursuit. The European immigrants who laid the foundations for the California wine industry knew well that great wine is made in the vineyard and they staked out claims that are now recognized as among the most favored spots on earth for great wine.

Napa Valley

Louis M. Martini was regarded as one of the savviest of vineyard men in California wine. The son of Italian immigrants who came to California shortly before the turn of the century, Martini got his start in the San Joaquin Valley. Although his first winery was built in Kingsburg in 1920, just about the time Prohibition

Through mid-May, the delicate young foliage will be vulnerable to frost damage. (PAGES 132–133): The red earth of Louis M. Martini's Monte Rosso Vineyard comprises 250 acres in the Mayacamas Mountains overlooking Sonoma Valley.

went into effect, he managed to do a profitable business anyway, selling grape juice and concentrates to home winemakers. The sherries and ports that he made were allowed to be sold for sacramental and medicinal purposes. Martini recognized that once Prohibition was over there would be a huge demand for good wine. He also realized that he was not in the best place to produce it. Scouting Napa Valley in 1932, he purchased property just south of the town of St. Helena and began building a winery in 1933.

Louis Martini was one of the great pioneers in the vineyard revival that followed Prohibition. Within a few years he had acquired some of the best vineyard land in the state: Monte Rosso Vineyard in the Mayacamas mountains and two properties in Carneros, the cool hills in southern Napa overlooking San Pablo Bay. Martini made a reputation for the firm, well-balanced red wines—Cabernet Sauvignon, Zinfandel, Pinot Noir—that came from these and other holdings in Napa and Sonoma.

Louis M. Martini died in 1974, but the winery that bears his name is still owned by the Martini family, operated by his son Louis P., and his three grandchildren, Carolyn, Michael and Patricia. Louis P. worked alongside his father all his life, except for a stint in the Air Force during World War II. The younger Louis's expertise in two areas is renowned: viticulture and the art of blending. Starting in the 1950s, his Special Selection and Private Reserve Cabernet Sauvignons, Pinot Noirs and Zinfandels won high praise from critics and collectors for three decades, and many of these wines remain superb today. Louis P. turned the winemaking over to Michael in 1977, but he continues to be actively involved, especially in the vineyards.

One sunny afternoon in June, Louis drove me up to the legendary Monte Rosso. We drove over the Mayacamas range on the Oakville grade, came down into Sonoma Valley and then climbed back up a winding mountain road to Monte Rosso. As the vines came in view, I saw immediately how the vineyard got its name, which means "red mountain" in Italian. The

sun reflected off the soil, bathing the landscape in a warm glow. The vivid red color, caused by the high iron content of the volcanic soil, was astonishing, accentuated by the lush green of the vines. This terra rosa is found in a few choice spots around the globe that produce exceptional wine, notably the Côte d'Or of Burgundy. Louis's father bought the property in 1938 when it was planted mostly in Burger, Riesling, Chasselas, Zinfandel and a little-known white variety called Folle Blanche. Slowly the Martinis began replacing the less desirable varieties with Cabernet Sauvignon, Gamay, more Zinfandel, Riesling and Chenin Blanc.

Stands of Zinfandel planted in the 1890s—twisted old vines with short thick trunks the size of small trees—still remain. The grapes from these wiry stumps produce richly concentrated juice that makes Monte Rosso Zinfandels collectors' items. The 250-acre vineyard is dryfarmed—that is, nonirrigated, watered only by rainfall. This stresses the vines, resulting in low yield and fruit that is more con-

centrated in flavor. The vines send their roots deep into the earth, probably thirty feet or more, in search of pockets of moisture. As they descend through the various layers of soil, the vine roots pick up nutrients that give Monte Rosso grapes their unique character. The Cabernet Sauvignons have an intense aroma and flavor of black currants, with an inherent balance of fruit and acidity that makes them very long-lived: Monte Rosso Cabernets from the 1940s still have life and vigor in them.

The other Martini vineyards, some eight hundred acres in all, each have their own distinctive character, and selected portions of top vintages are bottled under the names of the vineyards from which they are produced. Los Viñedos del Rio is in the cool Russian River district of Sonoma; Glen Oak Vineyard is in Chiles Valley, a group of hills to the east of Napa Valley proper but included in the Napa Valley appellation. The elder Martini was one of the earliest vintners to recognize the Carneros district as an important area for Pinot Noir and

Chardonnay and the first to make a substantial investment in vineyard land. In 1942 he bought a portion of the old Stanly Ranch, famed in its day for producing consistently superior wines, mostly red. La Loma Vineyard has 210 acres, primarily planted in Pinot Noir, with some Cabernet Sauvignon. Martini purchased another Carneros vineyard four miles away called Las Amigas, where Chardonnay and other varieties are planted.

Los Carneros, a series of hills near San Pablo Bay, is one of California's coolest wine-growing regions. Carneros has its own appellation but is a subregion of both Napa and Sonoma valleys, bisected by the county line. The name is Spanish for "sheep," but as far back as anyone can remember, it was principally dairy country. Only a few vineyards existed in Carneros until the early 1980s, but today it is literally carpeted in grapevines. Fog-bound and windswept, the Carneros is a marginal area for grapegrowing, but it can be superb for varieties like Pinot Noir that need to mature slowly.

Chardonnay does well here, too, but it is occasionally too cool for some grapes. Cabernet will not ripen every year in parts of Carneros (though it seems to on the Sonoma side of the line). Carneros grapes command high prices, and without question some of California's best Pinot Noirs and Chardonnays come from here as do, increasingly, Cabernet Sauvignon and Merlot.

The Martinis originally produced a full line of wines that included the "mountain" jug wines, fortified sherries and ports, and several oddball wines such as Napa Duriff, Gutedel and Red Pinot (Pinot St. George). In recent years the spectrum has narrowed to eleven varietal wines and four generics. Martini still produces Mountain Red and Mountain White, generic blends that are creditable everyday wines. But the winery is best known for Cabernet, Zinfandel and Pinot Noir, particularly those labeled Special Selection or bearing vineyard designation.

The Martinis' best-kept secret is a delicate sweet wine called Moscato Amabile. Louis M.

Sunset on Carneros. These cool hills south of Napa and Sonoma valleys are noted for fostering fine Chardonnay and Pinot Noir.

first made this wine in 1936, by accident really. He had some extra Muscatel juice and a few empty brandy barrels, so he put the grape juice in them, added a little yeast and covered it with a layer of cotton. It was December and the wine slowly fermented over the winter. In the spring, the story goes, when checking the barrels he found a delectable nectar, slightly effervescent from the carbon dioxide trapped in the cold wine. It was a great hit, and still is, but it is available only at the winery. As it tends to referment, the wine must be kept cold. Moscato Amabile fans bring ice packs and thermal bags to the winery to transport it home. Martini also produces a fine cream sherry.

Napa Valley has long been the home of outstanding Cabernet Sauvignons. A small arc of land nestled between mountain ranges, the valley is some thirty-five miles in length and a little over a mile wide at its narrowest point. Good Cabernets come from many parts of the valley: the hills, the mountains, and the valley floor from south to north. Several important districts for Cabernets have emerged over the last decade, such as the Stag's Leap District, Howell Mountain and Pritchard Hill. But many of the most distinctive Cabernets come from a strip of land against the western hills running from Oakville to St. Helena known as the Rutherford Bench. Cabernets grown here have a character all their own, with aromas of cedar or hints of mint and eucalyptus, dark fruit with cassislike flavors, great depth and balance that enable them to age well.

The prototype among Cabernets is Beaulieu Vineyard's Georges de Latour Private Reserve, which for over thirty years was made by André Tchelistcheff, California's most revered winemaker. Born in Russia, Tchelistcheff was trained in France as an oenologist and came to Napa Valley in 1937 to be winemaker at Beaulieu. His expert palate soon singled out Beaulieu's finest Cabernet vineyards on the Rutherford Bench, with their taste of what he termed "the Rutherford dust," a kind of *goût de terroir* (taste imparted from earth) that informs

most wines from many of the world's great vineyards. In time, other Cabernets with this signature emerged: Inglenook's Cask Reserve Cabernets, Freemark Abbey's Cabernet Bosché, Robert Mondavi Reserve, Heitz Cellars' Martha's Vineyard and Bella Oaks and, more recently, Rubicon and Spotteswoode.

The single most famous plot along the Rutherford Bench is Martha's Vineyard, now owned by Tom and Martha May. But the man who made it famous is Joseph Heitz, who buys the grapes from the Mays and makes the wine that has become legendary. From the first vintage of 1966, Heitz kept the grapes separate from his other Cabernet grapes and discreetly put "Martha's Vineyard" on a corner of the label to designate it as something special. It quickly gained a devoted following. Heitz Cellars Martha's Vineyard Cabernet is a big, rich wine, full of flavor that practically leaps from the glass. The aromas spring forth, spicy and berryish, redolent of eucalyptus and mint, which can be quite exaggerated in some vintages. The flavors are ripe and luxuriant, but the wine is not overburdened with tannin as are some of the big Cabernets. These wines age well, and they drink well just about every step of the way.

The original twelve acres that are now part of the forty-acre vineyard were planted in 1960 by Dr. Bernard Rhodes, a physician and wine collector from San Francisco, and his wife Belle. "I would like to claim that it [the vineyard] was a brilliant move and that we selected it because we knew it would make a unique wine," Dr. Rhodes recalls, somewhat ruefully. "Well, in fact we selected it because we wanted to live in

Mountain vineyards such as these owned by Sterling Vineyards on Diamond Mountain (OPPOSITE)—1,200 feet above Napa Valley —yield wines of intense flavor and depth, suitable to long aging. (LEFT): Mechanical harvesters, such as this one at work in Rutherford Hill's Napa Valley vineyards, are used increasingly worldwide. Not only can they accomplish the equivalent labors of forty human pickers, they also allow for harvesting at night when the grapes are cool, thus retaining a better quality of fruit and aroma. (PAGES 138–139): A sunny December day on Sonoma Mountain provides ideal conditions for pruning at Laurel Glen. Owner Patrick Campbell is in the red shirt.

the little house up on a knoll that looked out over the valley." Below the house was an old prune orchard, and it is common wisdom in wine country that land where prunes grow will be good for vineyards. Dr. Rhodes started investigating soil types and talked to professors from the University of California at Davis, who advised him that it was good land for Cabernet. They were surrounded by Cabernet plantings, actually: Just across the creek was the block of vineyard that makes Robert Mondavi's best Cabernet.

The Rhodeses planted twelve acres of Cabernet Sauvignon and lived there for only a couple of years before they decided to move back to Oakland. Vines take a minimum of three years to set a good crop, and the vineyard was not yet bearing in 1962 when the couple sold the property to Tom and Martha May. The Mays added an adjacent parcel of vineyard that they developed, bringing their total holding to forty acres, all Cabernet Sauvignon. Along the way the vineyard acquired its famous moniker, and

the rest is live history in the bottle.

Bernard Rhodes appears to have a nose for good Cabernet land. Just biding his time until he could move back to Napa Valley for good, in 1968 he and Belle bought another property farther north on the Rutherford Bench. It, too, had a prune orchard on it, which they operated for a year and then cleared to plant the vineyard. This time they had a better idea of what they wanted, something different from what they had done down at Oakville. They selected different clones of Cabernet and used tighter spacing in the vineyard, eight by ten feet instead of the old eight-by-twelve configuration. The soil was a little different as well, richer and deeper than the Martha's property. Joseph Heitz contracted to buy these grapes, too, and the first Bella Oaks Cabernet was from the 1976 vintage.

The Bella Oaks Cabernet makes its own statement. With none of the eucalyptus character of Martha's Vineyard, it is a classically structured Cabernet that has subtle complexities of

flavor needing time to develop. None of the vintages has yet reached its peak. Bella Oaks Cabernet commands thirty-five dollars for bottles from current vintages, more for older ones.

SONOMA

The ridge known as Sonoma Mountain lies between Santa Rosa and Glen Ellen. Laurel Glen Vineyard's thirty-five acres slope gently across the mountain 2,400 feet above sea level. A little to the southwest is the vineyard Jack London once owned, which still produces grapes. And to the east, across the Valley of the Moon, you can see the rolling contours of Monte Rosso. It is good land for Cabernet Sauvignon and Merlot, which are the primary grape varieties planted at Laurel Glen. Most of Laurel Glen angles to the northeast, which is important for even ripening, since the vines get the full force of morning sun but are inclined away from the intense heat of the afternoon sun that hits west-facing slopes.

Owner Patrick Campbell was solely a grower for nine years, selling his grapes to wineries like Chateau St. Jean, Veedercrest and Kenwood Vineyards, but in 1981 he decided it was time to establish his own label. He had definite ideas about the kind of wine he wanted, aiming for an estate-grown Cabernet Sauvignon, blended with Merlot and a little Cabernet Franc, producing a wine rich in flavor but elegantly balanced.

The grapes at Laurel Glen are handpicked and then hand sorted at the crusher, with Campbell checking every load that goes through; grapes that show signs of rot, or anything else he does not like, are thrown out. Many of the techniques used here are too labor-intensive to be practical at larger wineries, like punching down the "cap" of skins, pulp and seeds that forms on top of the juice during fermentation. Red wines ferment with the skins, for it is the skin of the grape that contains the color, tannin, and other flavoring elements that are extracted by the heat of fermentation. In the standard approach to winemaking, large hoses are used to pump the juice from the bottom of the tank over the skins, thus breaking up the cap and macerating the juice with the skins. In contrast, Campbell breaks it up by hand several times a day with a long wooden pole shaped like the plumber's friend at one end. It is hard work—the cap can be a couple of feet thick— but worth it, Campbell feels, because it provides a gentler action than pumping and therefore extracts less of the harsher tannins. Most of Campbell's techniques derive from time-honored practices employed in Bordeaux. During the two years the wine spends in French oak barrels, it is "racked" several times. This technique is accomplished by drawing the wine off the lees that have settled in the barrel and piping it into fresh barrels. Campbell believes in frequent racking to aerate the wine. Though air is wine's enemy, small amounts hasten the maturation process so that the wine is quite stable by the time it is bottled. The bottled wine rests about a year at the winery before it is released.

Production is about 5,000 cases of Caber-

Bernard and Belle Rhodes (TOP), proprietors of Bella Oaks Vineyard in Napa Valley, watch as vineyard manager Laurie Wood checks Bella Oaks Cabernet for ripeness. The juice is squeezed onto a grape hydrometer to measure sugar. (BOTTOM): The midnight blue of Cabernet Sauvignon at harvest, Laurel Glen Vineyard.

Although French oak barrels can cost upward of $350 apiece, a period of time in new oak is considered essential for the aging of the best wines. Here, a cooper shaves the inside of a barrel to renew the wood; this can be done to good effect once or twice before the barrel must be replaced.

net a year, which sells for about fourteen dollars a bottle. In a very short time, the wine has become one of the most highly regarded Cabernets in California. Impeccably well balanced, Laurel Glen Cabernet has luxuriant texture that makes it smooth even when quite young, but it is the spicy, blackberry aromas and flavors that make the wine so appealing.

LIVERMORE VALLEY AND MONTEREY

The Wente name in California wine goes back to 1883, when German immigrant Carl H. Wente settled on a fifty-acre plot in Livermore Valley, about sixty miles east of San Francisco. Livermore was mostly cattle ranches and grain fields back then, but by the early years of the new century over twenty wineries were in operation and there were twenty thousand acres of vineyards. Carl's son Ernest, who died in 1985 at age ninety-five, noted in his recollections of the early years that a grape glut drove many out of business in Livermore and Prohibition fin-

ished off the rest. Of the handful that still exist today, Wente and Concannon Vineyards are the most important. Since Concannon was sold in 1983 to a British distiller, Wente is one of the few California wineries still owned and operated by the family that founded it in the nineteenth century. The fourth generation—great-grandchildren of the founder—is now in charge: Eric Wente is president and winemaker, Carolyn is director of marketing and public relations, and Philip is in charge of vineyard operations.

Wente's original 50 acres has now grown to over 1,200, and the region is once again attracting new winegrowers. Livermore's warm climate, cooled by marine winds from the Pacific, and its gravelly, well-drained soil are quite good for certain varieties, particularly Cabernet Sauvignon, Petite Sirah, Sauvignon Blanc and Sémillon. Wente's Sauvignon Blanc and Sémillon vines derive from cuttings originally imported from Château d'Yquem, the illustrious chateau of the Sauternes region in France.

Wente has always been best known for its

white wines such as Chardonnay, Sauvignon Blanc and Gray Riesling, the latter being one of its most popular. Although whites predominate, the winery does produce creditable reds. In addition, they have recently made a big move into sparkling wine. In 1981 the Wentes purchased the old Cresta Blanca winery site, south of the town of Livermore, which is now a state historic landmark. They restored the white stucco cellars to serve as a sparkling-wine facility, as well as the old sandstone caves where they now age 20,000 cases of Wente Vintage Brut (produced from grapes from the Arroyo Seco region). Vineyards surrounding the buildings were replanted, and a visitors' center with an elegant restaurant was completed in 1986. The stunning complex has become the showplace of Livermore Valley, poised to carry the Wente heritage into the next century.

In addition to Livermore, the Wentes pioneered another California wine region—Monterey. In the 1960s, looking to expand production, the

Wentes began a search for soils and climates that could produce as successfully as those in Livermore, and their search led to land in the Arroyo Seco district of Monterey.

Monterey is among the youngest of California's wine regions. The broad, flat Salinas Valley, setting for John Steinbeck's *East of Eden*, used to be known as "the nation's salad bowl," where miles of lettuce, celery, broccoli and other vegetables grew. In the last twenty-five years, however, vineyards have usurped much of the land devoted to vegetable crops, and Monterey is now the largest of the coastal wine regions in terms of acreage, with 36,000 acres planted in vineyards. (Napa and Sonoma are next in size, with just over 30,000 acres each.) In 1962, Mirassou Vineyards, Paul Masson Vineyards, and Wente, all looking to escape the urban sprawl that was overtaking land in Santa Clara and Livermore, became the first wineries to plant vineyards in Monterey. Other familiar names from this area include Jekel Vineyards, Almadén, The Monterey Vineyard, Durney Vineyards and Chalone Vineyards. In the early years of California wine, the insufficient rainfall, a mere ten inches a year, caused Monterey to be shunned by winegrowers. But the vast watertable, fed by the underground Salinas River, is the largest of its kind in the country, and this provided the solution: irrigation. As early as 1935, professors at the University of California at Davis had identified Monterey's cool climate, with its daily breezes from Monterey Bay, as potentially good for growing grapes.

Monterey suffered growing pains in its first decade. The late-1960s' enthusiasm for the new region prompted a rash of planting that proved to be too much too soon in some areas, particularly in the north around the town of Gonzales. Some varieties planted here simply did not ripen. Others, especially reds, had a vegetal character that many wine drinkers found objectionable. Now that the vines have some age on them, and growers have come to understand the region better, Monterey is starting to live up to its original promise. White wines like Chardonnay, Riesling, Gewürztra-

As the wine ages, sediments build up on the inner surfaces of oak barrels. The tartrate-encrusted barrels pictured have nurtured Laurel Glen Cabernet during the eighteen to twenty months it must spend in wood prior to bottling.

VINEYARDS
OF
CALIFORNIA

Fresh figs and goat cheese are fitting accompaniments for Chalone Chardonnay.
(PAGES 146–147):
The broad expanse of the Salinas Valley, near Soledad in Monterey County. Once planted in lettuce, broccoli and other vegetables, the valley now abounds in Vitis vinifera.
(PAGES 148–149):
Moonrise at Chalone Vineyard.

miner and Pinot Blanc have intense fruit and crisp acidity that sets them distinctively apart from wines of other regions. Red wines, notably Cabernet Sauvignon, also show greater potential for quality, particularly those from vineyards along the benchlands of the western hills. Wineries from all regions of California buy grapes from Monterey, and the number of the area's own wineries is gradually increasing.

The Arroyo Seco district of Monterey has proved to be one of the best for wine grapes, especially Chardonnay and Riesling. Set in a basin southwest of Soledad, the area heats up through the morning hours but is cooled by afternoon winds from the Pacific. Arroyo Seco was designated a viticultural area in 1983 and is a frequently cited appellation on wine labels. Wente's Arroyo Seco vineyards comprise some six hundred acres planted with eleven varieties, the largest amount of which is Chardonnay. Wente's Arroyo Seco Chardonnay is one of the winery's best white wines.

A discussion of Monterey would not be complete without mentioning Chalone, one of the most influential wineries in California. Chalone inhabits a unique spot in Monterey, not on the valley floor but 2,000 feet above it in the Gavilan Mountains east of Soledad. The 110 acres of Chalone Vineyard nestle along a rolling plateau in the lee of natural rock walls, and the arid limestone-rich soil is superb for the Burgundian varieties Chardonnay and Pinot Noir. Vines were planted here in 1920 by William Silvear, who later sold grapes to Wente and Almadén. New owners revived the long-idle vineyard and began construction on a winery in the early 1960s, but in 1965, when that partnership dissolved, Richard Graff formed a corporation and bought Chalone. He realized its potential for producing Burgundian-style Chardonnay and Pinot Noir by using the traditional, hand-crafted methods perfected in Burgundy. Production has remained small at Chalone to make this possible. Only about 5,000 cases of their Pinot Noir are produced annually, but as one of the finest examples of this varietal in California, it

commands upward of twenty-five dollars a bottle.

Pinot Noir remains the winemaker's greatest challenge in California, the one that responds most to the human factor in winemaking—and the response is not always positive. This is a quirky, highly temperamental grape, not as stable as other red varieties, and often reacting unpredictably from vintage to vintage. One year it produces a lovely, rounded, complex wine, luscious in aroma and flavor; the next, the same vineyard's version can be tough, thin and acidic, and downright unpleasant to drink. Many wineries have abandoned the variety altogether, but a steadfast few remain dedicated, striving to understand and work with it. "If every year were the same," says Richard Graff, "it wouldn't be any fun. It's the different conditions that make it exciting to work with Pinot Noir."

Graff has spent nearly thirty years of patient effort with Pinot Noir. Over the years he has made numerous visits to Burgundy in quest of the elusive secret that produces the great red Burgundies. He has picked up much just by observing masters like André Noblet, the now-retired cellarmaster at the Domaine de la Romanée-Conti on the Côte d'Or. Patience and close attention ultimately paid off; Graff returned with techniques that he and his brother Peter, Chalone's winemaker, implemented for both Chardonnay and Pinot Noir. Many of these methods are now widely used by others. Chalone produces a few other wines, such as dry Chenin Blanc, dry French Colombard, and Pinot Blanc, but Chardonnay and Pinot Noir are the collectors' items.

Chalone Vineyard went public in 1986. Rather than try to expand the original vineyard, Graff and his partners instead decided to build new wineries, or acquire existing ones. To raise the needed capital, they sold shares of the corporation, which now has six hundred stockholders. Chalone has evolved into a small but high-profile empire that produces wines under four labels, allowing for an enviable diversity of style. These labels include: Chalone, whose

wines are the most complex and the longest-lived; Edna Valley Vineyard, another cool region near San Luis Obispo, producing only slightly lighter Chardonnay and Pinot Noir; Carmenet, which produces a claret-style red and a Sauvignon Blanc and is situated in the Mayacamas range above Sonoma; and the newest acquisition, Acacia Winery in Carneros, a young winery with a reputation for stylish Pinot Noir and Chardonnay, which tend to be the most immediately drinkable of those produced by the four labels.

SANTA YNEZ VALLEY

The hills that encircle the Santa Ynez Valley are golden most of the year, scored with cattle trails, studded with live oaks draped in Spanish moss. In startling contrast, the valley floor is a patchwork of vibrant greens that supports two happy pursuits: wine and horses.

Horses have a longer history in the valley than wine grapes, though the missions—La Purisima and Santa Inés, established in 1787 and 1801—had vineyards, as did Rancho del Refugio, a large ranch near the coast owned by the Ortega family. It was at Santa Inés Mission that one Joseph Chapman, an ex-pirate, learned about viticulture and winemaking. Originally a New Englander, Chapman married an Ortega and eventually went to Los Angeles and planted his own vineyard in 1826, becoming the first American known to do so in California. Meanwhile, the vineyards of Santa Ynez Valley with-

ered away until the 1970s brought about a significant renaissance.

The pioneer vintner of the modern era in Santa Ynez is A. Brooks Firestone. Brooks, grandson of Harvey Firestone, who founded Firestone Tire & Rubber, thrives on a hard day's work, but selling tires was not the way he wanted to expend his energies. Although groomed for the executive suite, he withdrew from the corporate scene—"I'm the classic executive drop-out," he admits—and began casting about for something that would claim both his energy and his enthusiasm. His father, Leonard Firestone, owned a three-hundred-acre vineyard and cattle ranch in Santa Ynez Valley and asked Brooks to explore its investment potential. The figures indicated that there wasn't much profit in selling grapes, but there was money to be made in selling wine *if* you were willing to make the initial outlay to build, equip and staff a winery, and *if* you could hang on until the venture could turn a profit (or just break even for that matter). These were big "ifs," but the wine boom was just taking off and the challenge

The 200-acre vineyard at Chalone (OPPOSITE) undulates across the Gavilan range some 2,000 feet above the Salinas Valley in Monterey County. Burgundian oak (LEFT) is used for aging Chardonnay and Pinot Noir at Chalone. The winery purchases a significant portion of new barrels every year. (BELOW): Fat, ripe clusters of Pinot Noir at the Firestone Vineyard in the Santa Ynez Valley.

intrigued Brooks and his wife, Kate, who has been fully involved in the vineyard since the start. The beauties of Santa Ynez Valley worked a little magic, too, no doubt. Already a skilled rider and enthusiastic horseman, Brooks found the prospect of life on the land appealing, a good place to raise children as well as grapevines and cattle.

Brooks Firestone went directly for expert advice on viticulture and wine: He hired André Tchelistcheff as consultant. Tchelistcheff was highly optimistic about Santa Ynez. The cool climate, the gravelly, well-drained soil laced with limestone in places, indicated excellent potential for fine wine.

To finance the venture, Firestone formed a partnership with his father and a family friend, the head of Suntory Ltd. in Japan. The Firestone Vineyard was planted in 1972 and construction on the winery began a year later. A handsome, modern redwood structure with soaring ceilings and stained-glass windows, it still manages to evoke a sense of early California in its tasting area and barrel room. From the beginning the focus was solely on premium varieties: Cabernet Sauvignon, Merlot, Chardonnay, Pinot Noir, Riesling and Gewürztraminer; Sauvignon Blanc has since been added. The first vintage was 1975 and the first wine released was Riesling, made in a crisp, lightly sweet style that has proved popular ever since.

It has taken a decade or more to determine which varieties do best here. Since phylloxera was unknown in the valley, the vines were planted on their own roots. The result, at first, was a rather aggressive varietal character for some grapes, mainly reds like Cabernet Sauvignon and Merlot, but as the vines have matured, much of that has disappeared. Where there were no vineyards in 1970, there are now over 10,000 acres and several other well-known wineries in Santa Ynez Valley, including such important ones as Zaca Mesa Winery, Brander Vineyard, Sanford Winery, Ballard Canyon Winery, Au Bon Climat and Austin Cellars.

Firestone's first winemaker was Tony Austin (who now has Austin Cellars). Austin fa-

vored the big, intense style that was typical of many California wines during the 1970s. His Cabernet Sauvignon and Pinot Noir were massively concentrated and full-bodied. Under present winemaker Alison Green, Firestone's style has moderated somewhat and the wines exhibit significantly greater balance and elegance.

Santa Ynez is particularly good for white varieties. Chardonnay, Sauvignon Blanc, Riesling and Gewürztraminer do extremely well here. Firestone's most consistently outstanding wines are their two styles of Riesling: a lightly sweet version that is delightful for sipping, and a late-harvest Riesling with the honeyed character of grapes affected by *Botrytis cinerea,* the same mold that creates the great Sauternes of France, where it is known as *pourriture noble,* or "noble rot." Botrytised grapes look quite pathetic when the mold has taken over; bruised and purple, they have a greenish fuzz in later stages that is decidedly unappetizing. But winemakers welcome it on certain varieties (Riesling, Sauvignon Blanc, Sémillon, Gewürztraminer) because of the miraculous transformation it works. Starting as little brown spots on the skins of the grape, it pierces the skin as it develops, allowing moisture to escape but concentrating the sugars and flavors into a marvelous nectar that is luscious and long lived. Harvest conditions in Santa Ynez are often conducive to botrytis—periods of high humidity alternating with warm, breezy afternoons—and Firestone has had a string of superb late-harvest Rieslings through the years.

"We probably haven't made our best wines yet," says Firestone; perhaps that is partly what keeps the challenge alive. Success always brings a temptation to expand, but the Firestones like the size of their wine estate and have resisted it. The 300-acre vineyard supplies all the grapes they need for a maximum production of about 80,000 cases a year. Settled on a ranch in the hills not far from the winery, Brooks and Kate live a life centered around wine and horses. Brooks has lately taken up polo with passion, a pursuit that has not, however, interfered with his duties as a vintner. The couple now

The aging cellars at Firestone (TOP); a collection of the wooden bungs used to stopper wine barrels (BOTTOM).

spends much of the summer traveling around the country with a string of ponies, presenting demonstrations of polo that are followed by wine tastings.

People sometimes forget how young the California wine industry is; it is only in the last decade that California has entered the ranks of the world's great wine regions, gaining as well a reputation for being the most exciting and dynamic among them. Part of what makes this so is the intense and tireless effort toward greater quality. California growers and winemakers constantly strive to realize more from the grape, in both the winery and the vineyard. Currently, the emphasis is on viticulture. Not only is there increasing focus on planting the right grape variety in the right spot, but new techniques for growing the grapes—new to California, at any rate—are being explored. These involve closer spacing within the vineyard, using rootstocks that produce better fruit and following methods of pruning and vine trellising that promote more efficient photosynthesis.

Some of this new impetus comes from the French, who, having recognized California's potential for fine wine, have become an increasingly visible presence in California. Several of the leading Champagne houses—Moët et Chandon, Mumm, Roederer, Laurent-Perrier, Taittinger, Deutz—now have operations in the cooler coastal regions, where they produce sparkling wines. Two of the top Bordeaux producers, Baron Philippe de Rothschild of Château Mouton-Rothschild and Christian Moueix of Château Petrus, have formed historic joint ventures with Napa Valley growers. Baron Philippe and Robert Mondavi, for example, teamed up to produce Opus One, an exceptional red wine that exhibits the opulence of California fruit tempered by the restraint of traditional Bordeaux winemaking techniques.

In 1986, the partners completed the first major new vineyard planted with closer spacing. Laid out one meter by two, roughly three feet between vines and six feet between rows, the spacing approximates that in the vineyards of Bordeaux. This is a dramatic departure from the traditional California spacing of eight by twelve feet; instead of some 450 vines per acre, there are 2,700 or more. The increased competition among the vines supposedly will intensify fruit and character and produce wines with better balance and more finesse. If it succeeds as hoped, it may ultimately revolutionize grape-growing in America, though not rapidly because of astronomical cost. It normally costs about $10,000 an acre to develop new vineyard land in California. The Opus One vineyard was more than triple that. Nevertheless, a few new vineyards are being planted in the new configuration, including those of such established operations as Simi in Sonoma and Caymus in Napa Valley.

There are those who say that California is just beginning to show the world what its best wines can be. Wines from the vintages of the mid-1980s, particularly 1985 and 1986, give ample evidence that this could well be so.

CHAPTER SIX

VINEYARDS OF THE NORTHWEST

OREGON FEVER STRUCK AMERICA IN THE 1840S, fired by the somewhat exaggerated reports that getting there was easy once the northern Rockies had been crossed. The 2,000-mile crossing was a formidable task for those who set out from Missouri and Kansas on the Oregon Trail with its bone-wearying haul up and down rocky terrain, along boulder-littered streams and over prairies knotted with sagebrush, but once through, they were told, it would be easy going on rivers to the sea and the green, fertile valleys of the Oregon Territory.

How rude was the shock that awaited! The reports had come from those who had *heard* of the river passages—the Snake River and the mighty Columbia—but who had not actually negotiated the swift and dangerous river gorges that exacted high toll in human lives and livestock. Some of the pioneer wagon trains that followed the Oregon Trail were reduced by half at trail's end. But the rewards of the trek sounded too enticing to ignore.

The whole Pacific Northwest was known as Oregon at that time: 250,000 square miles of prairie, forests, mountains, river valleys and plateaus. Its 1840 population was little more than a couple of hundred fur traders and a few settlers who had come up from California. All that changed in 1843. Bills were proposed in Congress offering to every male 18 or over 640 acres of free land plus another 160 acres for his wife and the same to each child if they settled in the Northwest. The bills were never passed, but on the expectation that they would be, a thousand emigrants set out for Oregon in 1843 and 1844.

Most of these settlers headed for the Wil-

lamette Valley, a broad expanse of prairie and wooded hills stretching 170 miles south of Portland and the Columbia River. Awaiting those who managed to get there was plenty of timber for building (how different from the plains of the Midwest, where the first houses were built from sod), and an abundance of water, forests filled with game and salmon leaping in streams and rivers. There was a lot of rain; the women in particular, according to pioneer diaries, despaired of lengthy periods of dreary weather, but the fecund soil and mild climate were ideal for crops, especially fruits and vegetables. It was a healthy climate for people, too, according to one doctor who, having settled in Oregon, complained of having so little opportunity to practice medicine that he hired out as a fiddler for barn dances.

Oregon, Washington and Idaho compose what we know today as the Pacific Northwest. Taken as a region, the Northwest is the second-largest area for growing vinifera grapes in the United States, totaling some 17,000 acres of vineyard; yet the modern wine industry here is scarcely two decades old. Attempts at wine-growing were sporadic in the early days of the Northwest, though some vinifera cuttings were brought up from California in the 1850s and labrusca vines had come west with the pioneers. Until the 1960s, in fact, the grapegrowing industry revolved mainly around labrusca varieties like Concord, used to some extent for wine but mostly for juices, jams and jellies. Other fruits were used for wine, and still are, the climate yielding intensely flavored raspberries, blackberries, loganberries and gooseberries, among other fruits. For cold-tender vinifera

Pinot Noir from The Eyrie Vineyards, near McMinnville, Oregon.

Outside the Côte d'Or of Burgundy, Oregon may be the world's best location for growing Pinot Noir, especially here in the red hills of Dundee where Eyrie is situated.

grapes like Chardonnay, Cabernet Sauvignon, Pinot Noir and others, this region was considered completely unsuitable by the viticultural minds of the day. Many of the notable breakthroughs in human achievement, of course, whether life saving or merely life enhancing, are those that fly in the face of accepted dogma. Predictably, a few intrepid souls bucked the advice handed down from viticultural specialists, with happy result.

Some experts today feel that the Pacific Northwest has the potential to be the foremost wine region in America—not in terms of quantity (California will continue to lead in volume of production for the foreseeable future), but in terms of quality. The Pacific Northwest lies on the same general latitudes as do Burgundy and Bordeaux, and it has the cooler-climate conditions essential for great wines. Granted, these latitudes in much of North America are too cold for winegrowing, but here the ameliorating effects of the Pacific Ocean, the Coast Range of Oregon and the Cascade Mountains that bisect Washington into two distinctly different climatic regions counteract the cold normally associated with such a northerly region.

Wine regions of the Northwest are frequently lumped together as if growing conditions in the three states were identical. In fact, they differ significantly in some respects, and varieties that do well in Oregon are not as successful in Washington, and vice versa.

OREGON

The most desirable climate for winegrowing is a cool one with a growing season that runs 100 to 120 days from bud break in the spring to the first frost of autumn. Oregon barely makes it some years, but it is just this factor that helps produce wines that have brought this state worldwide recognition. Because it is cool, the grapes take longer to ripen and they therefore develop more character than those in warmer regions like California, where high temperatures can result in overripeness and, consequently, higher alcohol.

Such a climate, however, presents the same problems that often occur in Burgundy. In some years it is too cool for the grapes to ripen sufficiently, or it rains at harvest, promoting rot or diluting the wine's flavor and character. It is ultimately something of a trade-off between the region's inherent potential for greatness in good years and the certainty that some years will have a very poor showing indeed. But this also provides an exciting challenge, and the success of an adventurous few is luring new aspirants every year. One of those successes is The Eyrie Vineyard in the Willamette Valley.

Back in the early 1960s, before the wine boom, a dental student named David Lett paid a visit to Napa Valley that changed the course of his life. After his trip to Napa, Lett decided to give up dentistry and enrolled in a graduate program at the University of California at Davis to study grapegrowing and winemaking. What particularly captured his fancy was Pinot Noir, the grape used for the great red Burgundies of the Côte d'Or. Comparing California Pinot Noirs with some of these wines, he was greatly disappointed. The California wines, for the most part, lacked the delicacy and complexity of the finer Burgundies.

After graduation from U.C. Davis in 1964, Lett spent nine months in Europe visiting French and German vineyards, talking with winemakers and research scientists, trying to figure out where he should establish a vineyard in the United States. He felt that California was too warm to produce the quality and finesse he sought. The question he repeatedly asked of European growers was, why is *this* grape variety planted *here*, in this particular climate?

"I finally uncovered what European winegrowers have known empirically for centuries," he recalls. "Any grape variety produces its best fruit when it is grown in a climate which is marginal to the maturation of the fruit, when maturation just coincides with the end of the growing season. Grapes grown in these marginal climates retain their most complex flavors. In good or great years, those flavors can be trans-

lated into great wines, more than making up for the struggle of the grapegrower in poor years." Recognizing this, Lett decided to go for the margin.

He considered various places to start a vineyard, including northern Portugal and New Zealand, before settling on the Willamette Valley in Oregon. Here was a cool climate—days with temperatures in the high seventies, nights in the fifties—that should bring out the best in Pinot Noir. In 1965 he acquired 1,000 Pinot Noir cuttings, set them out in a rented plot and began his search for land to buy to start his own vineyard. In 1966 he found the spot he wanted, twenty acres in the red iron-rich soil of the Dundee hills about thirty miles south of Portland. Nearby was a prune orchard, another good indication that it was prime land for grapes.

Lett and his wife, Diana, planted their new vineyard with Pinot Noir (using the rooted cuttings he had established earlier) as well as with Chardonnay. These were the first vinifera vines to be planted in the Willamette Valley since Prohibition. As they worked, David and Diana noticed a pair of red-tailed hawks circling overhead. Spotting the hawks' nest in a fir tree at the border of the vineyard, they took this as a good omen and named it The Eyrie (eye-ree) Vineyard. It is at the vineyard that the Letts made their home, but the winery is located in a converted turkey barn in the village of McMinnville, a few miles away.

Many people, including his former professors, thought Lett was crazy to try growing wine grapes in a place better known for green peas. The grapes would never ripen, they said; or they would be killed by frost in spring and autumn. Lett proceeded undeterred. He was fully aware that it would not be easy, having already taken into account some of the region's disadvantages. To counteract what was likely to be the greatest detriment, he planted the vineyard on a south-facing slope where there was less danger of frost. To give the grapes optimum potential for ripening, he pruned for low yield. Fewer bunches means there is more energy for existing fruit, which ripens sooner and can then be harvested ahead of autumn rains.

Like most of Oregon's vineyards, The Eyrie Vineyard is small—twenty-six acres, only six of which are devoted to Pinot Noir. Half of the vineyard is in Pinot Gris, a variety better known in Alsace and in northern Italy (Pinot Grigio), but not widely planted here. Here it produces a dry crisp white, which Lett makes because it goes so well with the fabled salmon of the Northwest. In addition to Chardonnay, he grows two other fairly obscure varieties, Muscat Ottonel, which makes a spicy white wine, and Pinot Meunier, a black grape grown in the Champagne region of France. Total production is small, about 7,000 cases of wine a year, but Lett likes it that way and has no plans to get bigger. At this size he can give the wines and vineyard the meticulous personal attention he feels is critical to produce the best wines.

Since its planting, there have been struggles and triumphs at the vineyard, but David Lett has emerged as one of America's leading pioneers with Pinot Noir. The first ten years were difficult and there were obstacles other than cold to overcome. He had been taught at Davis, for example, to ferment at low temperatures but then discovered that he could extract more color and flavor from Pinot Noir at warmer temperatures. Mildew was a problem until his friend Bernard Koblett, director of a viticultural research station in Switzerland, taught him the advantages of leaf-pulling in the vineyard. Peeling leaves off the sunny side of the vines opens up the canopy, promoting air circulation, thereby controlling mildew. Leaf-pulling has since become an important and widespread vineyard technique in many re-

In an attempt to foil an age-old enemy of the grapegrower—birds—the Eyrie Vineyard swathes its Pinot Noir vines in a special netting (TOP). The ultra-sharp, curved-blade knife used for harvesting grapes can be hard on the fingers (BOTTOM). Here, a picker wears duct tape for protection as he picks Pinot Gris.

A harvest worker
carries a stack of lug
boxes, each of which
can accommodate up
to forty pounds of
grapes.

velopment of our own identity in Oregon for *Oregon* wines." Still—and remarkably—in a blind tasting of red Burgundies and American Pinot Noirs held in 1979 in France, French tasters mistook Eyrie's 1975 Pinot Noir for one of their own. The French were incredulous when the discovery was made, so Robert Drouhin, a leading Burgundy shipper, restaged the tasting. The Oregon wine came within a fraction of points awarded the top wine, and when word of the outcome hit the wine world, the future of The Eyrie Vineyard—and Oregon Pinot Noir—was assured.

Although Oregon vineyards tend to be relatively small—most under 20 acres—the acreage overall amounts to 5,000, and Pinot Noir is the most widely planted grape. Of the several vineyards that produce fine Pinots, Knudsen-Erath Winery, Adelsheim Vineyard, Elk Cove Vineyards, Sokol-Blosser Winery, Amity Vineyards, Oak Knoll Winery, Ponzi Vineyards and Tualatin Vineyards are just the primary names. Newer ones, including Hidden Springs Winery, Adams Vineyard Winery and Rex Hill Vineyards, continue to emerge. Other varieties also do well in Oregon—mainly Chardonnay and Riesling. While the Willamette Valley is Oregon's largest and most concentrated area of wine grapes, there are other important regions, such as the Umpqua Valley near Roseburg (pioneered by Richard Sommers of Hillcrest Winery), and the Rogue River region in the southwest. East of the Cascades, which jut down into northeastern Oregon, a new wine area is emerging that is warmer and drier than western Oregon, more similar to the Northwest's largest wine region, the Columbia Valley in Washington.

gions. Lett's principal tenet is that the wine is made in the vineyard. He strives to get the right balance in the grapes themselves, avoiding the need to make adjustments during the winemaking process.

What he likes about Pinot Noir is its delicacy, a complex of subtleties that is elusive. The wine bears no single identifiable aroma or flavor but at its best is a mingling of spices, violets, roses, worn leather, smokiness, fruit and wood—a combination unique to Pinot Noir. Good Pinot Noir, that is; Lett is critical of many California versions for being coarse and heavy, since, he feels, "it's just too hot down there."

For years, before the wines had acquired their reputation, one of Oregon's biggest obstacles was marketing. Although Oregon growers knew that they were making world-class Pinot Noir, outside recognition was slow in coming. "The character of our Oregon Pinot Noir is different from that of California," Lett says, "but it is also different from Burgundy. We never intended to replicate French wines in Oregon. Our climate is unique enough to allow the de-

WASHINGTON

Practically all of Washington's 11,000 acres of vineyard are in the southeastern part of the state, an arid expanse of gently undulating hills created eons ago by lava flows. A few small vineyards are situated in isolated microclimates west of the Cascades, but the Washington coast is far

too rainy to be a successful winegrowing region on any scale.

The Cascades are articulated by many narrow valleys, crystalline mountain lakes and snow-covered peaks that offer challenge to trekkers and climbers. By blocking the marine air from the Pacific, these mountains create the climatic phenomenon known as a rain shadow, which extends across the vast Columbia Valley and severely limits precipitation. An average annual rainfall of ten inches or less made the region a desert until the early 1900s, when irrigation tapped the waters of the Columbia and Yakima rivers. Now it is close to ideal for crops of all sorts: fruits, nuts, hops, spices, vegetables, legumes and especially wine grapes.

Both vinifera and labrusca (mostly Concord) were planted in Columbia Valley following Prohibition, but the two often were blended, with poor results. Vinifera did not come into its own here until the 1960s. The two men who first recognized Washington's potential for good wine were from California, Leon Adams and André Tchelistcheff. During a visit to the region in 1966, in preparation for the first edition of *The Wines of America*, Adams tasted some homemade wines made entirely from vinifera. Impressed, he remarked to Victor Allison of American Wine Growers (a cooperative of growers in the Yakima Valley) that this was the direction Washington winegrowers should pursue. When Allison asked where they could get the technical expertise to do so, Adams suggested he contact André Tchelistcheff. Tchelistcheff, too, was impressed with the possibilities for Washington grapes and agreed to act as consultant for American Wine Growers, which launched the Chateau Ste. Michelle label with Cabernet Sauvignon, Sémillon, Pinot Noir and Grenache from the 1967 vintage.

In terms of size, Chateau Ste. Michelle and The Eyrie Vineyard represent opposite ends of the spectrum in the Northwest. Both, however, have played a critical role in the evolution of winegrowing in the region. Corporate-owned, and itself the proprietor of a staggering 3,000 acres of vineyard, Chateau Ste. Michelle pro-

duces over 700,000 cases of wine a year and could well reach a million cases by 1990. Purchased by U.S. Tobacco Company in 1973, Ste. Michelle uses three facilities: one at Grandview in the Yakima Valley (a subregion of the Columbia Valley along the Yakima River), another in the Columbia Valley along the banks of the Columbia River, and a third, its headquarters, is at the original site in Woodinville on the outskirts of Seattle. Winegrowing and winemaking are team efforts at Chateau Ste. Michelle, under the direction of Cheryl Barber for white wines and Peter Bachman for red wines. Consultant André Tchelistcheff comes to Ste. Michelle four or five times a year to taste the wines and offer advice.

Ste. Michelle's white varietals—Chardonnay, Sauvignon Blanc, Sémillon and Riesling—constitute the winery's greatest volume and are made at Woodinville. The grapes are crushed at the Paterson facility in Columbia Valley and the juice is then shipped by refrigerated truck to Woodinville. The red wines are made at the Yakima winery at Grandview, then aged in underground cellars at Paterson. Columbia Crest, Ste. Michelle's sister operation which overlooks the Columbia River near Paterson, is where Ste. Michelle's state-of-the-art technology is most fully put to use. Fermentation and storage areas are housed underground in a building that covers nine acres. The fermentation area alone is the length of two football fields. Above ground, a handsome chateau-like building houses tasting rooms, a retail shop, offices and dining rooms that look out over the 2,000 acres of vineyard.

From the air, the most startling topographical feature of Columbia Valley is the circles dotting the landscape near the Columbia River. Each of the winery's eighty-five such circles there covers a quarter section—120 acres—and is half a mile in diameter. The system is known as pivot irrigation and is used for several crops, but Ste. Michelle was the first to use it for irrigating vineyards. Water is pumped through a quarter-mile-long pipe that rotates slowly on wheels, dispensing a fine mist at timed inter-

Morning fog in the Willamette Valley (TOP). Stretching half the length of Oregon, the valley extends from the Columbia River to the mountains south of Eugene.
The Umpqua Valley (BOTTOM) in the southern part of the state was the first Oregon site in which vinifera was planted after Prohibition— but even then, not until 1961.

vals. It is an innovative approach that works very well for some crops, notably barley, corn, wheat and potatoes. But it is being phased out at Ste. Michelle's vineyards because the atmosphere of constant dampness promotes rot. It is now used primarily after harvest to soak the ground with moisture to protect the vines during dormancy.

A wet soil over winter can mean life or death to the vineyard in this arid region. Freezing temperatures rarely penetrate deeper than three feet, but if the soil is dry the cold will seep into air pockets and freeze the vine roots. By filling the soil with water to rooting depth (at least three feet), the soil will freeze solidly around the roots and protect them, not only from sudden killing freezes but from dehydration brought about by the cold and wind.

Temperatures are more extreme here than in the Willamette Valley, with warmer summers and colder winters. Frosts and freezes threaten periodically and have done considerable damage some years. In the winter of 1978, for example, temperatures plummeted so low that many vines died, greatly reducing the 1979 crop, particularly in red varieties. On the other hand, it did produce some very beautiful, concentrated Cabernet Sauvignons that will probably age nicely to the end of the century. Although summer days can reach eighty-five degrees or higher, nights are quite cool, a combination that results in high sugars and high acidity. Too much of either, however, can produce imbalance, but as the vineyards mature and growing techniques improve, these characteristics endow the wines of this area with exciting potential.

Southeastern Washington can grow more types of grapes than any region in the Northwest. Until now, the region has been known mostly for white varieties, especially Riesling, the most widely planted grape. Early on, the state pinned its hopes on Riesling and planted far too much of it in view of the fact that other varieties later proved equally successful. Washington Rieslings are brisk, lively wines, usually lightly sweet but nicely balanced with acidity.

Chenin Blanc, with its melony fruit, is similar in style and is also well suited to the cooler climate. Washington Chenins are lighter and more delicate than those from California. Drier wines from this state are steadily gaining favor. These include Chardonnay, Sauvignon Blanc and Sémillon, which often exhibit intense fruit but, again, tend to be lighter in style than those from California. They are particularly appropriate as accompaniments to the abundant seafood that characterizes Northwest cuisine.

Increasingly, however, it is the red wines that are creating excitement in Washington, particularly Cabernet Sauvignon. Chateau Ste. Michelle consistently produces elegant Cabernets that age well, especially the Reserve wines. Much of eastern Washington is too cold for Cabernet Sauvignon to ripen fully every year, and it has taken time to isolate the warmer spots where the variety will thrive. A late ripener, Cabernet matures in middle or late October. Ste. Michelle's best Cabernets, the Reserves, come from Cold Creek Vineyard, a vivid patch of green nestled against the arid treeless Rattlesnake Hills in Yakima Valley. The 672-acre vineyard benefits from a microclimate that traps warm air well into October, allowing Cabernet to develop fine character and balance. Cold Creek Vineyard was renamed Tchelistcheff Vineyard in 1986.

Other spots suitable to Cabernet have emerged in recent years. Excellent Cabernets are produced by Columbia Winery, Washington's second largest, and by smaller vintners such as Leonetti Cellar, Quilceda Creek Vintners, Hogue Cellars, Arbor Crest Winery and Neuharth Winery. Merlot is also grown in Washington, where it is made on its own or is blended with Cabernet. The region is considered by many to be too warm for Pinot Noir, though it has been tried and continued attempts are underway on a limited basis.

Washington's smaller growing regions extend farthest east into Walla Walla Valley (best known for sweet onions) and to the west along the Columbia River Gorge, where the river is joined by the Klickitat River near the Dalles.

Winds from the Pacific slice through here at sixty miles an hour at times, sweeping up into Columbia Valley without slowing down, but grapes can grow successfully in protected pockets on either side of the river, particularly Riesling and Gewürztraminer. There are also a few small wineries in western Washington but acreage is very limited and most get their grapes from Yakima or Columbia valleys.

IDAHO

Comprising about a thousand acres today, Idaho vineyards were planted in the 1970s, most in the Sunny Slope area west of Boise, with limited acreage farther north around Lewiston. The Sunny Slope region occupies high mountain valleys some 2,500 feet above the Snake River. The climate here is similar to that of the Columbia Basin in Washington, essentially near-desert conditions with warm days and cool nights, which accentuate flavor in the grapes while retaining the high acidity that gives the wines good structure. Within a few years of its first vintage in 1976, Ste. Chapelle (named after the famed chapel in Paris) surprised many with the rich, buttery Chardonnays and luscious late-harvest Rieslings it produced.

The Symms family, owners of Ste. Chapelle, are local fruit growers with 2,900 acres of apples, peaches, plums, nectarines and cherries. The vineyard, known as the Symms Family Vineyard and often so designated on Ste. Chapelle labels, is about 190 acres, planted primarily with Chardonnay, Cabernet Sauvignon and Riesling. Vineyard manager and winery president Richard Symms gives credit to the unique microclimate of the mountain valleys for producing high quality, intensely flavored fruit. Protected by the Rocky Mountains from the fierceness of arctic storms, the area nevertheless endures a long, cold winter, which pushes the vines into deep and lengthy dormancy. The long sleep over winter coupled with warm days and cool nights during the growing season are believed to contribute fruit intensity and balance.

Idaho's wine industry has suffered a few growing pains in its brief history. Several wineries have been sold, some have merged and reappeared in new incarnations. Petros Winery, for instance, has been through a succession of owners since 1979. Now owned by Peter Eliopulos, an investment counselor in Boise, Petros (Greek for Peter) plans on producing 50,000 cases, making it one of the larger northwestern wineries. The winery currently owns about 25 acres of Chardonnay and Riesling, but purchases most of its grapes from the Batt Vineyard, a well-established 160 acres of Chardonnay, Pinot Noir, Riesling and Gewürztraminer, also in the Sunny Slope area. Like most Idaho wineries, Petros also buys grapes from Washington vineyards. Two small wineries that have recently started production are Camas Winery in Moscow, near Lewiston, and Weston, in the Sunny Slope region at Caldwell.

Wineries of the Northwest are steadily gaining national prominence as production increases and the wines become more widely available. The 1980s have seen a significant difference in quality as well. Prior to 1980 few of the wines possessed the quality and stylishness to make a positive impact on American wine consumers. In recent years, however, numerous wines have emerged that demonstrate the enormous potential of the vineyards of the Northwest: Pinot Noir from Oregon; Sémillon, Merlot and Cabernet Sauvignon from Washington; Riesling and Chardonnay from Idaho. As vineyards have matured, viticulturists have gained a better understanding of how to work with nature's quirks, coaxing more character and flavor into the grape. At the same time, experience is bringing greater finesse to winemaking. The 1990s will undoubtedly see the promise of the 1980s fulfilled.

A Washington Fumé Blanc makes a fine companion to shellfish.

Seen from the air, irrigation circles near Paterson (TOP) create striking patterns. Though pivot irrigation—a system that sprays a fine mist of water through a quarter-mile-long pipe—will continue to be used for corn, potatoes and other crops, it is being phased out in the vineyard because the moisture promotes rot. Interior of Chateau Ste. Michelle's Grandview winery in Yakima Valley (BOTTOM); it is used exclusively for red wine production.

Grapes at the crusher (TOP) of Chateau Ste. Michelle's Paterson facility. Visible in the background is the Columbia River, Lewis and Clark's route to the Pacific. A gondola of grapes (BOTTOM) awaits its turn at the crusher.

CHAPTER SEVEN

VINEYARDS OF CANADA

WINEGROWING IN CANADA IS AN ASTONISHING mix of the old and the new, reflecting the entire gamut of twentieth-century winemaking on the North American continent, and it is undergoing as dramatic a transition here as it is in the state of New York. Still, Canadian wines are not well known in the United States, despite the millions of cases produced annually by the country's three largest wineries, Andrés, Bright's-Ste. Michelle and Chateau Gai.

Winegrowing in Canada is scarcely a hundred years old, but real progress has been made in the last dozen or so years toward creating wines of quality that are recognized internationally. This cold country, where a shot of liquor traditionally started the day's work for many hardworking farmers and other laborers, is gradually moving toward greater wine consumption, but the shift is a recent one.

The opportunity was there even during Canadian Prohibition (1917–1927), however, since wine could legally be made and sold on a limited basis in Ontario. But the wines were so bad, for the most part, that the exemption did more harm than good. One hears stories of how records kept at the time showed more vinegar than alcohol in many of the wines. (It has been said that the Liquor Control Board of Ontario was formed at the time to protect citizens from bad wine.)

By the end of Prohibition, something like fifty-three new winery licenses had been issued. Many wineries were officially put out of business and some of the larger wineries like Bright's, Chateau Gai and Jordan (now Jordan-Ste. Michelle and owned by Bright's), bought out the smaller wineries in order to obtain their licenses, thereby gaining outlets for selling. The law allowed each licensed winery to have only one direct sales outlet. It is estimated that from forty to forty-five wineries were purchased by half a dozen of the large, older firms and were then closed down, their licenses retained in order to expand the number of outlets the firms controlled.

The same forces that prompted change in the United States in the late 1960s brought the beginning of change to Canada. For nearly three decades after Prohibition was repealed, restrictive drinking laws did little to promote moderate consumption of alcohol. Women were barred from drinking places altogether, and alcohol was not permitted in restaurants. No new winery licenses had been granted since Prohibition and the industry lumbered along with mediocre to poor wines—often made from native varieties like Concord, or fortified with grain alcohol.

Canadians who traveled abroad in the 1950s and 1960s, however, were introduced to wine in a new way. Having encountered wine as a beverage served with meals and as an alternative to whiskey in France, Italy, Germany and elsewhere, they came home with a taste for something better than the traditional domestic wines. The liquor control boards, which operate independently in each province and control sales through state-owned stores, began to allow in more imported wines. Demand steadily increased, and French wines in particular experienced an enormous boost during the early 1980s when the devalued franc unleashed a flood of inexpensive wines. This situation played havoc with the Canadian wine industry.

Large oak casks are
used for fermenting
and storage at
Inniskillin.

Considerable good came of it, however. As producers grasped the fact that their competition was of higher quality at lower prices, the move toward making better-quality wines accelerated, paving the way for a new generation of growers and winemakers.

Even today, with the increasingly sound and stylish wines now made in Canada, there exist wines that continue to demonstrate the lack of experience and professionalism that has held the country's wine industry back. There is still wide use of imitative names like Burgundy or Sauternes for generic blends. Wineries more mindful of the bottom line than of quality cut corners by using grape concentrates from Europe or California; others add water either to ameliorate the aggressive flavor that is derived from inferior grape varieties, or to stretch the better ones to the limit the law allows. Sugar is often used to disguise undesirable flavors, fresh juice to "revitalize" older, tired wines.

To some extent these practices are understandable, due to the fact that the cold Canadian climate is not generally hospitable to the grape. Even in regions where it is more accommodative—such as southern Ontario not far from Niagara Falls, or in the Okanagan Valley in British Columbia—severe winter freezes every few years can kill the vines or damage the current year's crop. The most recent freeze of this sort was in 1985, and prior to that in December of 1980 and in the winter of 1978–1979. "Everything we do in the vineyard," says Ian Mavety, a grower in the Okanagan Valley, "is toward protecting the vines for winter." It involves such labor-intensive practices as hilling up the vines in winter or costly irrigation after harvest to insure that sudden freezes will not damage roots.

Although small vineyards and a couple of wineries exist in Nova Scotia, and there are wineries but no commercial vineyards in Québec and Alberta, Canada's wine industry essentially has two fronts: in the East, southern Ontario, and in the West, British Columbia. Canadian vineyards are found mainly along the shores of, or near, Lake Ontario, and on the slopes that

overlook the long deep lakes of the Okanagan Valley. These large bodies of water moderate the cold Canadian climate, allowing hardy varieties to survive. Native American species such as labrusca were originally the most widely planted, until many growers turned to hardy French hybrids such as Seyval Blanc, Chancellor, Vidal, Maréchal Foch and others. Today there is a steady move to vinifera, particularly varieties that do well in cool climates, such as Chardonnay, Riesling, Gewürztraminer, Pinot Blanc, Pinot Auxerrois (a white wine grape grown in Alsace) and Pinot Noir.

ONTARIO

One of the success stories of the modern era in Canadian wine is the Ontario winery Inniskillin, a few miles from the mighty roar of Niagara Falls. In terms of volume, Inniskillin is relatively small in the Canadian hierarchy, producing between 80,000 and 90,000 cases a year compared with the 1 to 5 million or more cases pro-

duced by the large wineries. But in terms of influence, it looms large on two counts: It was Canada's first estate winery (one that uses grapes from vineyards owned or controlled by the winery), and owner Donald Ziraldo was the first vintner since 1929 to receive a Canadian winery license.

The Ziraldo family owned a nursery business in the Ontario town of St. Catherines that supplied grape stock for both wine and table varieties. In the early 1970s, Donald Ziraldo, fresh out of the University of Ontario at Guelph with a degree in agriculture, met an Austrian chemist, Karl Kaiser, who had come to the Ziraldo nursery for vines to start his own vineyard.

Kaiser had learned about viticulture from his student work in a Cistercian monastery vineyard in Austria, and about winemaking from his wife's family. When her parents moved to Ontario, they persuaded the couple to immigrate, somewhat against Kaiser's wishes. He tried to get a job with one of the Ontario wineries, but there were no openings.

The Ziraldo family had long made wines at home from their own grapes, but in 1973 Donald Ziraldo and Kaiser decided to start a commercial winery. Ziraldo applied to the Liquor Control Board of Ontario for a winery license, but they did not take the young twenty-four-year-old seriously. No new licenses had been issued in over forty years; moreover, there were dozens of applications ahead of his, all from people trying to cash in on the success of Baby Duck, a sweet sparkling red made by Andrés. Ziraldo was persistent, however, and eventually the application landed on the desk of the L.C.B.O.'s new bureau head, Major-General George Kitching. Unlike his predecessors, Kitching was eager to see improvement in Canadian wines and was impressed with Ziraldo's aim of producing quality wines from better grape varieties. In April 1974, Kitching granted the license.

Ziraldo and Kaiser left immediately for Europe to visit vineyards and buy equipment. Later that year they planted sixty acres of vineyard at Niagara-on-the-Lake, mostly vinifera varieties like Riesling and Chardonnay, but also French hybrids. They took the name Inniskillin from the farm's original owner, who had been commanding officer of the Royal Inniskillin Fusiliers, a regiment that fought in the War of 1812.

Inniskillin wines won immediate acceptance with consumers, and the winery's reputation for stylish wines of balance and quality saw them through the difficult days when imports were plentiful and cheap. Today, Inniskillin continues to make some of Canada's most highly regarded wines, including an excellent Chardonnay with the steely, crisp character of a good French Chablis. They make fine Riesling and Gewürztraminer, as well as popular table wines labeled Brae Rouge and Brae Blanc, which are blended from French hybrids like Seyval Blanc and Foch. Also produced by the winery are some of Canada's first late-harvest wines, including superb German-style *Eiswein* (ice wine) made from grapes that have frozen on the vine.

Inniskillin sold off a large portion of the original vineyard to finance a new winery in 1978, but it retains control of the viticultural practices through long-term contract with the present owner. There are twelve acres at the winery site and Inniskillin is part owner of fifty-two acres situated two and a half miles west of the winery. Together, these three vineyards supply about a third of the grapes used for Inniskillin wines; the remainder are purchased from other Ontario growers.

Karl Kaiser is now making sparkling wines—from Chardonnay and Pinot Noir grapes—at Inniskillin. He is very optimistic about the future of Pinot Noir in Ontario, not only for sparkling wines but as a still wine. "We are a classic cool region for Pinot Noir," he says, "and as we discover the warmer areas where the grapes can ripen, we are hoping for great success with this variety. There are very few areas in the world that can grow Pinot Noir with finesse, but we believe this may be one of them." Kaiser's enthusiasm stems from the quality of Pinot grapes at a vineyard a few miles inland from the Niagara escarpment, a microclimate where Cabernet Sauvignon and Pinot Noir ripen ten to fifteen days earlier than at other locations, where autumn rains or early frost may prevent ripening altogether in some years.

Inniskillin has made notable strides in its thirteen years of existence. Ziraldo and Kaiser were the first to prove that vinifera are viable in the Ontario climate, and the first to demonstrate that a moderate-sized winery could compete with Canada's larger wineries. Inniskillin's success has also had considerable influence on new directions taken by some of these larger wineries, prompting them to institute experimental programs of their own. Other estate wineries have followed Inniskillin's lead as well, helping to move Canadian wines closer to international standards of quality and style. These include wineries like Ontario's Chateau des Charmes, Rief Winery and Vineland Estates, and Grand Pré in Nova Scotia.

Paul Bosc, an Algerian immigrant who arrived in Québec in 1963, was winemaker at Chateau-Gai for fourteen years before founding

his own winery, Chateau des Charmes, in 1977. Bosc, whose family had owned a vineyard in Algeria, was trained in oenology at the University of Dijon in Burgundy. Having seen Dr. Konstantin Frank's success with vinifera in New York, he was eager to try several varieties in Canada. He and a partner bought sixty acres on the Niagara Peninsula, planting Chardonnay, Pinot Noir, Riesling, Aligoté and Gamay Beaujolais. Careful not to overcrop—big yields are a mistake frequently made with vinifera, making them vulnerable to winter damage—Bosc pruned accordingly and was highly gratified by the success of his vineyard. His clonal experiments in developing hardier vines have proved useful to other Ontario growers. Chateau des Charmes makes popular generic blends like Cour Blanc and Sentinel Red as well as a *nouveau*-style Gamay Beaujolais (that is, made by the carbon maceration method; see glossary). Paul Bosc has made his reputation, however, with flowery-scented Rieslings and estate-bottled Chardonnays aged in French oak.

Ontario's newest estate wineries, Rief Winery and Vineland Estates, also produce highly regarded Rieslings and Chardonnays. Along with hybrids, both wineries grow varieties developed in Germany that were introduced to Canada as part of the Becker Project in British Columbia (see page 196), such as Bacchus and Siegfried Rebe.

NOVA SCOTIA

Nova Scotia seems very far north for wine grapes, but in fact it is on roughly the same latitudes as the Mosel Valley in Germany and the Champagne region of France. Nova Scotia vineyards now comprise 155 acres, all planted since 1977, mostly in the Annapolis Valley west of Halifax. It is cool here, but the nearby Bay of Fundy moderates winter cold and promotes a growing season sufficiently long to ripen early-maturing varieties. The pioneer grower is Roger Dial, who founded Grand Pré Wines in 1977. Born in California, Dial had worked at

Davis Bynum Winery in Sonoma to finance his education. When he moved to Nova Scotia, where he was a professor at Dalhousie University in Halifax, he became intrigued by the viticultural experiments at the agricultural station in Kentville and soon started winegrowing as a hobby. In 1970 he and a partner, Norman Morse, planted a few French hybrids and were so encouraged that in 1977 they planted sixty or so varieties from wine regions around the world to see which would best succeed.

Now considered one of Canada's leading estate wineries, Grand Pré has thirty-six acres planted with French hybrids, cool-climate vinifera like Chardonnay, Pinot Noir and Gewürztraminer and two *Vitis amurensis* varieties imported from the Soviet Union. The Russian varieties, native to the Amur River valley in eastern Siberia, both make sturdy red wines. Dial's biggest success has been with one of the French hybrids developed at Vineland that he calls L'Acadie Blanc. It is a dry, tartly crisp white named after the French Acadians who settled at Grand Pré in the eighteenth century and later were driven out by the British.

Grand Pré grew slowly for the first decade, mainly because of Nova Scotia liquor laws prohibiting direct sales from the winery. In June of 1986, however, the law changed, and the potential for future wine sales look very promising. "People here in Nova Scotia consume a lot of wine," says Dial, "and we expect to increase further. Our plan is to provide 18 to 20 percent of the market in the 1990s." To do so, Grand Pré will add 52 acres of vineyard in 1988 and ultimately plans to have 600 acres, producing about 100,000 cases of wine.

Roger Dial's enthusiasm for Nova Scotia winegrowing persuaded others to start vineyards in the Annapolis Valley, one of whom, Hanns Jost, has just started his own winery, Jost Vineyards, a little farther north near the town of Malagash. Dial expects to see other small wineries get underway soon.

Stained glass borders frame the shuttered windows at Inniskillin.

Okanagan Valley

In western Canada, the Okanagan (Oka-*nog*-gan) Valley in central British Columbia is emerging as the country's most dynamic region for winegrowing. Tucked away between the Rockies and Canada's coastal range, this little-known area is also one of the prettiest wine valleys on the globe. Approached from the south, winding around Mount Baldy on Highway 3, one suddenly comes upon breathtaking vistas of the long, narrow lake valley nestled between mountain ranges. It stretches a hundred miles northward, with four large lakes linked to one another, the deepest being Lake Okanagan.

The Okanagan Valley is Canada's principal fruit-growing region, with acres of apple, cherry and peach orchards dotting the valley floor and vineyards crisscrossing the flat benchlands overlooking the lakes. In spring, when the apple and cherry trees are in blossom, the Okanagan is enchanting, but it is also beautiful in autumn when the landscape turns golden, ac-cented with scattered patches of red sumac. Driving through Penticton at the southern end of Lake Okanagan, I immediately thought of Lake Geneva in Switzerland, with its broad scoop of water, its mountain backdrop and the picturesque towns along its shores.

The first white man to settle in the valley was Father Charles Pandosy, a priest who ar-rived in 1860 to work with the local Salish Indi-ans. He established a mission in the middle of the valley at what is now the region's largest city, Kelowna. Father Pandosy is said to have planted grapevines, since the mission needed wine for the Sacrament, though how the vines fared is not known. The region was slow to at-tract settlers because it was so remote; in 1890 there were a mere 400 people in the valley, but about 20,000 head of cattle.

The Okanagan is dry, arid country, with an average annual rainfall of about eleven inches, certainly not enough to support or-chards or vineyards without irrigation. Sum-mers are hot, especially on the eastern side of the

Gehringer Vineyard near Oliver, founded in 1985, is one of the Okanagan's most promising young wineries.

lakes, where the sun beats down late in the day; winters can get severely cold, just as they do three hundred miles south in the Yakima and Columbia valleys of Washington State. The Okanagan is similar in climate to southeastern Washington, in fact, although the latter region is warmer longer, allowing red varieties like Cabernet Sauvignon to ripen more easily.

The lakes of the Okanagan, like most large bodies of water, help to moderate the cold. Lake Okanagan itself never freezes because it is so deep—no one knows just how deep—but its depth is significant enough to provide a home for its own version of the Loch Ness monster. The creature, known as Ogopogo, lurks in the deep off the western shore of the lake and allegedly is still sighted from time to time. The lake's depth moderates temperatures by giving off moisture in summer and, in winter, by pulling the cold air down from the slopes. It also provides ample water for irrigation.

One of the biggest dangers for winegrowing in the Okanagan is autumn frost. The region has a long and late growing season that lasts well into November some years. If it arrives in October before the grapes are in, an early frost puts a rude halt to the ripening process. If the grapes are not ripe, they produce a thin, acidic wine with little character. This is one of the reasons that microclimates are so important here. Growers take pains to plant vineyards on upper slopes, trying to avoid low-lying areas that trap cold air. The wisdom of this was borne out on a chilly October morning at Sumac Ridge, one of the Okanagan's leading estate wineries. Sumac Ridge is the only vineyard I know that is situated on a golf course. The winery was started in the clubhouse basement, though it is now in an adjacent building. The tasting room, however, is still located in the club lounge upstairs, next to the clubhouse restaurant that overlooks fairways and vineyards. Golf carts double as vineyard transport and vineyards occupy the upper slopes that formerly were holes one, two and nine.

The vineyards that October morning were bathed in sunlight, but the low-lying green on the present first hole was white with frost. Vineyards could never survive in this spot; the grapes would freeze or simply could not ripen. Although the frost had disappeared by midmorning, the sun is too low in the sky this time of year to hit the slope, which tilts the wrong way for good exposure. It is fine, however, if you are swinging a golf club, and managing partner Harry McWatters finds the combination of vineyard and golf course to work superbly. It is an attractive setting for the winery and vineyard, and the club members, delighted with their on-premises winery, help promote Sumac Ridge wines.

Sumac Ridge, named for the colorful red sumac that proliferates in the Okanagan, produces some of the region's best wines. Their Gewürztraminer wins medals year after year for its clean, crisp varietal character and spicy aromas, as does a very good red made from Chancellor. Sumac Ridge also grows Perle of Csaba, a Hungarian vinifera little known in North America, though it deserves greater recogni-

tion. It makes a lightly spicy dessert wine with Muscat-like aromas and flavor. The winery also makes one of the better renditions of Okanagan Riesling, a white hybrid that originated in the Okanagan Valley and is totally unrelated to the true German Riesling. Though widely planted for its cold-hardy nature, this grape produces rather neutral wines without much to recommend them and is being phased out in many vineyards.

In 1977 British Columbia passed a law that brought dramatic change to the Okanagan: the "cottage winery" law. Although the term may seem somewhat misleading—implying that, like cottage industries, winegrowing is nothing more than a small household business—the true impetus behind the law was to strictly limit the cottage wineries' production. They may produce no more than 30,000 gallons of wine a year, or about 13,000 to 14,000 cases. They must own a minimum of 20 acres of vineyard and the winery must be situated on vineyard property. A cottage winery's yield is not to exceed 150 gallons per hectare (2.2 acres); larger British Columbian wineries like Bright's and Calona are allowed a maximum yield of 250 gallons per hectare. As a consolation, however, the cottage wineries, increasingly referred to as "estate wineries," pay minimal taxes.

Since 1977 only a handful of estate wineries have sprung up in the Okanagan, but they have done well and get a lot of attention, not only locally but in the rest of British Columbia, including Vancouver. Most of the interest at the moment centers on vinifera—Riesling being the most widely planted variety—but the severe winter cold makes growing many vinifera varieties difficult. Okanagan growers are currently experimenting with lesser known vinifera varieties like Pinot Gris, Pinot Blanc and Pinot Auxerrois, which are proving hardy enough to withstand the cold, better at least than tender varieties like Chardonnay or late-ripening reds like Cabernet Sauvignon and Merlot. German varieties like Riesling, Müller-Thurgau and Kerner also seem to do well, though they produce mostly sweet or off-dry wines that are often pleasant to drink but are not as versatile for accompanying food. Recogniz-

Gray Monk Cellars
is among the leading
estate wineries in the
Okanagan Valley of
British Columbia.

ing this, some growers are working with varieties that can produce dry wines. Ian Mavety, owner of Vaseaux Farms, south of Penticton, has forty acres on the rolling plateaus above Vaseaux Lake, now planted mostly in hybrids. But Mavety is gradually converting the vineyard to vinifera and is particularly keen on the Pinot varieties: Pinot Blanc, Pinot Auxerrois and Pinot Noir. "Everybody here is planting the German varieties—Müller-Thurgau and Rieslings," he says. "It's a lighter, sweeter style that is popular now, but I think the market is limited. We haven't begun to tap the potential for French style, the drier wines."

Mavety sells most of his grapes to Bright's in the town of Oliver, but he sees an expanding future for the estate wineries and an increasing demand for quality grapes. "The estate wineries are significant because they are limited in what they produce, so they can go for quality," says Mavety. Clearly he expects to be ready with the kinds of grapes he thinks they will want.

One of the Okanagan's newest estate wineries is Gehringer Vineyards, owned and operated by the Gehringer brothers, Walter and Gordon. Set on a bench back against Mount Cobo on the western side of the valley south of Oliver, the Gehringer vineyard benefits from a southeastern exposure that is shaded from the blistering late afternoon sun in August. It can reach 110 degrees on the opposite shore, so hot that the photosynthesis process that ripens the grape is shut down. This has been a problem for some of the larger vineyards on the eastern shore, including Inkameep Vineyards, operated by local Indians who sell grapes to Bright's and Andrés. At Gehringer, the vineyards get direct sun from the early morning until about mid-afternoon, and the rocky soil also absorbs heat, radiating it upward at night, much like the fabled slate soil of the Mosel Valley in Germany.

Thirty-two-year-old Walter Gehringer was the first Okanagan vintner to graduate from Germany's famous wine school at Geisenheim. He worked at Bright's until 1985 and then joined his younger brother, Gordon (also trained at Geisenheim), to produce the vineyard's first vintage. It was a happy moment for the Gehringers when their first Pinot Auxerrois was awarded a gold medal at the 1986 harvest festival in Kelowna. Gehringer produces very attractive wines, balanced, stylish and elegant, the kind of wines that will greatly enhance the Okanagan's reputation as a significant growing region. In addition to Pinot Auxerrois, a crisp and appealing off-dry white wine, Gehringer makes sweet whites from Verdelet and Ehrenfelser, and a fruity red blended from Baco Noir and other red French hybrids that is quite good. They call it Burgundy at the moment, but it deserves a better name that reflects its own identity and appellation.

Gray Monk Cellars, north of Kelowna, is becoming increasingly well known for fine whites made in an off-dry or lightly sweet style, particularly Gewürztraminer, Riesling, Pinot Gris and Pinot Auxerrois. George and Trudy Heiss, owners of Gray Monk, were hairdressers in Edmonton, Alberta, before Trudy's father, who had started a vineyard a few years before, persuaded the couple to make the move and become winegrowers in the Okanagan in 1971.

The Heisses began with hybrids but soon moved to vinifera varieties, including Pinot Gris, which is how the winery got its name. George Heiss was born in Austria, where one name for the Pinot Gris grape is Grauer Mönch, meaning "gray monk." Since the Heisses decided to concentrate mainly on that variety, it seemed quite logical to adopt the name for the winery and vineyard.

Gray Monk's white stucco winery occupies a spectacular site on a steep hillside overlooking Lake Okanagan. The surrounding vineyard has a west-facing exposure, an advantage at the cooler northern end of the valley in that the vineyards get the benefit of afternoon sun.

Uniacke is another small estate producing reputable wines. Owned by David and Susan Mitchell, Uniacke produces wines from hybrids and vinifera. A former geologist, David Mitchell does especially well with the Pinot varieties, making attractive Pinot Noir Blanc and Pinot Auxerrois. The name Uniacke is Gaelic for "unique" and was taken from a royal citation bestowed on one of Mitchell's maternal ancestors in the fourteenth century: The knight was dubbed *uniacke*, or "without peer," for loyal service to the king of England.

Among the larger wineries of the region, Bright's and Mission Hill Vineyards produce some of the better wines. Both wineries, like most of Canada's large wineries, buy vinifera grapes and wine from Washington State and California for blending. Bright's, however, also purchases grapes from top local growers like Ian Mavety of Vaseaux Farms and the Heisses of Gray Monk. Founded in Ontario in 1874, Bright's produces some 700,000 gallons of wine at their Okanagan winery near Oliver. In charge here are general manager John Bremmer and winemaker Lyn Stark, two native British Columbians who have had considerable influence in the region, having served as consultants to some of the smaller wineries. Some of the notable work at Bright's is with "exotics," little-known European varieties that they hope will eventually prove practical on a larger scale. These include cold-hardy Russian varieties like Matsvani, Sereksyia Charni and Rkatsiteli.

Other large wineries in British Columbia, like Andrés, Calona, Jordan-Ste. Michelle (now owned by Bright's) and Casabello produce a broad range of wines that include fortified, dessert and sparkling wines as well as table wines, some of which are good, others mediocre. The large firms are obviously aware of the increasing demand for better wines and the recognition that has come to the smaller wineries that produce them. We should, therefore, see a general upgrading of quality among the large producers in the years ahead.

Okanagan winegrowers get important technical support from the government's agricultural research station in Summerland. Its help, for example, in coordinating the Becker Project had considerable impact on the region. In 1976, Dr. Helmut Becker, an internationally known grape scientist at the Geisenheim Institute in Germany, was invited to come and help determine which varieties were best suited

to the Okanagan climate. As a result, Dr. Becker later sent more than thirty varieties to be planted in experimental plots at chosen sites. Included were some of the varieties mentioned earlier, such as Kerner, Ehrenfelser, Bacchus, Siegfried Rebe and Scheurebe.

Experimental batches of wine from these vineyards are produced each year by Dr. Gary Strachan, chief oenologist at Summerland Station, and these wines are later presented for evaluation at a tasting for growers. In addition to wines from the Becker Project, Dr. Strachan has also experimented with other vinifera varieties. Some of his most dramatic successes have been with red grapes that supposedly cannot ripen here, and he has produced several reds that may one day dispel that notion. His 1985 Cabernet Sauvignon, Malbec, Grenache and Syrah—from varieties not grown commercially in the Okanagan—exhibited extraordinary color and intensity of fruit, and a depth of character indicating excellent potential for aging.

In this and other respects, the future appears rather open-ended for the Okanagan. There are barely 3,000 acres of vineyard at present. Some 35,000 are arable for fruit trees or grapevines, however. The potential is there for the Okanagan to become Canada's leading wine region, but one gets the feeling that the Okanagans are not entirely convinced of it. As the success of a few continues and increases, however, and it undoubtedly will, we should be hearing a good deal more from the Okanagan Valley.

CHAPTER EIGHT

VINEYARDS OF MEXICO

SINCE MEXICO HAS THE OLDEST WINEGROWING tradition on the continent, one that dates back almost five centuries, it may seem curious that we hear so little about its wines. But Mexico's modern wine industry is still in its infancy. Annual per capita wine consumption is a mere two-tenths of a liter of wine—not even half a bottle. The most popular drinks in Mexico are beer, *pulque* and soda pop, and the country is also one of the largest producers of brandy in the world.

Until fairly recently, most of Mexico's vineyards were planted in varieties like Ugni Blanc or Thompson Seedless, ones that produce wine more suitable for distilling than for drinking. Only in the last decade has Mexico begun to move into the modern era of winegrowing, by planting better grape varieties like Cabernet Sauvignon, Chenin Blanc or Chardonnay, and by modernizing the wineries; but the centuries-long delay had more to do with politics than with viticulture.

Initially, Mexico seemed headed for certain success with the vine. The first visionary to recognize and act on the New World's potential for winegrowing was conquistador Hernando Cortez in the sixteenth century. When Cortez and his party journeyed inland from the Gulf of Mexico to meet the Aztec ruler Montezuma, they first traveled through inhospitable jungle and rugged mountain terrain. Eventually, however, they reached the Aztecs' fertile highland valleys, which, much to their amazement, were lush with corn, fruits and other crops.

Though the country was extremely arid, the Indians had established an intricate canal system to irrigate the crops. Chroniclers of the day, like Baltasar Obrégon, recorded how the valleys flourished and that people ate well, their meals including roast chickens "as large as peacocks." The conquistadors were especially intrigued by the thick stands of maguey cactus; they watched with fascination as the Indians harvested it to make the native drink *pulque*. As soon as the maguey flowered, the young juicy shoot was cut off at its base with a machete. The hollow that remained formed a sort of natural chalice into which the juice flowed and then fermented. The milky beverage, lower in alcohol than wine, eventually became the national drink of Mexico.

The conquistadors did not find *pulque* especially to their taste. They were delighted, however, to find wild grapes growing in abundance, and they used them for the first wines ever made in the New World. But, as we have seen elsewhere, wines made from native grapes proved disappointing to European palates, which were accustomed to wines made from *Vitis vinifera*. As governor of Mexico from 1521 to 1527, Cortez set about remedying the situation by instituting a law requiring the larger haciendas to plant a thousand vinifera vines a year for five years. Cortez requested that each shipment from Spain include vine cuttings, which were then distributed to the plantations and missions. The policy worked well; so well that, within fifty years, the colony of New Spain no longer depended on the mother country for wine. Vineyards also became widely established in areas of northern Mexico. The first commercial winery was founded in the Valle de Parras (*parras* means vine trellises) in 1593 by a Spanish officer, Captain Francisco de Urdiñola.

The young colony's success spawned jeal-

Prickly pear cactus front a venerable vineyard in Mexico.

ousy back home, and politics intervened. Threatened by the loss of revenue and the prospect of serious competition to their own wines, Spanish producers prevailed upon Philip II to halt the colony's young industry. In 1595 Philip issued his infamous edict prohibiting wine production and the raising of olive trees (another major Spanish product) in Mexico. He went even further by commanding that existing vines and trees be ripped out. Although this order caused Mexican vineyards to be destroyed in some places, many haciendas quietly continued to farm their vineyards and to make wine for use on the estate.

The missions, however, were the great preservers of the vine. Wine was vital to their operations, not only for the Sacrament but also for medicinal uses. Those in the more remote regions received only sporadic supply shipments and were thereby forced to become as self-sufficient as possible. Many of these outposts were hospitals established by Augustinian monks and became important centers of community as well as of religious activity. As Robert Ricard notes in *The Spiritual Conquest of Mexico*, the hospitals also served "as free provisioning centers" where natives, colonists and travelers could find whatever they needed or wanted: meat, oil, lard, sugar and, among other items, wine. Winegrowing also spread gradually from Mexico to other Latin American countries—Peru, Chile, Argentina—and, of course, northward into the American Southwest and California, but in Mexico the growth of viticulture was effectively choked off by the repressive grip of Spanish law.

Wine was a significant impetus for Mexico's thrust for independence in the early nineteenth century. In fact, one of the principal goals of the revolution Padre Miguel Hidalgo began in 1810 was to end the prohibition against winegrowing and thereby revive Mexican viticulture and winemaking. Hidalgo, father of Mexican independence, openly defied Philip II's law, which was still being rigorously enforced, by teaching Indians at the mission in Dolores to plant vines. More than once, local

Spanish officials came and tore out the vines.

Though Mexico won its independence in 1811, the vine's progress in Mexico was further delayed by the long period of disorder and confusion that followed the revolution. It wasn't until the 1860s that a winery was started in the state of Coahuila, which borders Texas; in 1888 Bodegas de Santo Tomás was founded in Baja California, the long fingerlike peninsula that stretches south of California. The first significant efforts at growing any grape other than the Mission were also started around this time, aided in part by one of California's leading vintners, James Concannon of Livermore Valley. Concannon, an Irish immigrant who founded Concannon Winery in 1883, shipped over a million cuttings of vinifera varieties to estates throughout Mexico, and vineyards began to flourish in many of the northern regions, but again, progress was thwarted by politics.

In 1910 civil war erupted. During this ten-year period of strife, many vineyards were neglected, some were destroyed. For several decades the industry languished. In the 1940s, large international distillers such as Seagram's, Spanish brandy producers like Domecq and Osborne, and Martell Cognac set up operations in Mexico mainly to produce brandy, though they also produced some wine. Beer and *pulque* became entrenched as the leading fermented beverages in Mexico, while brandy and other hard alcohols were considered the sophisticated drinks.

In the last ten years, however, subtle but significant shifts have been set in motion. Consumption of *pulque* has been on the decline, and a new generation of young adults has come of age at a time when wine, rather than liquor, holds the international spotlight. Efforts with better grape varieties that were planted in the last twenty years or so have resulted in better wines. The cumulative effect of these developments is encouragement to Mexican vintners, who are finally beginning to see brighter prospects for the future.

Wine grapes grow in several areas of Mexico, but the three most important growing re-

Baja California is home to several Mexican wineries, including two owned by the Cetto family. Pictured here are the crusher (LEFT) and the fermentation vats (RIGHT) of Vinícola L. A. Cetto.
(PAGES 196–197): About thirty miles inland from the Pacific Coast of Baja California vineyards contribute to the greens of the Guadalupe Valley, a near-oasis area in the midst of the arid hills east of Ensenada.

gions are in the states of Querétaro, about a hundred miles north of Mexico City; Zacatecas, in the north-central part of Mexico; and Baja California. Most Mexican wineries are quite large in capacity, producing millions of gallons of wine a year. They make a broad range of products, including brandy, table wine, fortified and sparkling wines and vermouth. Mexican wine labels use terms like *tinto* for red wines, *blanco* for whites and *rosada* for rosé. Some of the large old firms, regrettably, have appropriated European geographic names (Burgundy, Sauternes, Chablis) for some of their blended generic wines, but the better wines are labeled with varietal names. A number of Mexican wines, for example, bear such names as *Vino Tinto de Cabernet Sauvignon* or *Vino Blanco de Chenin Blanc*. There is a good deal of variation in quality, ranging from rather mediocre to soundly made, balanced wines that are pleasant but unexceptional.

Baja is Mexico's oldest and largest wine region, with sizable vineyards planted around Tecate, just south of the California border, in the Guadalupe Valley east of Ensenada, and south of Ensenada toward San Vicente. The climate in Baja is Mediterranean, dry and warm, desertlike in terms of moisture (annual rainfall is about eleven inches), though not especially hot. Summer days inland average eighty degrees, but are somewhat cooler near the coast, where fog and Pacific breezes affect temperatures; the nights in Baja drop to sixty degrees.

Bodegas de Santo Tomás, which owns vineyards south of Ensenada in the Santo Tomás Valley as well as in Guadalupe Valley, is Mexico's oldest surviving winery. It also was one of the first to modernize, a move accomplished with the aid of wine consultant Dmitri Tchelistcheff (son of California's André Tchelistcheff), who served as technical director for several years during the 1970s. Tchelistcheff

encouraged the planting of better grape varieties like Chenin Blanc, Cabernet Sauvignon, Riesling and Pinot Noir, and introduced such techniques as cold fermentation, which produced fresher, more attractive white wines, and bottle fermentation for sparkling wines based on the traditional method used in Champagne. Santo Tomás, troubled by financial difficulties in recent years, is now under new management and a retrenchment of its wine program is underway.

Another modern winery is Casa Pinson Hermanos, founded by Pedro Pinson in the late 1970s. Casa Pinson purchases grapes from the Guadalupe Valley as well as from growers in the Valle del Rocio of Querétaro in central Mexico. Pinson's Baja wines—dry and sweet whites and a medium-bodied Ruby Cabernet—are bottled under the Don Eugenio label and have limited distribution in Texas and other parts of the southeastern United States.

Amid the dry hills east of Ensenada, about fifty miles south of the American border, the Guadalupe Valley appears as a kind of oasis. Green vines carpet the valley floor and curve up into the surrounding hills. Driving overland from the Pacific Coast, one is constantly reminded that Mexico remains a country with a foot in two eras, presenting a startling contrast of the ancient with the modern. For many of those who live here, life has changed little in the last fifty years. Antique trucks lumber along dusty roads, carting produce or chickens. Burros laden with packs or pulling wooden carts trudge the roadsides. Only thirty miles inland there are no telephones, though there is electricity; the smallest shack will sometimes have a television antenna.

Rising above the vineyards of the Guadalupe are two of Mexico's most modern wineries, owned by the Cetto and Domecq families. The Domecq name is best known to Americans for its Spanish sherry and Spanish brandy—indeed, the company's brandy distillery on the outskirts of Mexico City is the largest in the world. In the last fifteen years, however, Do-

mecq has become a leading wine producer in Mexico. The firm owns 2,000 acres of vineyard in the Calafia Valley, the heart of the Guadalupe, growing such premium varieties as Cabernet Sauvignon, Sauvignon Blanc, Zinfandel, Chenin Blanc, and Sémillon. Vineyards were planted here in 1972 and the winery, a handsome stucco structure with an arched facade and red-tile roof, has a capacity of 5 million gallons. According to winemaker and head oenologist Camilo Magoni, Domecq produces over a million cases of wine a year. The Domecqs brought Professor Emile Peynaud, France's leading oenologist, to Baja to serve as consultant for the first few vintages. Professor Peynaud was particularly influential in improving white wines, emphasizing freshness, crispness and good balance.

The vineyards in Calafia are about equally divided between red and white varieties. Domecq reds, such as Cabernet Sauvignon and Zinfandel, are robust wines—sturdy, dry and a little austere but not overly tannic—wines suit-

ed to beef, roast chicken and other meats. Domecq also grows Gamay, Merlot, Ruby
Cabernet, Petite Sirah, and two Italian varieties, Barbera and Nebbiolo, the latter producing a dark, tannic, full-bodied wine of the
Barolo style. A Reserve Cabernet Sauvignon, labeled Chateau Domecq, is made only in years
when the grapes are especially good. Aged in
American oak barrels, Chateau Domecq is
somewhat firmer and more tannic than the regular Cabernet, though it is not an especially
concentrated wine.

The whites are light, fruity and attractive,
especially the Dry Chenin Blanc, which is clean
and fresh and very well balanced. Riesling, Sauvignon Blanc and Colombard are also produced.
Though some vineyards of the Guadalupe are
dryfarmed (without irrigation), Domecq has
the financial resources to irrigate by tapping underground water from mountain springs. This
allows them to get larger yields than dryfarmed
vineyards and pushes the harvest back by about
two weeks. Magoni would like to make Char-

donnay, but the climate in the Calafia Valley is
a little too warm to get the best quality, so Domecq is attempting to grow Chardonnay near
the coast—with some difficulty because there is
little water for irrigation. It helps, in starting a
new vineyard, to be able to irrigate so the vines
are not overly stressed in the beginning. Domecq wines are widely distributed in Mexico
and have had considerable influence in demonstrating that Mexico is capable of producing
creditable wines.

The Cetto family has two operations in
Baja, one directly across the valley from Do-
mecq and another in Tecate, at which Camilo
Magoni is winemaker. The Cetto family pro-
duces wine in Aguascalientes, including one of
Mexico's best brands, Castell Celva, which con-
sists of varietals like French Colombard, Chenin
Blanc, Ruby Cabernet and Cabernet
Sauvignon.

Two of Mexico's most promising new regions
are Aguascalientes and Querétaro in the north-

Certainly at similar latitudes elsewhere (North Africa, for instance), the climate is subtropical. But vineyards here are more than a mile high and the extreme elevation—over 6,000 feet—moderates conditions to accommodate premium varieties like Chardonnay, Cabernet and Riesling. The hottest months are April and May. During the major part of the growing season, in July and August, it is much cooler, thereby permitting the grapes to mature slowly and develop more character. Winters are very cold here, with a long period of dormancy for the vines. This, too, is considered beneficial for a good crop, though sometimes a mid-April freeze can be damaging in years with early springs. The high elevation also has another effect according to Francisco Domenech, winemaker at Cavas de San Juan near San Juan del Rio in Querétaro. "Our wines age much faster in wood here," says Domenech. "They lose their attractiveness and tend to oxidize quickly. Instead of the 60-gallon barrel, we have to use larger containers holding 250 gallons."

Although the winery released its first wines in 1964, the Domenechs began experimenting with better grape varieties in the late 1950s. With cuttings procured from California, France, Germany and Spain, they planted some 120 varieties, which were eventually narrowed to eight: Cabernet Sauvignon, the largest planting; Ugni Blanc, used for brandy; Chenin Blanc; Gewürztraminer; Riesling; Merlot and small amounts of Chardonnay and Pinot Noir. The best wines, varietals like Cabernet Sauvignon, Chenin Blanc and Riesling, appear under the Hidalgo label. Cavas de San Juan also makes sparkling wines from Chardonnay and Pinot Noir.

Francisco Domenech is one of the new breed of winemakers in Mexico who were trained either at the University of California at Davis or at the viticultural school in Montpellier, France. Domenech went to Davis, where he learned some of the latest techniques in wine production and growing. Another Davis-trained winemaker is Dr. Eduardo de la Cerna, whose Los Pioneros (The Pioneers) Cabernet Sauvignon exhibits concentrated flavors and a depth of character that is unusual in Mexican Cabernets. These winemakers have brought a new level of expertise to Mexican wines and have had significant influence in terms of upgrading quality.

Mexico appears to be on the verge of tremendous expansion in the next decade. At the moment the major problem is educating consumers about wine. "This is a baby market," says Paco Domenech. "People here are not used to drinking wine, or even the idea of wine. We have to teach them everything. At the moment, because of the soda pop market, the public taste is for semisweet wines, but we are just beginning to see greater demand for better wines that people drink with food."

Mexico's serious economic problems have also taken their toll in recent years. The feeling now, however, is that the decline has stopped and a stronger middle class is showing interest in wine. With restrictive tariffs on imported wines, Mexican vintners are finally being encouraged to expand their market. They have made a great leap in the last ten years, and it is quite possible that in the next ten Mexico will take its place among the leading wine-producing countries of the world.

Domecq's popular Calafia Bianco is a blend of several white grapes including Chenin Blanc and French Colombard.

The Northeast

NEW YORK

Finger Lakes Region

Canandaigua Wine Company, Inc.
116 Buffalo Street
Canandaigua, NY 14424
(716) 394–3630

Glenora-on-Seneca*
Dundee, NY 14837
(607) 243–5511

Great Western Winery
Hammondsport, NY 14840
(607) 569–2111

Hermann J. Wiemer Vineyard*
P.O. Box 4, Route 14
Dundee, NY 14837
(607) 243–7971

Heron Hill Vineyards, Inc.*
Hammondsport, NY 14840
(607) 868–4241

The Taylor Wine Company
Hammondsport, NY 14840
(607) 569–2111

Vinifera Wine Cellars*
(Dr. Konstantin Frank)
RD 2
Hammondsport, NY 14840
(607) 868–4884

Wagner Vineyards*
Route 414
Lodi, NY 14860
(607) 582–6450

Widmer's Wine Cellars, Inc.
West Avenue & Tobey Street
Naples, NY 14512
(716) 374–6311

Erie–Chautauqua Region

Schloss Doepken Winery
RD 2, East Main Road
Ripley, NY 14775
(716) 326–3636

Hermann J. Wiemer, Vintner
Hermann J. Wiemer Vineyard

Peter Johnstone, Vintner–Winemaker
Heron Hill Vineyards

John Hutchinson, Winemaker
Wagner Vineyards

Woodbury Vineyards*
RD 1, South Roberts Road
Dunkirk, NY 14048
(716) 679–WINE

Hudson Valley Region

Benmarl Wine Co., Ltd.*
Highland Avenue
Marlboro, NY 12542
(914) 236–4265

Brotherhood Corp., Inc.
35 North Street
Washingtonville, NY 10992
(914) 496–3661

Clinton Vineyards, Inc.
Schultzville Road
Clinton Corners, NY 12514
(914) 266–5372

Royal Wine Corporation
Dock Road
Milton, NY
(914) 795–2240

West Park Wine Cellars*
Burroughs Drive
West Park, NY 12493
(914) 384–6709

Long Island

Hargrave Vineyard
Alvah's Lane, Box 924
Cutchogue, NY 11935
(516) 734–5158

Lenz Vineyards*
Box 28, Main Road
Peconic, NY 11958
(516) 734–6010

Pindar Vineyards
P.O. Box 332, Main Road
Peconic, NY 11958
(516) 734–6200

MASSACHUSETTS

Chicama Vineyards*
Stoney Hill Road
West Tisbury, MA 02575
(617) 693–0309

Louis Fiore, Vintner
West Park Wine Cellars

Gary Galleron, Winemaker
Lenz Vineyards

The Matthiesen Family
Chicama Vineyards

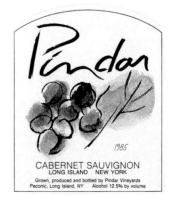

Commonwealth Winery*
22 Lothrop Street
Plymouth, MA 02360
(617) 746–4138

RHODE ISLAND

Diamond Hill Vineyards
3145 Diamond Hill Road
Cumberland, RI 02864
(401) 333–2751

Prudence Island Vineyards,
Inc.
Sunset Hill Farm
Prudence Island, RI 02872
(401) 683–2452

Sakonnet Vineyards
Box 572, 162 West Main Road
Little Compton, RI 02837
(401) 635–4356

CONNECTICUT

Clarke Vineyard
RD 2, Taugwonk Road
Stonington, CT 06378
(203) 535–0235

Crosswoods Vineyards, Inc.*
75 Chester Maine Road
North Stonington, CT 06359
(203) 535–2205

Di Grazia Vineyards & Winery
131 Tower Road
Brookfield Center, CT 06805
(203) 775–1616

Haight Vineyard, Inc.
Chestnut Hill
Litchfield, CT 06759
(203) 567–4045

Hamlet Hill Vineyards
Pomfret, CT 06258
(203) 928–5550

Hopkins Vineyard
Hopkins Road
New Preston, CT 06777
(203) 868–7954

PENNSYLVANIA

Allegro Vineyards
RD 2, Box 64
Brogue, PA 17309
(717) 927–9148

SOUTHEASTERN NEW ENGLAND TABLE WINE
AMERICA'S CUP WHITE
PRODUCED & BOTTLED BY
SAKONNET VINEYARDS, LITTLE COMPTON, RI
CONTAINS SULFITES
1986

George Sulick, Jr., Winemaker
Crosswoods Vineyards

NEW JERSEY

Alba Vineyard
RD 1, Box 179AAA
Milford, NJ 08848
(201) 995–7800

Four Sisters Winery
RD 1, Box 258
Route 519
Belvedere, NJ 07823
(201) 475–3671

Gross' Highland Winery
306 East Jim Leeds Road
Absecon, NJ 08201
(609) 652–1187

Kings Road Vineyard
RD 2, Box 352B
Milford, NJ 08848
(201) 479–6611

Tewksbury Wine Cellars
Route 2
Lebanon, NJ 08833
(201) 832–2400

Tomasello Winery, Inc.
225 White Horse Pike
Hammonton, NJ 08037
(609) 561–0567

The South

MARYLAND

Boordy Vineyards*
Hydes, MD 21082
(301) 592–5015

The Chaddsford Winery
Route 1, Box 229
Chadds Ford, PA 19317
(215) 388–6221

Fox Meadow Farm
RD 2, Box 59
Chester Springs, PA 19425
(215) 827–9731

Naylor Wine Cellars, Inc.
RD 3, Box 424
Ebaugh Road
Stewartstown, PA 17363
(717) 993–2431

York Springs Winery
Route 1, Box 194
York Springs, PA 17372
(717) 528–8490

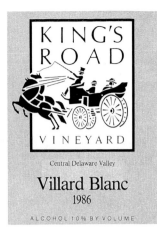

KING'S ROAD VINEYARD
Central Delaware Valley
Villard Blanc
1986
ALCOHOL 10% BY VOLUME

NAYLOR
PENNSYLVANIA
CHARDONNAY
Dry Oak Aged
White Table Wine
PRODUCED AND BOTTLED BY
NAYLOR WINE CELLARS, INC.
RD 3, STEWARTSTOWN, PA 17363

Allegro Vineyards
RESERVE
CABERNET SAUVIGNON
YORK COUNTY
TABLE WINE
Produced and Bottled by
Allegro Vineyards,
Brogue, Pa. 17309
1983

Byrd Vineyards
Church Hill Road
Myersville, MD 21773
(301) 293–1110

Catoctin Vineyards, Inc.
805 Greenbridge Road
Brookeville, MD 20833
(301) 774–2310

Montbray Wine Cellars Ltd.*
818 Silver Run Valley Road
Westminster, MD 21157
(301) 346–7878

VIRGINIA

Barboursville Winery, Inc.*
Route 777
Barboursville, VA 22923
(703) 832–3824

Chermont Winery
Route 1, Box 59
Esmont, VA 29937
(804) 286–2211

Ingleside Plantation
Vineyards*
P.O. Box 1038
Oak Grove, VA 22443
(804) 224–8687

Meredyth Vineyard*
P.O. Box 347
Middleburg, VA 22117
(703) 687–6277

Montdomaine Cellars, Inc.
Route 6, Box 168A
Charlottesville, VA 22901
(804) 971–8947

Oakencroft Vineyard*
Route 5
Charlottesville, VA 22901
(804) 295–8175

Deborah Welsh, Winemaker
Oakencroft Vineyard

Piedmont Vineyards
P.O. Box 286
Middleburg, VA 22117
(703) 687–5528

Prince Michel Vineyard
Star Route 4, Box 77
Leon, VA 11715
(703) 547–3707

Rapidan River Vineyards, Inc.
Route 4, Box 199
Culpeper, VA 22701
(703) 399–1855

THE CAROLINAS

Biltmore Estate Wine Co.*
One Biltmore Plaza
Asheville, NC 28803
(704) 274–1776

Truluck Vineyards
Route 3
Lake City, SC 29560
(803) 389–3400

FLORIDA

Lafayette Vineyards*
Route 7, Box 481
Tallahassee, FL 32308
(904) 878–9041

THE DEEP SOUTH

Chateau Elan*
Route 1, Box 563–1
Hoschton, GA 30548
(404) 867–8286

Claiborne Vineyards*
302 North Highway 49W
Indianola, MS 38751
(601) 887–2327

Laurel Hill Vineyard*
1370 Madison Avenue
Memphis, TN 38104
(901) 725–9128

The Winery Rushing*
P.O. Drawer F
Merigold, MS 38759

The Heartland

OHIO

Breitenbach Wine Cellars
RR #1
Dover, OH 44622
(216) 343–3603

Chalet Debonne Vineyards
7743 Doty Road
Madison, OH 44057
(216) 466–3485

Grand River Wine Company*
5750 Madison Road
Madison, OH 44057
(216) 298–9838

Markko Vineyard*
RD 2, South Ridge Road
Conneaut, OH 44030
(216) 593–3197

Meier's Wine Cellars
6955 Plainfield Pike
Silverton
Cincinnati, OH 45236
(513) 891–2900

MICHIGAN

Boskydel Vineyard
Route 1, Box 552
Lake Leelanau, MI 49653
(616) 256–7272

Fenn Valley Vineyards*
Route 4
6130 122nd Avenue
Fennville, MI 49408
(616) 561–2396

Good Harbor Vineyards
Route 1, Box 891
Lake Leelanau, MI 49653
(616) 256–7165

Grand Traverse Vineyards*
12239 Center Road
Traverse City, MI 49684
(616) 223–7355

L. Mawby Vineyards
4519 Elm Valley Road
Suttons Bay, MI 49682
(616) 271–3522

St. Julian Wine Company
P.O. Box 127
Paw Paw, MI 49079
(616) 657–5568

MINNESOTA

Alexis Bailly Vineyard
18200 Kirby Avenue
Hastings, MN 55033
(612) 437–1413

WISCONSIN

Wollersheim Winery
Highway 188
Prairie Du Sac, WI 53578
(608) 643–6515

MISSOURI

Carver Wine Cellars*
Box 1316
Rolla, MO 65401
(314) 364–4335

The Welsch Family
Fenn Valley Vineyards

Judy and Bob Slifer, Vintners
Montelle Vineyards

Bobby Cox, Vintner–Winemaker
Pheasant Ridge Winery

Montelle Vineyards*
Route 1, Box 94
Augusta, MO 63332
(314) 228–4464

Stone Hill Wine Company*
Route 1, Box 26
Hermann, MO 65041
(314) 486–2221

ARKANSAS

Cowie Wine Cellars
Route 2, Box 799
Paris, AR 72855
(501) 963–3990

Mt. Bethel Winery
U.S. Highway 64
Altus, AR 72821
(501) 468–2444

Wiederkehr Wine Cellars,
Inc.*
Route 1, Box 14
Altus, AR 72821
(501) 468–2611

The Southwest

TEXAS

Fall Creek Vineyards*
Fall Creek Ranch
Box 68
Tow, TX 78672
(915) 379–5361

La Buena Vida Vineyards
WSR Box 18–3
Springtown, TX 76082
(817) 523–4366

Llano Estacado Winery
P.O. Box 3487
Lubbock, TX 79452
(806) 745–2258

Messina Hof Wine Cellars
Route 7, Box 905
Bryan, TX 77802
(409) 779–2411

Pheasant Ridge Winery*
Route 3, Box 191
Lubbock, TX 79401
(806) 746–6033

Ste. Genevieve Vineyards*
Box 687
Fort Stockton, TX 79736
(915) 395–2417

David Johnson, Winemaker
Stone Hill Wine Company

Al Wiederkehr, Vintner
Wiederkehr Wine Cellars

Ed and Susan Auler, Vintners
Fall Creek Vineyards

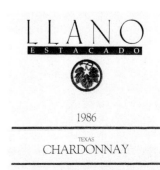

Texas Vineyards, Inc.
P.O. Box 33
Ivanhoe, TX 75447
(214) 583–4047

Val Verde Winery
139 Hudson Drive
Del Rio, TX 78840
(512) 775–9714

NEW MEXICO

Blue Teal Vineyards*
P.O. Box 489
Lordsburg, NM 88045
(505) 542–8881

La Chiripada Winery*
P.O. Box 191
Dixon, NM 87527
(505) 579–4675

La Vina Winery
Box 121
Chamberino, NM 88027
(505) 882–2092

St. Clair Vineyards*
P.O. Box 112
Deming, NM 88031
(505) 546–6585

Sangre de Cristo Wines
Route 2, Box 20–A
Sapello, NM 87745
(505) 425–5077

ARIZONA

Sonoita Vineyards*
P.O. Box 36344
Tucson, AZ 85718
(602) 455–5893

R. W. Webb Winery, Inc.
4352 East Speedway
Tucson, AZ 85712
(602) 887–1537

California

Beaulieu Vineyard
1960 St. Helena Highway
Rutherford, CA 94573
(707) 963–1451

Chalone Vineyard*
P.O. Box 855
Soledad, CA 93960
(415) 441–8975

Patrick and Michael Johnson, Vintners
La Chiripada Winery

Gordon and Rocky Dutt,
Vintner–Winemakers
Sonoita Vineyards

Richard Graff, Vintner
Chalone Vineyard

The Firestone Vineyard*
P.O. Box 244
Los Olivos, CA 93441
(805) 688–3940

E & J Gallo Winery
600 Yosemite Boulevard
Modesto, CA 95353
(209) 579–3111

Heitz Wine Cellars* (Martha's
Vineyard, Bella Oaks
Vineyard*)
500 Taplin Road
St. Helena, CA 94574
(707) 963–3542

Laurel Glen Vineyard*
P.O. Box 548
Glen Ellen, CA 95442
(707) 526–3914

Louis M. Martini*
P.O. Box 112
St. Helena, CA 94574
(707) 963–2736

Robert Mondavi Winery
(Opus One Vineyard*)
P.O. Box 106
Oakville, CA 94562
(707) 963–9611

Rutherford Hill Winery*
200 Rutherford Hill Road
Rutherford, CA 94573
(707) 963–9694

Sterling Vineyards*
P.O. Box 365
Calistoga, CA 94515
(707) 942–5151

Wente*
5565 Tesla Road
Livermore, CA 94550
(415) 447–3603

The Northwest

OREGON

Adelsheim Vineyard
Route 1, Box 129D
Newberg, OR 97132
(503) 538–3652

Elk Cove Vineyards
Route 3, Box 23
Gaston, OR 97119
(503) 985–7760

Alison Green, Winemaker
The Firestone Vineyard

Patrick Campbell, Vintner–Winemaker
Laurel Glen Vineyard

Bill Jaeger, Vintner
Rutherford Hill Winery

Philip, Carolyn and Eric Wente
Wente

The Eyrie Vineyards*
P.O. Box 204
Dundee, OR 97115
(503) 864-2410

Knudsen–Erath Winery
Worden Hill Road
Dundee, OR 97115
(503) 538-3318

Oak Knoll Winery
Route 6, Box 184
Hillsboro, OR 97123
(503) 648-8198

Ponzi Vineyards
Route 1, Box 842
Beaverton, OR 97007
(503) 628-1227

Sokol–Blosser Winery
P.O. Box 199
Dundee, OR 97115
(503) 864-2282

Tualatin Vineyards
Route 1, Box 339
Forest Grove, OR 97116
(503) 357-5005

WASHINGTON

Arbor Crest
E. 4506 Buckeye
Spokane, WA 99207
(509) 484-9463

Chateau Ste. Michelle*
One Stimson Lane
Woodinville, WA 98072
(206) 488-1133

Columbia Winery
1445 120th Avenue NE
Bellvue, WA 98005
(206) 453-1977

Leonetti Cellar
1321 School Avenue
Walla Walla, WA 99362
(509) 525-1428

Neuharth Winery
P.O. Box 1457
Sequim, WA 98382
(206) 683-9652

Quilceda Creek Vintners
5226 Snohomish–Machias Road
Snohomish, WA 98290
(206) 568-2389

David Lett, Vintner–Winemaker
The Eyrie Vineyards

Snoqualmie Winery
1000 Winery Road
Snoqualmie, WA 98065
(206) 888-4000

MONTANA

Mission Mountain Winery
Dayton, MT 59914
(406) 849-5524

IDAHO

Camas Winery
521 North Moore Street
Moscow, ID 83843
(208) 882-0214

Petros Winery*
9600 Brookside Lane
Boise, ID 83703
(208) 939-4200

Ste. Chapelle Winery*
Route 4, Box 775
Caldwell, ID 83605
(208) 459-7222

Weston
Route 4, Box 731
Caldwell, ID 83605
(208) 454-1682

Canada

ONTARIO

Andrés Wines Ltd.
P.O. Box 550
Winona, Ontario
Canada L0R 2L0
(416) 643-4131

Chateau des Charmes*
P.O. Box 280
St. David's, Ontario
Canada L0S 10
(416) 262-4219

Inniskillen Wines, Inc.*
Niagara Parkway
Niagara-on-the-Lake, Ontario
Canada L0S 1J0
(416) 468-2187

Reif Winery
RR #1, Niagara Parkway
Niagara-on-the-Lake, Ontario
Canada L0S 1J0
(416) 468-7738

Karl Kaiser, Winemaker
Inniskillen Wines

Vineland Estate Wines Ltd.
RR #1, Moyer Road
Vineland, Ontario
Canada L0R 2C0
(416) 562–7088

NOVA SCOTIA

Grand Pré Wines*
Box 18
Grand Pré, Nova Scotia
Canada B0P 1M0
(902) 542–2042

Jost Vineyards
Malagash, Nova Scotia
Canada B0K 1E0
(902) 257–2248

BRITISH COLUMBIA

Bright & Co. Ltd.*
P.O. Box 1650
Oliver, British Columbia
Canada V0H 1T0
(604) 498–4981

Calona Wines Limited
1125 Richter Street
Kelowna, British Columbia
Canada V1Y 2K6
(604) 762–3332

Gehringer Vineyard*
Oliver, British Columbia
Canada V0H 1T0
(604) 498–3537

Gray Monk Cellars Ltd.*
Box 63
Okanagan Center, British
Columbia
Canada V0H 1P0
(604) 766–3168

Mission Hill Vineyards
P.O. Box 610
Mission Hill Road
Westbank, British Columbia
Canada V0H 2A0
(604) 768–5125

Sumac Ridge Estate Winery
Ltd.*
P.O. Box 307, Highway 97
Summerland, British Columbia
Canada V0H 1Z0
(604) 494–0451

Uniacke Estate
Lakeshire Road
Kelowna, British Columbia
(604) 764–8866

Mexico

Bodegas de Santo Tomas
Avenida Miramar 666
Ensenada, Baja California
Mexico
4–08–36

Casa Pinson Hermanos*
Calz. al Desierto de los Leones
#4152
Mexico 01060
595–70–22

Cavas de San Juan*
76800 San Juan del Rio
Queretaro, Mexico
91–467–20120

Pedro Domecq Mexico
Avenida Mexico 101 Coyoacan
Mexico 21, D.F.
554–54–11

Vinícola L.A. Cetto, S.A.
Apartado Postal 292
Tijuana, Baja California 22000
Mexico

Vinicola de Tecate
Avenida Pueblo No. 1050
Tecate, Baja California
Mexico
91–668–23–61

George Heiss, Jr., Vintner–Winemaker
Gray Monk Cellars

North American vineyards grow a variety of wine grapes that primarily fall into three categories: the native American species such as Vitis aestivalis, Vitis labrusca, Vitis rotundifolia (Muscadine) and others; the European species Vitis vinifera; and varieties hybridized in France from crossings of vinifera and American varieties. The latter are known as French-American, or simply French, hybrids. There are also varieties hybridized from vinifera crosses that have been developed in the U.S. and Germany, as well as several bred from native American species. The following alphabetical listing includes the wine grapes most commonly grown, now or previously, in North American vineyards.

ALEXANDER. An early American grape thought to have been derived from crossing wild native grapes with vinifera planted in the Philadelphia vineyard established in 1684 by John Alexander, William Penn's gardener. Also known as the Cape grape.

ALICANTE-BOUSCHET. V.VINIFERA. A thick-skinned, purple-juiced variety grown mainly in California's San Joaquin Valley. Frequently used for blending in red wines to add color.

ALIGOTÉ. V.VINIFERA. A secondary white variety grown in Burgundy. It produces good but simple white wines that are less distinctive in character than those made from the leading Burgundian white variety, Chardonnay. Limited plantings in California and the Pacific Northwest.

AURORE. French hybrid used for white and sparkling wines in the East, primarily New York State. Often exhibits some foxy (wild grape) flavors.

AUXERROIS. *See* Pinot Auxerrois.

BACCHUS. V.VINIFERA. A vinifera hybrid white developed in Germany from Riesling, Sylvaner and Müller-Thurgau. Grown in Canada, primarily in the Okanagan Valley of British Columbia.

BACO NOIR. A French hybrid producing vivid red wines; grown primarily east of the Rockies.

BARBERA. V.VINIFERA. A red grape from the Piedmont in northern Italy, Barbera is widely grown in California's Central Valley and more recently in Texas.

BLANC DUBOIS. A new white Muscadine variety introduced in 1987 by Florida plant geneticists, it was named for French grape breeder Emile Dubois, who worked in Tallahassee in the 1880s.

BURGER. V.VINIFERA. A lesser but large-yielding white variety used mostly for blending jug whites in California.

CABERNET FRANC. V.VINIFERA. Red variety from Bordeaux where it constitutes a considerable portion of Saint-Emilion vineyards. Increasingly grown in California and other states for blending with Cabernet Sauvignon; occasionally seen as a varietal.

CABERNET SAUVIGNON. V.VINIFERA. The leading red variety in the Médoc region of Bordeaux and the coastal regions of California, particularly Napa and Sonoma. Increasingly grown in other states, including Washington, Idaho, Virginia, Texas, Georgia and Arkansas.

CARDINAL. A vinifera cross developed by the University of California at Davis for warm climates; grown primarily in California's inland valleys.

CARIGNANE. V.VINIFERA. A black grape yielding hearty red wines that are used mainly for blending. Grown in warmer climates like southern France and the inland valleys of California.

CARLOS. V.ROTUNDIFOLIA. A white Muscadine variety developed in North Carolina and grown mainly in the Southeast, notably Florida and Mississippi.

CARMINE. V.VINIFERA. A red vinifera hybrid—from Carignane, Cabernet Sauvignon and Merlot—developed at the University of California at Davis for warm climates.

CARNELIAN. V.VINIFERA. Red vinifera hybrid (Carignane, Cabernet Sauvignon and Grenache) bred in California for high yield in warm climates. Also grown in Texas.

CASCADE. A French hybrid red grown mainly in the East, especially New York, where it is used for blending.

CATAWBA. V.LABRUSCA. One of the earliest grapes of American origin, it was widely grown in Ohio until it succumbed to black rot; now grown mainly in New York, where it is used to make sweet or off-dry whites. Pronounced labrusca flavor.

CAYUGA. A hybrid developed at the Geneva experimental station in New York; produces fruity, attractive off-dry whites.

CENTURION. V.VINIFERA. A red hybrid developed in California with limited plantings in the San Joaquin Valley.

CHAMBOURCIN. A French hybrid grown in the East and Midwest to produce claretlike reds or *rosé*.

CHAMPANEL. V.RIPARIA. A native red variety often used as rootstock, occasionally for blending.

CHANCELLOR. A popular French hybrid red grown widely east of the Rockies and in Canada. Capable of yielding well-balanced, flavorful red wine.

CHARDONNAY. V.VINIFERA. Leading grape for dry white wines. Widely grown in wine regions around the world, notably Burgundy and California, as well as in virtually every other region of North America.

CHASSELAS. V.VINIFERA. Also known as Golden Chasselas and as Fendant in Switzerland. A lesser white variety, primarily used for blending.

CHELOIS. A French hybrid grown in the East and Midwest; occasionally produces a fruity, medium-bodied red.

VIRGINIA
Blush de Michel

1986 VINTAGE VIN ROSÉ
Grown, vinted and bottled by VaVin, Inc., Leon, Virginia
Contains sulfites   Alc. 10.5% by vol.

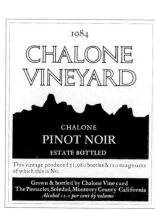

1984
CHALONE
VINEYARD

CHALONE
PINOT NOIR
ESTATE BOTTLED

This vintage produced 31,980 bottles & 120 magnums
of which this is No.

Grown & bottled by Chalone Vineyard
The Pinnacles, Soledad, Monterey County California
Alcohol 12.0 per cent by volume

1986
UNIACKE
ESTATE WINERY & VINEYARDS
Okanagan Riesling
CEDAR CREEK VINEYARD
OKANAGAN MISSION

WHITE WINE • 750 ml   11% ALC.VOL • VIN BLANC
PRODUCT OF CANADA   PRODUIT DU CANADA

CHENIN BLANC. V.VINIFERA. A white grape used to make fruity, occasionally dry, but usually lightly sweet, wines. Used for Vouvray and other Loire Valley whites, as a varietal and as a blending grape in California, the Northwest and Texas.

CHEVRIER. An old Bordeaux name for Sémillon (*q.v.*).

COLOBEL. A French hybrid *teinturier*, or color grape, used for blending in red wines to increase color. Not widely planted in North America.

COLOMBARD. *See* French Colombard.

CONCORD. V.LABRUSCA. A native American grape developed in the mid-1800s by Ephraim Bull of Concord, Massachusetts. Still widely planted outside California, its pronounced foxy flavor now causes it to be used more for juice and jam than for wine. Still the basis of some sweet kosher wines.

CONQUISTADOR. V.ROTUNDIFOLIA. A red Muscadine developed at Florida State University, released in 1983, and grown primarily in the South.

COUDERC NOIR. A French hybrid used for hearty reds and *rosé*; not widely grown.

CYNTHIANA. V.AESTIVALIS. Considered by some to be the same as the Norton grape (*q.v.*). Grown in the Ozark highlands of Arkansas and Missouri where it produces an attractive, claret-style red with some aging potential and no foxy flavor.

DE CHAUNAC. A red hybrid developed in Ontario and grown in Canada and the eastern U.S., especially the Finger Lakes region of New York. It produces a large yield and is disease resistant, but to date it has produced mostly mediocre reds and *rosés*.

DELAWARE. V.LABRUSCA. A native pink variety with some aestivalis in its parentage. Bred for cold climates, it makes a crisp, usually sweet, pink or white wine and has traditionally been used for champagne.

DIAMOND. V.LABRUSCA. Also known as Moore's Diamond, this neutral white with labrusca

SERVE VERY COLD
1983
BLANC de BLANCS
BRUT
100% New York State
Chardonnay Champagne
Naturally Fermented in this Bottle

Produced and Bottled by
Woodbury Vineyards, Dunkirk, New York
BWNY661   12% ALCOHOL BY VOLUME

Gray Monk cellars

Pinot Auxerrois
KABINETT

750 ml.   PRODUCT OF CANADA   10.2% alc. / vol.
WHITE WINE   PRODUIT DU CANADA   VIN BLANC
GRAY MONK CELLARS ESTATE WINERY
OKANAGAN CENTRE, BRITISH COLUMBIA, CANADA

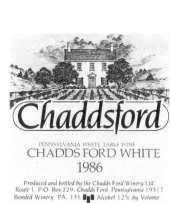

Chaddsford

PENNSYLVANIA WHITE TABLE WINE
CHADDS FORD WHITE
1986

Produced and bottled by the Chadds Ford Winery Ltd.
Route 1, P.O. Box 229, Chadds Ford, Pennsylvania 19317
Bonded Winery, PA. 131   Alcohol 12% by Volume

overtones is not widely planted. Generally used for sparkling wines.

DUTCHESS. V.LABRUSCA. Developed in the Hudson Valley in the 1860s, Dutchess has little of the foxy labrusca aroma and flavor; produces light, crisp, white wines, mainly in the Northeast.

EHRENFELSER. V.VINIFERA. A vinifera hybrid bred in Germany and grown in Canada to make a lightly sweet white wine.

ELVIRA. A white variety developed in Missouri from labrusca and riparia. Not widely planted; used mostly for blending.

EMERALD RIESLING. V.VINIFERA. A white variety developed at the University of California at Davis by crossing Riesling and Muscadelle. Grown mainly in the San Joaquin Valley and west Texas.

FLORA. V.VINIFERA. A cross between Gewürztraminer and Sémillon; used primarily to make sweet wines or for blending.

FOCH. *See* Maréchal Foch.

FOLLE BLANCHE. V.VINIFERA. White grape known as Gros Plant in the coastal region of the Loire Valley. Very limited planting in California, but Louis M. Martini makes a crisp white varietal with it.

FOX. Thomas Jefferson and other early American grape growers referred to certain native American varieties as "fox grapes," which may be the origin of the term "foxy" for the wild-grape flavor typical of native labrusca varieties.

FRANKEN RIESLING. *See* Sylvaner.

FRENCH COLOMBARD. V.VINIFERA. A high-yielding white variety grown in California and the Southwest; mainly used for blending but also bottled as a varietal.

FUMÉ BLANC. *See* Sauvignon Blanc.

GAMAY BEAUJOLAIS. V.VINIFERA. Originally thought to be related to the true Gamay of

1985 Finger Lakes
Chardonnay

Beaujolais, but actually a clone of Pinot Noir. Used in California to make a light, fruity red wine.

GAMAY NOIR À JUS BLANC. V.VINIFERA. The true Gamay grape of Beaujolais. Limited acreage in U.S. is gradually increasing in California, New York, the Southwest and other regions.

GEWÜRZTRAMINER. V.VINIFERA. A spicy white variety producing mainly an aromatic white in dry or off-dry styles, as well as occasionally sweet late-harvest versions. Originating in Germany and Alsace, it is best suited to cool areas and is grown in California, the Northeast, the Northwest and Southwest.

GRAY RIESLING. V.VINIFERA. Not the true German Riesling but a lesser white known in France as Chauché Gris. In California it is used primarily for blending.

GRENACHE. V.VINIFERA. A red grape suited to warm regions like the Rhone Valley. In central California it is mainly used for blending or to produce *rosé;* occasionally seen as a varietal.

GRIGNOLINO. V.VINIFERA. An Italian variety grown in the Piedmont to make light red and dry *rosé*. Little seen in the U.S., though Heitz Cellars makes a Grignolino Rosé.

GUTEDEL. *See* Chasselas.

HERBEMONT. Rare native red grape with some vinifera parentage (through cross pollination). Propagated in South Carolina as early as 1788 by Huguenot Nicolas Herbemont. Survived solely at Val Verde winery in southern Texas until recent plantings were introduced in central Tennessee.

HORIZON. New French hybrid white grape developed at the experimental station in Geneva, New York. Produces fruity white wine similar to Cayuga.

ISABELLA. V.LABRUSCA. Fruity red variety with strong labrusca flavors; grown mostly in New York (it is named for Isabella Gibb of Brooklyn) but the acreage is in decline.

IVES NOIR. V.LABRUSCA. Once widely grown in Ohio and New York, this native red variety has fallen from favor because of strong foxy flavors.

JACQUEZ. *See* Lenoir.

JOHANNISBERG RIESLING. *See* Riesling.

KAY GRAY. A new white hybrid bred to withstand severe cold.

KERNER. V.VINIFERA. A white vinifera cross developed in Germany to be highly cold- and disease-resistant. Limited plantings exist in the Okanagan Valley of British Columbia.

LANDOT. A French hybrid red, sparsely grown in the Northeast and Midwest.

LENOIR. (Also called Jacques, Jacquez, or Black Spanish). An American hybrid known in the late 1800s for producing spicy, sturdy red wines. Grown almost exclusively at Val Verde Winery in Texas.

LÉON MILLOT. A black French hybrid capable of producing concentrated reds. Developed by Kuhlmann, it is similar to Maréchal Foch.

MAGNOLIA. V.ROTUNDIFOLIA. A bronze-colored Muscadine hybridized in 1961 in North Carolina. Grown primarily in the Southeast and produced as a sweet white or varietal.

MALBEC. V.VINIFERA. A red wine grape long grown in Bordeaux for use in blending. Limited plantings in California for similar use.

MALVASIA. V.VINIFERA. One of the world's oldest varieties; used to make mostly sweet white wines in places like Spain, Yugoslavia, Madeira and parts of Italy. Small quantities have been planted in the warmer inland regions of California.

MARÉCHAL FOCH. A French hybrid red developed by Eugene Kuhlmann for use in cold climates. Grown mainly in the Northeast and the Heartland, producing either concentrated or light fruity reds, depending on how it is vinified.

MATSVANI. A Russian variety grown experimentally in the Okanagan Valley of British Columbia; produced as a dry white varietal by Brights.

MELON. V.VINIFERA. The white Muscadet of the Loire Valley, sometimes mistaken for Pinot Blanc in California. Has appeared as a varietal from Beaulieu Vineyard in Napa Valley.

MERLOT. V.VINIFERA. A principal red variety from Bordeaux, especially the Pomerol district; increasingly important in California both as a blending grape (with Cabernet Sauvignon) and as a varietal on its own. Notable for berryish fruit and soft texture, it is also grown in Virginia, New York (Long Island) and Washington.

MICHURNITZ. V.AMURENSIS. A red variety imported to Canada from the Amur Valley in the Soviet Union. Now grown only at Grand Pré winery in Nova Scotia.

MISSION. V.VINIFERA. Brought from Spain in the 1500s, this was the first European variety to be established in the New World. Franciscan friars who established the California missions planted it, thereby giving it the name. Very little remains in California, where it is used for blending (mostly in fortified dessert wines).

MISSOURI RIESLING. V.LA-BRUSCA. No relation to the true German Riesling, this native white variety was bred in Hermann, Missouri in the late nineteenth century. Holds regional interest in Missouri where it produces sweet or off-dry whites.

MÜLLER-THURGAU. V.VINIFERA. A vinifera cross of Riesling and Sylvaner developed in Germany. Grown to a limited extent in the Pacific Northwest and Canada, it makes a crisp, off-dry white.

MUNSON. A group of American hybrids developed by T. V. Munson, a nineteenth-century grape breeder in Missouri and later in Texas. The red variety known as *Munch* is still grown in Missouri.

MUSCADELLE DE BORDELAIS. V.VINIFERA. A white variety grown in Bordeaux where it is used to a limited extent in Sauternes. Very small acreage exists in California.

MUSCAT BLANC (CANELLI). V.VINIFERA. The preferred muscat for dessert wines, sparkling wines (Italy's Asti Spumante), and occasionally a crisp, dry white.

MUSCAT HAMBURG. V.VINIFERA. Also known as Black Muscat, it is used to make sweet red dessert wines such as Quady's Elysium.

MUSCAT OF ALEXANDRIA. V.VINIFERA. Spicy, aromatic white grape used to make dessert wines. Not widely grown outside California's central valley.

MUSCAT-OTTONEL. V.VINIFERA. Known mostly in Alsace, Hungary and other parts of Eastern Europe, where it produces whites with mild muscat aroma and character. Small quantities are grown in Oregon, British Columbia and New York State.

MUSTANG. V.CANDICANS. An American red variety native to Texas and the Southeast. T. V. Munson called it an excellent grape for making potent, sturdy red wine, but very little survives today.

NAPA GAMAY. V.VINIFERA. Long thought to be related to the true Gamay, and used to make Beaujolais-style wines in California, this red variety has recently been identified as the Valdiguie grape of the Midi region of France.

NIAGARA. V.LABRUSCA. Also known as the "white Concord," this native white grape was widely grown in New York and Ohio. Still popular as a table variety, the labrusca flavor limits its use for wine today.

NOAH. V.LABRUSCA. A native white variety planted in France after phylloxera struck in the late 1800s, it was never popular in Europe because of its strong labrusca flavor.

NOBLE. V.ROTUNDIFOLIA. A black Muscadine variety bred in

North Carolina and introduced in 1971. Made in the Southeast as a red varietal or as *rosé*, usually sweet.

NORTON. V.AESTIVALIS. Originally known as the Virginia Seedling and developed by Dr. Daniel Norton of Richmond. Now grown in Missouri and Arkansas where it produces a sturdy and appealing claretlike red that some growers call Cynthiana. Controversy remains as to whether the two varieties are the same.

OKANAGAN RIESLING. V.VINIFERA. An old Hungarian variety—no relation to true Riesling—that is widely grown in the Okanagan Valley of British Columbia. Produces a mild, neutral-flavored white; it is being phased out at many of the better vineyards.

ORANGE MUSCAT. V.VINIFERA. A muscat with orange aroma and flavor. Very limited acreage in San Joaquin Valley.

ORLANDO SEEDLESS. A new American hybrid developed in Florida as a seedless table variety that may also be desirable for white wine.

ORTEGA. A vinifera cross between Müller-Thurgau and Siegerrebe. Grown experimentally in the Okanagan Valley, it was developed in Germany and named for philosopher José Ortega y Gasset.

PERLE OF CSABA. V.VINIFERA. A little-known Hungarian variety with mild Muscat aroma and flavor. The only significant North American plantings are in the Okanagan Valley of British Columbia, where it produces a delicate, lightly sweet white that is quite appealing.

PETIT VERDOT. V.VINIFERA. A red grape grown in Bordeaux for blending. Very small acreage in California.

PETITE-SIRAH. V.VINIFERA. Originally imported as Syrah to California in the last century, it is actually the Durif, a minor red grape of the Rhone. Produces deeply colored red wines of a lusty character, rather than a noble one like the Syrah.

PINOT AUXERROIS. V.VINIFERA. A white member of the Pinot grape family from Alsace, grown mainly in the Okanagan Valley of British Columbia. Shows promise as a cold-climate white of delicate fragrance.

PINOT BLANC. V.VINIFERA. A white variety grown increasingly in California, the Northwest, Northeast and Canada. Popular as a dry white.

PINOT GRIS. V.VINIFERA. A pinkish white variety also known by such names as Tokay d'Alsace (France), Rülander (Germany), and Pinot Grigio (Italy). Grown in Oregon and the Okanagan Valley of British Columbia, it produces a very crisp white. Shows promise for other cool climates.

PINOT MEUNIER. V.VINIFERA. Best known as a minor red variety of the Champagne region; small acreage found in California and Oregon.

PINOT NOIR. V.VINIFERA. The noble red grape of Burgundy has proven difficult in North America but recent successes in Oregon, California and North Carolina are promising; may also be suitable to parts of the Southwest and New York.

PINOT ST. GEORGE. V.VINIFERA. A lesser red variety occasionally produced as a varietal in California.

RAVAT NOIR. A French hybrid crossed with Pinot Noir to produce a light red wine; grown mostly in the northern states.

RAYON D'OR. A French hybrid white that produces fruity, spicy wine used mostly for blending in table and sparkling wines of the Northeast.

RIESLING. V.VINIFERA. An aristocrat among the world's wine grapes. (The term Riesling in this volume refers exclusively to the true German Riesling of the Rhine and Mosel valleys.) Also known as White or Johannisberg Riesling, it produces a wide range of white wines, from dry and steely (Alsace) to lightly sweet to unctuously sweet late-harvest wines that are rare and costly. Widely grown in North America

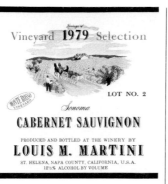

MONTELLE
1984
AUGUSTA APPELLATION
Cynthiana
dry red
table wine
Knoernschild Vineyard

Awarded Owl Seal by
Augusta Wine Board

CONTAINS SULFITES
PRODUCED & BOTTLED BY MONTELLE VINEYARDS, INC.
AUGUSTA, MISSOURI • B.W. NO. 100 • ALC. 12% BY VOL.

Ste. CHAPELLE
BOTRYTIS
SYMMS FAMILY VINEYARD
1986
Johannisberg Riesling
IDAHO
Late Harvest
PRODUCED AND BOTTLED BY STE. CHAPELLE, INC.
CALDWELL, IDAHO BWID-8. ALCOHOL 7.3% BY VOLUME.

(where it sometimes produces quite ordinary wines), Riesling does best in cooler climates like New York and the Northwest.

ROSETTE. A French hybrid red that yields mostly *rosé*. Limited acreage is found in Canada, New Mexico and a few other spots.

ROUGEON. A French hybrid red with good color but not much structure; grown in the Northeast and the Heartland.

RUBY CABERNET. A vinifera hybrid developed by the University of California at Davis by crossing Cabernet Sauvignon and Carignane. Bred for warm climates and grown mostly in the San Joaquin Valley and Texas.

RÜLANDER. *See* Pinot Gris.

SAINT-EMILION. *See* Ugni Blanc.

SAUVIGNON BLANC. V.VINIFERA. The crisp, tart white grape of the Loire Valley (Sancerre, Pouilly-Fumé). Also known as Fumé Blanc, it produces a dry, full-bodied white with herbaceous character often described as "grassy." Frequently considered an alternative to the more expensive Chardonnay. Grown in California, the Northwest, Texas and the Southwest.

SCHEUREBE. V.VINIFERA. A vinifera cross of Riesling and Sylvaner developed at Geisenheim, Germany, producing mostly sweet white wines; often late-harvest. Limited acreage in California, Canada, New York.

SCUPPERNONG. Best known of the Muscadines and the first to be made into wine in colonial America. Though it is still found in both wild and cultivated forms in parts of the South, newer Muscadine varieties like Carlos, Magnolia and Noble are assuming equal importance.

SÉMILLON. V.VINIFERA. A white grape that is an important component of Sauternes and white Graves in Bordeaux; also used for blending with Sauvignon Blanc for which it is increasingly grown in California and the Northwest. Also seen as a varietal.

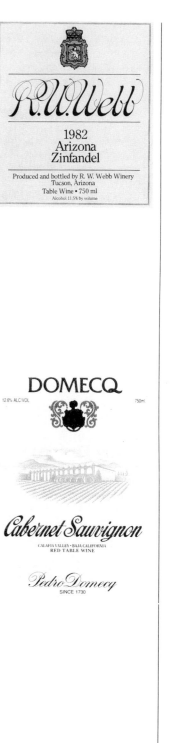

214

SEVERNYI. V. AMURENSIS. A spicy dark-red variety native to the Amur Valley in eastern Siberia; now grown in Nova Scotia at Grand Pré.

SEYVAL BLANC. The leading French hybrid white, widely grown east of the Rockies, especially in the Northeast, Maryland, Virginia and eastern Canada. Produces a crisp dry to off-dry, often stylish, white wine that is good with food.

SIEGERREBE. V. VINIFERA. An experimental early ripening hybrid with Gewürztraminer in its parentage. Brought to the Okanagan Valley as part of the Becker Project and planted in small trial plots.

STEUBEN. An American Muscadine originally developed for table use but occasionally used to make a sweet *rosé* with spicy flavors and slight muscat aroma.

STOVER. A white grape hybridized in Florida and used for blending with stronger Muscadine varieties.

SUWANNEE. A relatively new Florida-bred white hybrid with muscat character. It shows promise for Southern vineyards as a blending grape.

SWENSON. A group of American hybrids developed by Elmer Swenson of Minnesota, most of which were bred for very cold climates.

SYLVANER. V. VINIFERA. Similar to Riesling but lacking that grape's character and depth. California names for it include Franken Riesling, Monterey Riesling or Sonoma Riesling. Also grown in Canada.

SYMPHONY. V. VINIFERA. A vinifera cross of Muscat of Alexandria and Grenache; developed by Harold Olmo at the University of California at Davis. Produces mostly sweet wines and has a promising future, though very little planted as yet.

SYRAH. V. VINIFERA. The top red variety of the northern Rhone Valley, used to make Hermitage. Very little grown in North America but shows some promise in California and the Southwest.

THOMPSON SEEDLESS. Best known as a white table variety, but enormous quantities are used for bulk wines in the San Joaquin Valley and the Southwest. Also used for distilling into brandy.

UGNI BLANC. V. VINIFERA. Also known as Saint-Emilion and Trebbiano; generally used for bulk or jug wines in California.

VERDELET. A French hybrid white grown in the Northeast and the Heartland.

VIDAL BLANC. A French hybrid white increasingly grown east of the Rockies, especially in the Heartland, where it shows promise as an attractive fruity dry white or, when botrytis-affected, a late-harvest dessert wine.

VIGNOLES. Formerly known as Ravat 51, it is considered an excellent white hybrid for cool areas.

VILLARD BLANC. A French hybrid white suited to warmer climates and used primarily for blending.

VILLARD NOIR. A French hybrid red that grows well in warmer climates, producing light, fruity red wine.

VIRGINIA SEEDLING. Original name for the Norton grape (*q.v.*).

WEISSBURGUNDER. *See* Pinot Blanc.

WHITE RIESLING. *See* Riesling.

ZINFANDEL. V. VINIFERA. Often called California's mystery grape as its origins are uncertain (now believed to be from southern Italy). Produces hearty flavorful red wines, though in recent years more white Zinfandel is produced than red. Grown mostly in California, with scattered plantings elsewhere, notably Texas.

ACID. Grapes contain a number of organic acids, the primary ones being tartaric (q.v.) and malic. A proper degree of acidity gives the wine liveliness and acidity; if it is too high, however, the wine becomes sharp and tart, and too low a degree will make it dull and flabby.

APPELLATION. Designation of origin, as in Napa Valley, Pecos County, Willamette Valley. Those officially designated by the U.S. government are known as Viticultural Areas (q.v.).

AVA (AMERICAN VITICULTURAL AREA). See **VITICULTURAL AREA.**

BALANCE. A term used to denote the proportions of a wine's constituents such as fruit, acidity, tannin, alcohol, and their relation to one another. A wine is said to have balance when these elements are harmoniously related.

BARREL. In this book, barrel refers to a sixty-gallon oak container used for aging wine.

BLANC DE BLANCS. A French term meaning white wines made entirely from white grapes.

BLANC DE NOIRS. White wine made from black (or red-wine) grapes. The pulp and juice of most black grapes is pale or white.

BODY. The weight or feel of the wine in the mouth. Fuller-bodied wines usually have higher alcohol content than the average 11 to 12 percent.

BOTRYTIS CINEREA. The Latin name for the mold that attacks grapes under moist conditions. Beneficial on certain varieties such as Riesling, Sauvignon Blanc, Sémillon, Scheurebe and others where it results in richly sweet, luscious wines, it can be harmful to many varieties including most red ones. Known in France as *la pourriture noble*, ("noble rot"), notably in Sauternes.

BOUQUET. The complex of fragrances that develops in a wine as it ages and matures. Different from aroma, which refers to the fragrances of a young, undeveloped wine.

BRIX. A measurement used to determine grape solids (mostly sugars) present in pulp or juice. Checking Brix at harvest helps the grower decide if the grapes are ready to pick. White grapes are generally picked when in the range between 16 and 23 Brix, red when between 21 and 23, though this varies according to variety and region.

BRUT. Generally, the driest in a line of Champagnes or sparkling wines.

BUD BREAK. Grower's term for the moment in spring when the buds on the vine start to unfurl.

BULK PROCESS. A method of producing secondary fermentation for sparkling wines in large tanks rather than in individual bottles as in the *méthode champenoise* (q.v.).

BUNG. The wooden stopper which seals the bungholes of the barrels or casks used for aging wine.

CARBON DIOXIDE. The gas (CO_2) that is a byproduct of fermentation. For still wines it escapes, but for sparkling wines it is retained to create the bubbles.

CARBONIC MACERATION. A method of fermentation that makes use of whole grapes rather than crushed ones. It is used, sometimes only partially, to make light, fruity red wines and is commonly employed for wines in the nouveau style (q.v.).

CARBOY. A glass container used for fermentation or storage in wineries; usually of five-gallon capacity.

CASK. An oak container used for storing or aging wine; usually two hundred gallons or larger.

CHAPTALISATION. A procedure used in attempts to increase alcohol content—and therefore, body—by adding sugar to the grape juice prior to its fermentation. Although legal in many American regions, especially cool ones, it is prohibited by law in California.

CHARACTER. A winetasting term used to indicate a wine of more than simple drinkability—one with distinctive attributes of color, taste and bouquet.

CLEAN. A wine with no off-odor or off-flavor.

CLONE. An asexually propagated vine developed to adapt to a specific climate or soil. A given variety may have several clones developed at certain sites (the Volnay clone of Pinot Noir, for example).

COLD FERMENTATION. Fermenting grape juice at low temperatures in stainless steel, temperature-controlled tanks to preserve fruit character and aroma.

COMPLEX. A descriptive term for wines that have multifaceted flavor and bouquet.

CORKED; CORKY. A flaw that makes a wine smell of cork rather than wine; usually the result of a defective cork.

CROSS. Cross breeding one variety with another to obtain specific desireable characteristics. Emerald Riesling, for example, is a cross of Riesling and Muscadelle.

CROWN GALL. A bacterium that invades the vine at points of trunk injury. A tough, fibrous gall forms impeding the passage of nutrients and eventually causing the vine to die. Very common in Eastern vineyards due to winter cold which causes trunk splitting.

CRUSH. The winegrower's term for harvest; the crushing of the grapes.

CUTTING. A stalk cut from the vine that is used for propagation.

CUVÉE. A blend of wines, most commonly used in reference to sparkling wines.

DECANT. To transfer a wine from the bottle to another container (decanter, carafe, etc.) either to separate it from sediment accumulated during aging, or to aerate it.

DRY. Without perceptible sweetness. A wine in which all or most of the sugar has been fermented into alcohol is termed dry.

EARTHY. Characteristics of aroma or flavor arising from the soil in which the grapes were grown. Also used to describe wines of a rather rustic character.

ENOLOGY. The study and science of winemaking.

ESTATE-BOTTLED. A term for wines made from grapes grown by, or under the supervision of, the winery that produces the wine. Not necessarily a guarantee of superior quality.

EXTRA DRY. Term used for sparkling wines that are not as dry as Brut (q.v.).

FERMENTATION. The conversion of sugars into alcohol through the action of yeasts.

FILTER. Clarification by means of a filtering machine which removes solid matter.

FINING. Clearing a wine of solids by using clarifying agents such as gelatin, egg whites or bentonite.

FINISH. A winetaster's term for the aftertaste of a wine.

FORTIFIED WINES. Wines that have brandy added to them, such as sherries, port and similar wines.

FOXY. An aggressive wild-grape flavor common to certain native American species, especially labruscas such as Concord, Catawba, Niagara. Probably originated with a native grape the early Colonists called the Fox grape.

FREE-RUN. The juice that runs freely from the grapes before pressing.

FRUIT SET. The newly formed fruit that immediately follows a vine's flowering.

FRUITY. A tasting term for the grape, but not an indication of sweetness.

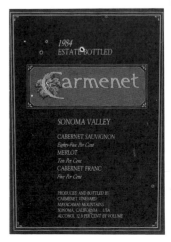

GENERIC WINES. Blended wines, often named for a well-known district such as American chablis or burgundy. Rarely do they relate in any way to the original prototype. The trend is away from such names and toward more general terms such as Premium Red or regional names like Texas Blush.

GRASSY. Winetaster's term for the herbacious, new-mown-grass character of Sauvignon Blanc.

GREEN. A tasting term signifying raw or unripe; young wines may overcome such rawness with time.

HARD WINES. Wines that are extremely firm; usually high in tannin.

HYBRID. The result of cross breeding two species or varieties. French-American hybrids, for example, are bred by crossing American species with European vinifera.

JEROBOAM. A large bottle, the equivalent of six normal-size bottles or four Champagne bottles.

LABRUSCA. A native American grape species developed mainly in the Northeast (including Concord, Niagara, Catawba, Isabella).

LATE HARVEST. A designation used on sweet wines to indicate extra-ripe grapes.

LEES. Sediment that drops to the bottom of a wine vat during and after fermentation; it consists of pulp, spent yeasts, seeds and pigment.

LIGHT WINES. Wines low in alcohol and/or viscosity.

MADERIZED. A term used for oxidized white wine which turns amber in color (like Madeira, from which the word is derived). See also **OXIDIZED.**

MAGNUM. Equivalent of two regular bottles. The metric magnum (one and a half liters) is used for generic or jug wines.

MALOLACTIC FERMENTATION. The conversion of malic acid to lactic acid, an effect which softens acidity and frequently adds

extra nuances of flavor. Considered highly desirable for cool-climate reds and some whites.

MELLOW. Descriptive term for a wine that has lost its sharp edges and has become smooth and rounded, sometimes with a hint of sweetness.

MÉTHODE CHAMPENOISE. The traditional and painstaking method used for making Champagne; applied to sparkling wines made by this method.

METHUSELAH. A large bottle containing the equivalent of eight bottles of Champagne.

MICROCLIMATE. A growing site with special conditions of climate and exposure that make grapegrowing possible in an area that is otherwise difficult. Suitable microclimates are often near bodies of water or on protected hillsides.

MILDEW. A fungus that attacks vines and grapes. Spraying with fungicides can be effective against it.

MUST. Crushed grapes and juice.

NEBUCHADNEZZAR. Largest of the oversize bottles, with a capacity of twenty regular bottles.

NEMATODE. A soil parasite that feeds on vine roots.

NOSE. Winetaster's term for a wine's bouquet (q.v.), as in "This wine has a powerful nose."

NOUVEAU. The French term that originated with Beaujolais nouveau, the first wine of the vintage. Now widely used for light, fruity reds that are released within a couple of months of the vintage.

OAKY. Descriptive term for a wine that smells of the oak barrel in which it was aged.

OENOLOGY. British spelling of enology (q.v.).

OVERCROPPING. Allowing higher fruit yield than the vine is capable of bringing to maturity. Results in neutral flavor or characterless wines and is unhealthy for the vine.

OXIDIZED. Wines that have spoiled or turned brown with

sherrylike character, due to oxygen. Since aging is a process of oxidation, all wines oxidize eventually. The trick is to catch them at the optimum moment along the way.

PH. A laboratory term for measuring acidity in the form of hydrogen ions present. For wine, the desirable pH ranges from 3.0 to 3.7. Anything higher may result in a wine that has stability problems; if lower, it is undrinkably acidic.

PHYLLOXERA. The root louse that feeds on vine roots and almost totally destroyed European vineyards in the late-nineteenth century. Native American species are phylloxera-resistant, thus today most of the world's vines have been grafted onto American rootstocks.

POMACE. The residue of skins, seeds and stems left after pressing.

POURRITURE NOBLE. See **BOTRYTIS CINEREA**.

PPM. Parts per million: a measuring unit that is the equivalent of one milligram per liter.

PRESS WINE. Wine collected from the final pressing of the grapes.

PROPRIETARY. A brand name, as opposed to generic or varietal labeling. Examples: Scrimshaw White, Opus One, Primavera.

RACKING. Separating wines from the lees (q.v.) or sediment (q.v.) by siphoning them into fresh barrels or tanks.

RESIDUAL SUGAR. The amount of sweetness remaining after fermentation, and increasingly seen on American wine labels. A reading of 1.5 to 2 percent is lightly sweet; 6 to 10 percent is rich, luscious and very sweet.

RICH. A descriptive term denoting generous or concentrated flavors, texture or body.

SALMANAZAR. An oversized bottle, equivalent to twelve bottles, or a case.

SEDIMENT. The solid materials that precipitate out of the wine after fermentation or settling. Red wines continue to throw sediment as they age, creating a

harmless, tasteless but gritty substance that makes them best when decanted.

SOLERA. The Spanish system of blending and aging sherry in a series of tiered barrels, with older sherries added to younger wines to give them character and consistency.

SOUR. A term used by inexperienced tasters to describe wines that are either very dry or overly acidic.

STRUCTURE. The way a wine is held together, or built, in terms of its various components (fruit, acids, tannin, etc.). The structure may be simple, or intricate and complex.

SULFUR DIOXIDE. A chemical (sulfur and oxygen, or SO_2) that protects wines from oxidizing (q.v.) or browning, and is used in virtually all wines made anywhere in the world. Because of modern hygiene and technology, however, less is required today than was formerly. Sometimes noted on labels as "sulfites."

TABLE WINE. The designation for any wine under 14 percent alcohol. Also a more general term for wines that accompany food.

TANNIN. Compounds found in skins, seeds and stems of grapes which add astringency to wines (mostly reds) and help preserve them during aging. The impression of tannin is somewhat harsh, bitter or mouth-puckering. Over time it breaks down and the wine softens.

TART. Descriptive term for wines high in acidity.

TARTARIC ACID. One of the principal acids found naturally in grapes. When subjected to cold temperatures it precipitates out of the wine and forms tiny crystals of potassium bitartrate which are sometimes found in white wines or clinging to corks. Quite harmless.

TEINTURIER. Grapes that are heavily pigmented and often used to deepen the color in red wines.

VARIETAL. Wines named for the principal grape used in making them, such as Cabernet Sauvignon or Chenin Blanc. By law, such wines must contain at least 75 percent of the grape variety on the label.

VARIETAL CHARACTER. Bouquet and flavor characteristics typical of the grape used to make the wine.

VINIFICATION. The process of turning grapes into wine.

VITICULTURAL AREAS. Also known as AVAs (American Viticultural Areas), these are winegrowing regions officially designated by the U.S. Bureau of Alcohol, Tobacco & Firearms, the government agency that regulates alcoholic beverages. In order to use an AVA on a label, 95 percent of the wine must come from that region.

VITIS VINIFERA. European species of wine grapes, including Cabernet Sauvignon, Chardonnay, Riesling, Pinot Noir, Sauvignon Blanc and numerous others.

WOODY. A tasting term for wines that show evidence of considerable time in wood; may be astringent or dried out.

YEASTS. The one-celled organisms that act as agents of transformation, making bread dough rise or converting sugars into alcohol.

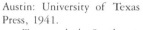

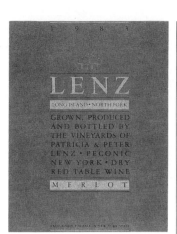

BIBLIOGRAPHY

Abbott, John. *History of Hernando Cortez.* New York: Harper & Brothers, 1855.

Adams, Leon D. *The Wines of America. 3d ed.* New York: McGraw-Hill, 1985.

Adlum, John. *A Memoir on the Cultivation of the Vine and the Best Mode of Making Wine.* Hopewell, N.J.: Booknoll Reprints, 1971.

Aspler, Tony. *Vintage Canada.* Ontario: Prentice-Hall, 1983.

Bancroft, Hubert Howe. *History of Mexico.* New York: Bancroft Company, 1914.

Bear, James A., Jr., ed. *Jefferson at Monticello.* Charlottesville: University Press of Virginia, 1967.

Betts, E. M. and J. A. Bear. *Family Letters of Thomas Jefferson, 1743-1826.* Charlottesville: University Press of Virginia, 1966.

Blue, Anthony Dias. *American Wine: A Comprehensive Guide.* New York: Doubleday & Company, 1985.

Cather, Willa. *O Pioneers.* New York: Houghton Mifflin, 1937.

Chorlton, William. *The American Grape Grower's Guide.* New York: C. M. Saxton, Barker & Company, 1860.

Cortes, Hernando. *Dispatches of Hernando Cortes.* New York: Wiley & Putnam, 1843.

deChambrun, Clara L. *Cincinnati: Story of the Queen City.* New York: Charles Scribner's Sons, 1939.

Dobie, J. Frank. *The Longhorns.*

Austin: University of Texas Press, 1941.

———. *Texas and the Southwest.* Austin: Texas Folklore Society, 1927.

Eichenlaub, Val. *Weather and Climate of the Great Lakes Region.* Notre Dame, Indiana: University of Notre Dame Press, 1979.

English, Sara Jane. *The Wines of Texas.* Austin: Eakin Press, 1986.

Fegan, Patrick W. *Vineyards & Wineries of America.* Brattleboro, Vt.: Stephen Greene Press, 1982.

Fehrenbach, T. R. *Lone Star: A History of Texas and the Texans.* New York: Macmillan, 1968.

Galet, Pierre. *A Practical Ampelography.* Translated by Lucie T. Morton. Ithaca: Cornell University Press, 1979.

Haley, James E. *The XIT Ranch of Texas and the Early Days of the Llano Estacado.* Chicago: Lakeside Press, 1929.

Hedrick, U. P. *Manual of American Grape-Growing.* 2d ed. New York: Macmillan, 1924.

Husmann, George. *American Grape Growing and Wine Making.* New York: Orange Judd, 1885.

Jackisch, Philip. *Modern Winemaking.* Ithaca: Cornell University Press, 1985.

Jefferson, Thomas. *Garden Book.* Philadelphia: American Philosophical Society.

Lawrence, R. de Treville, ed. *Jefferson and Wine.* The Plains, Va.:

Vinifera Wine Growers Association, 1976.

Lewis, Meriwether and William Clark. *The History of the Lewis & Clark Expedition.* 3 vols. 1893. Reprint. Edited by Elliott Coues. New York: Dover Publications, 1979.

Lichine, Alexis. *New Encyclopedia of Wines and Spirits.* 3d ed. New York: Knopf, 1984.

Meredith, Ted Jordan. *The Wines & Wineries of America's Northwest.* Kirkland, Wash.: Nexus Press, 1986.

Miller, Mark. *Wine: A Gentleman's Game.* New York: Harper & Row, 1984.

Morgan, Dale. *Overland in 1846.* Georgetown, California: Talisman Press, 1963.

Morton, Lucie T. *Winegrowing in Eastern America.* Ithaca: Cornell University Press, 1985.

Muench, Frederick. *School for American Grape Culture.* Translated by Elizabeth H. Cutter. St. Louis: Conrad Witter, 1865. Facsimile reprint edition available at Mount Pleasant Vineyards, Augusta, Mo. 63332.

Munson, T. V. *Foundations of American Grape Culture.* 1909. Reprint. Denison, Tx.: Denison Public Library, 1975.

Nichol, Alexander. *Wine and Vines of British Columbia.* Vancouver: Bottesini Press, 1983.

Parkman, Francis. *The Oregon Trail.* Madison: University of Wisconsin Press, 1969.

Prescott, William Hicking. *History of the Conquest of Mexico.*

Vol. 3. New York: Harper & Brothers, 1843.

Robinson, Jancis. *Vines, Grapes and Wines.* New York: Knopf, 1986.

Russell, Marian. *Land of Enchantment: Memoirs Along the Santa Fe Trail.* Albuquerque: Branding Iron Press, 1954.

Schlissel, Lillian. *Women's Diaries of the Westward Journey.* New York: Schocken Books, 1982.

Schreiner, John. *The World of Canadian Wine.* Vancouver: Douglas & McIntyre, 1985.

Starr, Kevin. *Americans and the California Dream, 1850–1915.* New York: Oxford University Press, 1973.

Teiser, Ruth and Catherine Harroun. *Winemaking in California.* New York: McGraw-Hill, 1983.

Thompson, Bob. *The Pocket Encyclopedia of California Wines.* rev. ed. New York: Simon & Schuster, 1985.

Vine, Richard P. *Commercial Winemaking.* Westport, Conn.: AVI Publishing, 1981.

Wagner, Philip M. *Grapes Into Wine: The Art of Winemaking in America.* New York: Knopf, 1976.

———. *A Wine-Grower's Guide.* 3d ed. New York: Knopf, 1984.

Wines & Vines Buyer's Guide, 1987. San Rafael, Calif.: Hiaring Company, 1987.

Winkler, A. J. *General Viticulture.* 2d ed. Berkeley: University of California Press, 1974.

INDEX

(Numbers in *italics* refer to pages with illustrations.)

Acacia Winery (CA), 151

Adams, Leon, 24*n*, 35, 73, 168

Adlum, John, 14, 63, 82

Agricultural Research Station (Leesburg, FL), 74

Agriculture, U.S. Dept. of, 78

Albermarle Harvest Wine Festival (VA), 70–71

Alexis Bailly Vineyard (MN), 87

Alicante Bouschet, 16, 126

Allison, Victor, 168

Almadén (CA), 126, 143,144

Alta California, 123, 126

American Wine Growers, 168

Arizona, 119–121

Arkansas, 14

  University of, 19

  Wiederkehr Wine Cellars, 96, 97, 98–99

Arroyo Seco district (Monterey, CA), 143, 144

Auler, Ed and Susan, 103, 104, *105,* 107–109

Austin Cellars (CA), 152

Baja California, 194, 195, *196–197*

Barbera (grape), 107

Barboursville Winery (VA), 65

Barnwell, Claiborne, 75, 78

Batt Vineyard (ID), 175

Bayou Rouge (Claiborne), 78

Beaulieu Vineyards (CA), 17, 126, 137

Becker, Helmut, 65, 190–191

Becker Project, 185, 190–191

Bella Oaks Vineyard (CA), 140–141

Benmarl (NY), 44, 46

Bennett, Nelda, 47, 48

Biltmore Estate Wine Co. (NC), 24, *25,* 72–73, *75, 76–77,* 79

Blanc de Blancs, 35, 39–40, 44

Blanc du Bois (grape), 74

Blue Teal Vineyards (NM), 119

Bodegas de Santo Tomas (Mexico), 194, 195, 198

Boordy Vineyards (MD), 72

Bosc, Paul, 182, 185

Botrytis cinerea (noble rot), 38, *43,* 152

Bremmer, John, 190

Bright's–Ste. Michelle (Canada), 179, 186, 188, 190

British Columbia, *see* Okanagan Valley

Brotherhood Winery (NC), 44

Bull, Ephraim Wales, 14, 33

Bully Hill winery, 40

Burgess, Jeanne, 74

Byers, Clayton, 96

Cabernet Franc, 72

Cabernet Sauvignon(s), 17, 27, 31, 40, 51, 56, 123

  grape, 30, *53, 66, 67, 141*

  from Heartland, 83

  from Mexico, 199, 201

  from Napa Valley, 134, 135, 137, 140–141

  from Northwest, 170

  from Santa Ynez Val., 152

  from Sonoma, 141–142, *143*

  from South, 63, 65, *70,* 72, 78, 79

  from Southwest, 109, 119, 121

California, 11, 14, 16, 17, 28, 43, 157

  after Prohibition, 126–127, 130–131

  early winemaking in, 123, 126

  Univ. of, *see* University of California (Davis)

  see also Mayacamas Mountains; Monterey region; Napa Valley; Santa Ynez Valley; Sonoma

Campbell, Patrick, 137, *138–139,* 141

Canada, 16, 179–191

  see also Nova Scotia; Okanagan Valley; Ontario

Canandaigua (NY), 36, 44

Carmenet (CA), 151

Carneros district (CA), 134–136, 151

Carver, Larry, 88

Casa Pinson (Mexico), 198

Cascade (grape), 85

Catawba, 33, 34, 35, 82

Cavas de San Juan (Mexico), 201

Cecil, William Vanderbilt, 72–73

Cetto family, 195, 199

Chadwick Bay (NY), 44

Chalone Vineyard (CA), 27, 127, 143, 144, *145, 148–150,* 151

Chancellor (grape), 36, 86

Chapman, Joseph, 151

Chardonnay(s), 30, 31, *43*

  from California, 135, 144, *145*

  grape, 36, 37, 66

  from Heartland, 83, 85–86, 88

  from New York, 39–40, 43, 46–48

  from Northwest, 162, *163,* 170

  from South, 63, 65, 72

  from Southwest, 109

Chateau des Charmes (Ontario), 182, 185

Chateau Elan (GA), 74

Chateau Gai (Canada), 179

Chateau Ste. Michelle (WA), 168, 170, *171, 174, 176, 177*

Chenin Blanc(s), 30, 78

  from Northwest, 170

  from Southwest, 109, 121

Chicama (MA), *52,* 53, 56

Childs, Tom, 104

Claiborne Vineyards (MS), 75, 78

Clinton Vineyards (NY), 46

Cold Creek Vineyard (WA), 170

Colle (VA), 62–63

Colorado, 121

Columbia Crest (WA), 168

Commonwealth Winery (MA), 56

Concannon, James, 194

Concannon Vineyards (CA), 142, 194

Concord (grape), 33, 34, 35, 159, 168

Connecticut, 58–59

  Crosswoods, *see* Crosswoods Vineyard

Connell, Hugh and Susan, 56, 57

Cooper, Clarence, 119

Cortez, Hernando, 11, 14, 193

Cottage Vineyards (NY), 46

Cox, Charles Robert, III, 109, 112

Crosswoods Vineyard (CT), 11, *12–13, 32,* 33, 53, *54–55,* 56–58

Davies, Jack, 127

Deford, Robert, 72

de la Cerna, Eduardo, 201

Delaware (grape), 33, 36

Dial, Roger, 185

Diamond Hill Winery (RI), 56

Domenech, Francisco, 201

Domenech, Paco, 201

Drouhin, Robert, 167

Dutt, Gordon, 119, 121

Edna Valley Vineyard (CA), 151

Eliopulos, Peter, 175

Erie–Chautauqua region (NY), 43–44

Eyrie Vineyards (OR), 24, *158,* 159, 160, *161,* 162, *163– 166,* 167, 168

Fall Creek Vineyards (TX), 19, *22–23,* 104, *105,* 107–109

Faulkner, William, 75

Feder, Ben, 46

Fenn Valley Vineyards (MI), 83, *84,* 85–87

Finger Lakes region (NY), 26, 27–28

  Glenora-on-Seneca, 28, *29,* 39–40

  Heron Hill Vineyard, 37–38

  Riesling grapes from, *16,* 36, 37, *38, 43*

  Wagner Vineyards, *41,* 42–43, 46

  Wiemer, 40, *41,* 42

Finger Lakes Wine Cellars (NY), 40

Fiore, Louis, 47–48

Firestone, A. Brooks, 151–152, *153,* 157

Firestone, Kate, 152, *153,* 157

Firestone, Leonard, 151, 152

Fitch, Bill and Joanne, 96

Flemer, Carl, 65

Florida, 30, 73–74

  University of, 19

Fournier, Charles, 35

Franciscan order, 14, 101, 123

Frank, Konstantin, 35–36, 40, 63, 83, 185

Fumé Blanc, 121, *174,* 175

Furness, Mrs. Thomas, 63

Galleron, Gary, 48, *49*

Gallo, Ernest and Julio, 126

Gallo winery (CA), 17, 127

Gehringer Vineyards (Okanagan), *187,* 189–190

Geisenheim Institute (Germany), 189, 190

Georgia, 11, 26, 74

Gewürztraminer, 38, 43, 51

Gifford, James, 40

Glen Oak Vineyard (CA), 134

Glenora-on-Seneca (NY), 28, *29,* 39–40

Gold Seal (NY), 35

Graff, Peter, 144

Graff, Richard, 127, 144

Grand Pré Wines (Nova Scotia), 182, 185

Grand River Wine Co. (OH), 83

Grand Traverse Vineyards (MI), 87

Gray Monk Cellars (Okanagan), *188,* 190, *191*

Great Western (NY), 34, 36

Green, Alison, 152, *153*

Guadalupe Valley (Mexico), 195, *196–197,* 198–199

Guth, Gerhard, 65

Haight Vineyard (CT), 58

Hanzell (CA), 127

Haraszthy, Agostón, 126

Hargrave, Alex and Louisa, 48

Hatch, Peter, 71–72

Heiss, George and Trudy, 188, 190

Heitz, Joseph, 127, 137, 140

Heitz Cellars (CA), 56, 127, 137

Held, Betty Ann, 89

Held, Jim, 89, 95, 96

Held, Jonathan, 89, 95, 96

Held, Patricia, 95

Held, Thomas, 95

Heron Hill Vineyard (NY), 37–38

Hidalgo, Miguel, 194

Hollerith, Joachim, 65

Hudson Valley (NY), 44–46

  West Park, *see* West Park Wine Cellars

Husmann, George, 14

Idaho, 159, 175
Ingle, John, 37
Inglenook Vineyards (CA), 17, 126, *130*
Ingleside Plantation Winery (VA), 63, 65
Inniskillin winery (Ontario), *178*, 179, *180*, 181–182, *184*

Jaeger, Hermann, 101
Jamestown colony, 14, 63
Jefferson, Thomas, 14, 61–63, 70–72
Jeffersonian Grape Growers Society (VA), 70–71
Johnson, David, 95
Johnson, Michael, *10*, 11, 115, 118
Johnson, Michelle, *115*
Johnson, Patrick, 115, 118
Johnstone, Peter, 37–38
Jones, Richard, 119
Jost, Hanns, 185

Kaiser, Karl, 181, 182
Kansas, 99
Keuka Lake (NY), 34, 35, *37*
Kitching, George, 182
Koblett, Bernard, 162
Krug, Charles (CA), 126, 127

La Buena Vida (TX), 103
La Chiripada Winery (NM), *10*, 11, *24*, 113, *114*, 115, 118
Lafayette Vineyards (FL), 74, 79
La Loma Vineyard (CA), 135
Las Amigas Vineyard (CA), 135
Laurel Glen Vineyard (CA), *27*, 137, *138–139, 140, 141–142, 143*
Laurel Hill Vineyards (TN), 79
La Viña Winery (NM), 119
Lenz, Patricia, *47*, 48
Lenz, Peter, 48, *49*, 51
Lenz Vineyards (NY), *47*, 48, *49*, 51
Lett, David and Diana, 160, 162, 167, 169
Liquor Control Boards of Canada, 179, 182
Liso, Vito, *118*
Livermore Valley (CA), Wente Bros. in, 17, 126, 127, 142–143
Llano Estacado Winery (TX), 103, 112–113
Long Island (NY), 48–49, *50*, 51, 58
Longfellow, Henry Wadsworth, 82
Longworth, Nicholas, 82
Los Viñedos del Rio, (CA), 134
Lucie Kuhlmann, 119

Magoni, Camilo, 198, 199
Markko Vineyard (OH), 82–83
Martha's Vineyard (MA), *52*, 53, 56
Martin, N.B., 65
Martini, Louis M., 17, 126, 130–

131, 134–135, 137
Martini, Louis P., 131
Maryland, 72
Massachusetts, 14, 33, 51–53
  Chicama, *52*, 53, 56
  Commonwealth Winery, 56
Mathiesen, George and Catherine, 53, 56
Mavety, Ian, 180, 189
May, Tom and Martha, 137, 140
Mayacamas Mountains (CA), 127, 151
Mazzei, Filippo, 61–63
McPherson, Clinton, 112
McWatters, Harry, 187
Meier's Wine Cellars (OH), 81, 82
Meredyth Vineyards (VA), 63
Merlot(s), 49, 51, 57, 58
  from Heartland, 83
  from Northwest, 170
  from South, 63
Messina Hof Wine Cellars (TX), 102, 103
Mexico, 11, 14, 101, 123, *192*, 193–201
Michigan, 11, 26, 81, 87
  Fenn Valley Vineyards, 83, *84*, 85–87
  University of, 81
Miller, Mark, 44, 46
Minnesota, 87, 99
Mirassou Vineyards (CA), 126, 143
Mission (grape), 101, 123
Mission Hill Vineyards (Okanagan), 190
Mississippi, 14, 30
  Claiborne Vineyards, 75, 78
  State Univ. (Starkville), 19, 74, 78
Mississippi Delta, 74–75, 78
Missouri, 11, 14, 81, 87–88
  Stone Hill, *see* Stone Hill Winery
Mitchell, David and Susan, 190
Mitchell, Jim and Lolly, 56
Mondavi, Robert, 127, 157
Montbray Wine Cellars (MD), 72, 79
Montelle Vineyards (MO), 95, 96
Monte Rosso Vineyard (CA), 131, *132–133*, 134
Monticello (VA), 14, *60*, 61–63, *64*, 65, 71–72
Mortensen, John, 74
Morton, Lucie T., 65, 71
Mowbray, G. Hamilton, 72
Muench, Frederick, 95–96
Munson, Thomas Volney, 14, 101
Muscadine, 73–74, 78

Napa Valley (CA), 17, 28, 127, *128–129*, 143, 157, 160
  Bella Oaks Vineyard, 140–141
  Cabernet Sauvignon from, 137, 140–141

Heitz Cellars, 56, 127, 137
  Martini vineyards in, 131, 134–135, 137
New Hampshire, 53
New Jersey, 59
New Mexico, 14, 19, *20–21*, 113, 119, 121
  La Chiripada, *see* La Chiripada Winery
  St. Clair Vineyards, 113, *116–117*, 118–119
New York, 11, 34
  Erie–Chautauqua region of, 43–44
  Lenz Vineyards, *47*, 48, *49*, 51
  Long Island region of, 48–51, 58
  see also Finger Lakes region; Hudson Valley
New York State Agricultural Experimental Station (Geneva), 35, 44
Niebaum, Gustave, 126
Noblet, André, 144
North Carolina, 72, 73
  Biltmore Estate, *see* Biltmore Estate Wine Company
Norton (grape & wine), 63, *94*, 95–96, 99
Norton, Daniel, 14, 63, 96
Nova Scotia, 185

Oakencroft Vineyard (VA), 65, 66, *67, 68–69*, 70, *71*
Ohio, 14, 81–83
Okanagan Valley (British Columbia), 26, 180, 186–187, 188–189
  Gehringer Vineyards, *187*, 189–190
  Gray Monk Cellars, *188*, 190, *191*
  larger wineries in, 190–191
  Sumac Ridge, 187–188
O'Keefe, Edward, 87
Ontario, Canada, 180–181
Oregon, 159, 160, *161, 169*
  Eyrie, *see* Eyrie Vineyards
Orlando Seedless (grape), 74

Pandosy, Charles, 186
Panoz, Donald, 74
Paul Masson Vineyards (CA), 126, 143
Pennsylvania, 14, 59
Petros Winery (ID), 175
Peynaud, Emile, 198
Pheasant Ridge Winery (TX), *28*, 109, 112
Philip II, king of Spain, 14, 194
Piedmont Vineyards (VA), 63
Pierce, Gene, 39–40
Pike's Peak Vineyard (CO), 121
Pinot Gris, 162, *166*, 190
Pinot Noir(s), *24*, 31, *151*
  from California, 135, 144, 152, 160, 167
  from Canada, 182
  from New York, 42, 43

from Northwest, *158*, 159, 160, *161*, 162, *166*, 167, 170
  from South, 73
Pinson, Pedro, 198
Pool, Robert, 44
Prince Michel Vineyards (VA), 65
Prohibition, 14, 16, 17, 19, 35, 89, 99, 126, 130–131, 179
Prudence Island Winery (RI), 56

Rancho del Refugio (CA), 151
Rapidan River Vineyards (VA), 65
Ravat, 36, 37, 96
Ray, Martin, 17, 127
Recht, Jacques, 65
Reed, Robert, 112
Ressler Vineyards (NY), 58
Rhode Island, 56
Rhodes, Bernard and Belle, 137, 140, *141*
Ridge Vineyards (CA), 127
Rief Winery (Ontario), 182, 185
Riesling(s), 30, 59
  from California, 152
  from Canada, 188
  grape, *16*, 30, 36, 37, *38, 43*
  from New York, 36, 38, 39, 40, 43
  from Northwest, 170
  from Southwest, 109
Roberts Vineyard (AZ), 121
Rogan, Felicia Warburg, 65, 66, 67, 70
Rogan, John, 65, 66, 71
Royal Winery (NY), 44
Rushing, Sam and Diane, 78
Rutherford Hill vineyards (CA), *137*

S.G.R.C., 103–104
St. Clair Vineyards (NM), 113, *116–117*, 118–119
Ste. Geneviève Vineyards (TX), 103–104, 107
Sakonnet Vineyards (RI), 56
Santa Ynez Valley (CA), 151, *154–155*
  Firestone Vineyard, 151–152, *153–156*, 157
Sauvignon Blanc(s), 30, 31
  grape, 38, 104, *105*
  from Northwest, 170
  from Southwest, 107, *108*, 109
Sax, Charles, 99
Schoonmaker, Frank, 127
Schramsberg (CA), 126, 127
Scuppernong, 14, 63, 73, 74
Sémillon(s), 38
  from Northwest, 170
  from Southwest, 109
Seneca Lake (NY), 34
  wineries on, 38–43
Seyval Blanc(s), 43
  grape, 36, 37
  from New York, 46
  from South, 65, 70, 72
Shaulis, Nelson, 39
Skinner, Ray, 79

Slifer, Bob and Judith, 96
Smith, Archie, 65
Sonoita Vineyards (AZ), *100*, 101, 119, *120*, 121
Sonoma (CA), *31*, 123, 126, 127, 143, 157
  Laurel Glen, *see* Laurel Glen Vineyard
South Carolina, 72, 73
Spring Ledge Vineyard (Glenora), 39
Sterling Vineyards (CA), *136*, 137
Stone Hill Winery (MO), *80*, 81, *88*, 89, *90–93*, 95
Strachan, Gary, 191
Sumac Ridge (Okanagan), 187–188
Summerland Station, 190–191
Summum winery (UT), 121
Symms Family Vineyard (ID), 175

Tabor Hill Vineyard (MI), 83
Taylor (NY), 34, 36
Tchelistcheff, André, 17, 126, 137, 152, 168
Tchelistcheff, Dmitri, 195, 198
Tchelistcheff Vineyard (WA), 170
Tennessee, 78–79

Tennessee Viticultural and Oenological Society, 79
Texas, 11, 14, 34, 42, 101 103, 112–113, 121
  Fall Creek, *see* Fall Creek Vineyards
  Pheasant Ridge Winery, *28*, 109, 112
  Texas A&M Univ., 19, 103, 107
  University of, 19, 103–104, 107
Tower, David, 56
Truluck Vineyards (SC), 73

Uniacke (Okanagan), 190
Univ. of California (Davis), 19, 95, 98, 127, 140, 160, 201
  climatic classifications of, 104, 107, 130
Utah, 121

Vallejo, Mariano G., 126
Valverde winery (TX), 103
Vaseaux Farms (Okanagan), *186*, 189
Vidal Blanc, 182, *183*

Vignes, Jean-Louis, 126
Vine, Richard P., 78
Vineland Estates (Ontario), 182, 185
Vinicola L.A. Cetto (Mexico), *195–198*, 199
Virginia, 11, 14, 26, 34, 63–65
  early winegrowing efforts in, 61–63
  Oakencroft, *see* Oakencroft Vineyard
Vuignier, Vincent and Noël, 118

Wagner, Bill, 41, 42
Wagner, Philip, 72
Wagner Vineyards (NY), *41*, 42–43, 46
Washington (state), *18*, 19, 159, 160, 167–168, 187
  Chateau Ste. Michelle, 168, 170, *171, 174*
Webb, R.W., 121
Welsch, Bill, 86–87
Welsch, Doug, 83, 85–86, 87
Welsh, Deborah, 65, 66
Wente Bros. (CA), 17
  in Livermore Valley, 126, 127, 142–143
  in Monterey, 143–144, 145
Wente family, 142
West Park Wine Cellars (NY), 14, *15, 35*, 44, *45*, 46–48
White Mountain winery (NH), 53
Widmer (NY), 36
Wiederkehr, Alcuin, 98–99
Wiederkehr, Johann Andreas, 98
Wiederkehr Wine Cellars (AR), 96, 97, 98–99
Wiemer, Hermann J. (NY), 40, *41*, 42
Winery Rushing, (MS), 78
Wisconsin, 87, 99
Wollersheim family, 87
Wood, Laurie, *141*
Woodbury Vineyards (NY), 44

Zellerbach, James, 17, 127
Zinfandel(s), 16
  from California, 123, *124–125*, 126, 134
Ziraldo, Donald, 181–182
Zonin, 65

ACKNOWLEDGMENTS

The author gratefully acknowledges the generous efforts and assistance of numerous people who aided me in producing this book. I am particularly grateful to editor Leslie Stoker for her patient guidance and shepherding of the project, as well as to editors Roy Finamore and Brian Hotchkiss. Special thanks also to Sarah Longacre and David Diamond for their tireless efforts in the photo department.

The author and photographer gratefully acknowledge and thank Margery Motzkin for her tireless efforts in producing the photographs in this book and for actually taking many of the aerial photographs when the photographer proved too large for the cockpits of countless aircrafts. We also thank Teresa King for producing the extraordinary balloon photography on pages 128–129.

People throughout the continent were helpful to the author and photographer in preparing this book. We would like specifically to thank the following:

In New York: James Tresize, New York Wine/Grape Foundation, Penn Yan; Peter Johnstone, Heron Hill Vineyards, Hammondsport; Gene Pierce, Glenora Wine Cellars, Dundee; Hermann J. Wiemer, Dundee; Professor Robert Pool, Cornell University Research Station, Geneva; William Wagner, Wagner Vineyards, Lodi; Ann Bierbower, Pedro Domecq, Larchmont; Theodore N. Kaplan, New York City; Patricia and Peter Lenz, Lenz Vineyards, Peconic; Joe Hemmingway, New York City; Bruce Stark, New York City; Henry Tobin, New York City; Rosita Sarnoff, New York City; The International Wine Center, New York City; Louis Fiore and Nelda Bennett, West Park Wine Cellars, West Park.

In Connecticut: Hugh and Susan Connell, Crosswoods Vineyard, North Stonington.

In Massachusetts: David Tower, Commonwealth Winery, Plymouth; The George Matthiesen Family, Chicama Vineyards, Martha's Vineyard.

In New Jersey: Charles Tomasello, Tomasello Winery, Hammondton; Tewksbury Wine Cellars, Lebanon.

In Maryland: G. Hamilton Mowbray, Montbray Wine Cellars, Westminster.

In Virginia: John and Felicia Rogan, Oakencroft Vineyard, Charlottesville; Deborah Welsh, Oakencroft Vineyard, Charlottesville; Jacques Recht, Ingleside Plantation, Oak Grove; Lucie T. Morton Garrett, Middleburg; Archie Smith III, Meredyth Vineyard, Middleburg; Cynda Godwin and Peter Hatch at Monticello, Charlottesville; Bruce Zoecklin, Virginia Polytechnic Institute, Blacksburg; Virginia Wineries Association, Oak Grove.

In Florida: Jeanne Burgess, Lafayette Vineyards, Tallahassee; Professor John Mortensen, University of Florida, Agricultural Research Center, Leesburg.

In Georgia: Dee Ann Stone, Atlanta; Bruce Galphin, Atlanta; Donald Panoz, Chateau Elan, Hoschston.

In Mississippi: Claiborne and Marian Barnwell, Claiborne Vineyards, Indianola; S. Duke Goza, Oxford; Samuel Rushing, Winery Rushing, Merigold; Dr. Richard P. Vine, Mississippi State University, Starkville.

In Tennessee: Ray Skinner, Laurel Hill Vineyard, Memphis; Gavin Gentry, Memphis.

In Arkansas: Alcuin Wiederkehr, Altus; Henry J. Sax, Altus; Bartelle and Constance Mullis, Pine Bluff.

In Michigan: The Welsch Family, Fenn Valley Vineyards, Fenn Valley; Joe Borello, Grand Rapids; Ray and Eleanor Heald, Ann Arbor; Edward O'Keefe, Chateau Grand Traverse, Grand Traverse; Professor Gordon S. Howell, Michigan State University Research Station, Fenn Valley.

In Missouri: Nancy Meyer, Webster Groves; Jim and Betty Ann Held, Stone Hill Wine Cellars, Hermann; Robert and Judith Slifer, Montelle Vineyards, Augusta; Scott Todabush, Mount Pleasant Vineyards, Augusta; Joe Pollack, St. Louis Post-Dispatch, St. Louis; David Kay, St. Louis; Larry Carver, Carver Wine Cellars, Rolla.

In Ohio: Ohio Wine Producers Association, Austinburg.

In Pennsylvania: Sam Hughes, Philadelphia; Pennsylvania Grape Industry Association, Brogue; Tim Crouch, Allegro Vineyards, Brogue.

In Texas: Ed and Susan Auler, Fall Creek Vineyard, Tow; Charles Robert Cox, Pheasant Ridge, Lubbock; Steve Hartman, University of Texas, Midland; Charles O. McKinney, University of Texas, Midland; Mary Sanger and Danny Presnal, Texas Department of Agriculture, Austin; Monet Stallé, Austin; Tom Childs, Ste. Genevieve, Fort Stockton; Billy Carr, Midland; Rebecca Murphy, Dallas; Professor George Ray McEachern, Texas A & M University, College Station.

In New Mexico: Michael and Patrick Johnson, La Chiripada, Dixon; Anderson Valley Vineyards, Albuquerque; Vito Liso, St. Clair Vineyards, Deming.

In Arizona: Professor Gordon Dutt, Sonoita Vineyards, Sonoita.

In California: Patrick Campbell, Laurel Glen Vineyard, Glen Ellen; Joseph and Alice Heitz, Heitz Wine Cellars, St. Helena; Tom May, Oakville; Dr. Bernard and Belle Rhodes, Bella Oaks Vineyard, Rutherford; William and Lila Jaeger, St. Helena; Louis P. Martini, Louis M. Martini Winery, St. Helena; Zelma Long, Simi Winery, Healdburg; Richard Graff, Chalone Vineyard, Soledad; Carolyn Wente, Livermore; Sterling Vineyards, Calistoga; Rene di Rosa, Winery Lake Vineyard, Napa; André Tchelistcheff, Napa; Brooks and Kate Firestone, The Firestone Vineyard, Los Olivos; Alison Green, The Firestone Vineyard, Los Olivos; Andrew Bassi, Los Angeles; Dr. Avron Weinreich, Los Angeles.

In Oregon: David and Diana Lett, The Eyrie Vineyards, McMinnville; Richard Erath, Knudsen–Erath Vineyards, Dundee.

In Washington: Bob Betz and Corky Merwin, Chateau Ste. Michelle, Woodinville; Gary Ballard, Chateau Ste. Michelle, Patterson; Michael Hogue, The Hogue Cellars, Prosser; Gerald Warren, Seattle.

In Idaho: Richard Symms, Ste. Chapelle, Caldwell; Michael Januik, Petros Winery, Boise.

In Canada: Gary Strachan, Summerland Research Station, B.C.; John Levine, B.C.; Doug Sperling, Kelowna, B.C.; Harry McWatters, Sumac Ridge, Summerland, B.C.; Walter Gehringer, Gehringer Vineyard, Oliver, B.C.; John Bremmer, Bright & Co., Oliver, B.C.; Ian Mavety, Vaseaux Farms, B.C.; Donald Ziraldo and Karl J. Kaiser, Inniskillin Wines, Inc., Ontario; Professor Roger Dial, Grand Pré Wines, Nova Scotia; Ted Ottley, Toronto.

In Mexico: Pedro Domecq, Baja California; Camillo Magoni, Baja California; Frederick Pinson, Baja California; Francisco Domenech, Cavas de San Juan, Querétaro; L.A. Cetto, Vinicola de Tecate, Baja California.

In Washington, D.C.: Dorothy Koester, Bureau of Alcohol, Tobacco & Firearms.